SUCCESS

IN THE

WORKPLACE

A STUDENT GUIDE

Compiled by

Margaret Brand

Ann Olney Sparkes

Eastern Townships School Board

Copp Clark Pitman Ltd.
A Longman Company

ISBN 0-7730-5004-3

Editing/June Trusty
Cover Design/Stephen A. MacEachern
Design Consultation/Jo-anne Slauenwhite
Illustrations/Dave McKay
Typesetting/Carol Magee
Printing and binding/Alger Press Limited

Canadian Cataloguing in Publication Data

Main entry under title:

Success in the workplace

ISBN 0-7730-5004-3

1. Success in business.   2. Vocational guidance.
I. Brand, Margaret.   II. Olney Sparkes, Ann.

HF5386.S83 1990   650.1   C90-094712-8

3   4   5   5004-3   94   93   92

Copp Clark Pitman Ltd.
2775 Matheson Boulevard East
Mississauga, Ontario
L4W 4P7

Printed and bound in Canada

A C K N O W L E D G M E N T S

The original *Work and Employability Skills* modules, on which this textbook is based, were prepared by the Eastern Townships School Board with the encouragement, advice, and assistance of many individuals and groups. The following are particularly thanked for their contributions.

H. Auger	P. Marcoux
R. Beasse	T. Matthews
D. Belden	R. McConnachie
N. Bilodeau	W. McGee
J. Boluk	L. Miller
S.P. Chadha	J. Mulholland
S. Cochrane	M. Mildon
G. Dallaire	D. Nixon
K. Danaher	R. Orr
L. Doyle	J. Perry-Gore
A. Edwards	A. Quick
D. Farrell	C. Rodger
D. Fidler	L. Roy
J. Garneau	I. Smith
G. Goddard	R. Stymiest
P. Grant	M. Taylor
M. Anaka-Hogue	

Thanks are due to reviewers Murray Shannon, Centre Wellington District High School; Brenda Hodge, Lincoln City Board of Education; and Shelley Smith, TVO.

Appreciation is also expressed to Paulette Proulx, Assistant to the National Co-ordinator of Education, Canadian Federation of Labour, for reviewing Chapter 22, ''Labour Unions.''

C O N T E N T S

UNIT 5: INFORMATION FOR THE WORKPLACE
▼▼▼

UNIT 6: CREATING WORK OPPORTUNITIES
▼▼▼

SUCCESS

IN THE

WORKPLACE

A STUDENT GUIDE

U N I T

1

You and the World of Work

INTRODUCTION
▼ ▼

Unit 1 will assist you to assess your interests and personal qualities. Learning the relationship between personal values, decision making, and the setting of goals will help you to understand the importance of setting short- and long-term goals. The chapter on occupational trends explains some of the ways in which the workplace is changing and draws your attention to some of the types of skills that employers need now and will need in the future. Careful study of this unit will provide you with the tools to make choices for a winning future.

Self-Concept

OBJECTIVES

After completing this chapter you should be able to:

- Explain what you like and what you don't like about yourself.
- Appreciate your own achievements more.
- Define the characteristics you value in other people.
- Understand that many jobs require people with certain characteristics.
- Identify occupations that your characteristics might suit.

INTRODUCTION

Who are you? You might answer this question with your name and some information about your family and school. Such information helps to identify you to others, but have you ever realized that you also need ways to identify and explain yourself to yourself?

The way you see yourself is called your *self-concept*. You begin to develop a self-concept early in life and keep revising and reassessing it as you continue to change and have different experiences.

Developing a self-concept is like looking in a mirror, because it depends so much on how you believe others see you. You imagine how you appear to other people, and your experience in a situation might confirm or deny that. If the experience doesn't confirm it, you might change your self-concept to match the experience. For example, perhaps you think of yourself as a bit of a ''loner.'' Then someone persuades you to try bowling as a hobby and you find that you really enjoy being part of a team. The probable result is that you'll adjust your self-concept.

How does the idea of self-concept relate to the world of work? You've probably heard people say, ''I'm a teacher,'' ''I'm an office manager,'' in describing their social roles. What you do in the world of work forms a large part of your self-concept as an adult. It's important, then, for you to explain yourself to yourself as well as possible. Then the person you truly are can identify occupations that will satisfy and reward you, and contribute most to your self-concept. The following exercises will help you to analyse how you see yourself.

1. IDENTIFYING YOUR SELF-CONCEPT

Answer the following questions and give examples that illustrate your answers.

1. How is it helpful for us to compare ourselves with other people?
2. Is it sometimes harmful to compare ourselves with others?
3. With whom do you compare yourself?
4. Whom do you admire most?
5. Why do you admire this person?
6. Do you try to be like this person?
7. What is a social role?
8. Describe your social roles.

2. WORDS THAT DESCRIBE ME

1. From the list of words that appears at the bottom of this page and the top of the next page, choose ten words that best describe you and write these in your notebook.
2. Which of the words you've chosen would you like to change? Think of, or find in the list, more positive words that could be substituted for the words you'd like to replace. The words you choose can be opposites, or antonyms, such as:

    nervous/calm   stubborn/adaptable   clumsy/graceful

    Or the words can be synonyms and have the same meaning but convey a more positive impression. Think about how behaviours and actions can be described with a positive tone when they're appropriate and with a negative tone when they're seen as unacceptable, as the following word sets illustrate.

    stubborn/persistent   distrustful/cautious

3. Choose ten words from the list that do *not* describe you well. Would you like to be able to use any of these words in a description of your-self in the future?
4. Make a list of ten words that describe the type of person you'd like to be.

Self-Descriptive Words

able	belligerent	clumsy
adaptable	bitter	cold
adventurous	bold	communicate well
agitated	bossy	complex
agreeable	calm	compulsive
aggressive	capable	confident
alert	carefree	conforming
ambitious	careless	congenial
anxious	cautious	considerate
apathetic	certain	controlled
assertive	cheerful	co-operative
authoritative	clever	courteous

cranky	hardworking	pugnacious
creative	honest	punctual
credible	hospitable	reflective
curious	humble	reliable
dependable	humorous	responsible
determined	imaginative	risk-taking
devious	independent	rude
diligent	initiator	self-confident
disagreeable	intelligent	self-reliant
distrustful	involved	sensitive
dogmatic	kind	sincere
domineering	likable	social
easygoing	logical	stubborn
energetic	lonely	sympathetic
enthusiastic	loyal	tactless
expressive	modest	talkative
flexible	nervous	tense
forgiving	optimistic	thorough
frustrated	orderly	timid
good friend	outgoing	tolerant
graceful	patient	touchy
grateful	persistent	unappreciated
greedy	physically fit	vain
gregarious	polite	versatile
grumpy	proud	well-groomed

3. MY ACCOMPLISHMENTS AND SATISFACTIONS

What things have you done that gave you pleasure and pride? Which activities give you satisfaction? What recognition have others given your accomplishments?

In your notebook, set up a table using the column heads explained below. Then refer to the lists of possible categories that follow these heads for ideas on the types of items you should use to complete your table. In some cases, you might insert an entry in either the first or second column only but, in every case, fill in the two final columns.

1. *Activities:* Name the activities and give specific examples.

2. *Achievements:* Name events in which you've participated, prizes, club offices, or awards you've received. Also describe any personal improvements you've made, such as improving your study habits, helping out more at home, cutting down on junk food—anything that has made you feel good about yourself.

3. *Responses of Others:* Explain whether the person is a relative, friend, acquaintance, employer, teacher, etc., and describe how that person reacted to your accomplishment.

4. *Your Reaction:* How did *you* feel about the activity or achievement? Did you feel proud? more self-confident? eager to become even better?

Possible Categories

Home:	**School:**	**Community:**
• Chores	• Subjects	• Volunteer activities
• Family	• Languages learned	• Part-time work
• Activities	• Clubs	• Hobbies
• Hobbies	• Sports	• Other
	• Other extracurricular activities	

Adapted from Ontario Ministry of Education. *One Step at a Time: Educational and Career Explorations,* 1984, p. 25.

CASE STUDY

Last summer I needed money to buy a mountain bike. I didn't have a job but I had some things of my own I could sell if I could find someone to buy them. I decided it would be a good idea for my family to have a garage sale to sell all of the family's unwanted items. My parents agreed I could have half the profits of the sale if I did all the organizing and assumed all the costs of running it. We set a date three weeks away so we would have enough time to advertise our sale.

That weekend I went to some garage sales to get ideas about pricing and ways to set up the sale. During my research I discovered that there were more customers when several garage sales were set up on the same street.

I decided to ask all the neighbours if they'd like to take part in our garage sale. I explained that if we co-ordinated our efforts we would all benefit. We could share the cost of the advertising, have a lot more customers, and have extra traffic on the street for only one day. Nine of our neighbours decided they'd like to participate. I made and distributed the posters and wrote the advertisement we put in the local newspaper.

The garage sale was a huge success. I earned $190 for my mountain bike. My parents and neighbours got some extra money and everyone had a good time. I increased my self-confidence and realized that I enjoyed selling. Someone liked one of the posters I made so well that she's hiring me to make some posters for her. One of my neighbours' friends whom I met that day offered me a part-time job for the summer working in her mobile canteen.

QUESTION

In your notebook, set up a table with the following column heads. Under each heading, list what skills the writer used to arrange and stage the garage sale.

1. *Skills with Information:* For example, researching sale methods, pricing of goods, etc.

2. *Skills with People:* For example, with parents, neighbours, sale customers, etc.

3. *Skills with Things:* For example, with posters, merchandise, etc.

4. MY SUCCESS STORY

Choose one of the accomplishments that you included in Exercise 3 on page 4, selecting one in which you played a principal role. In three or four paragraphs explain what you did, how you did it, your reward, and how you felt. Make sure that you give yourself full credit for your accomplishment. Write in the first person and use plenty of specific verbs to help identify the skills you used.

5. A THINKING ASSIGNMENT

Pick six of the following ten questions and answer them in short paragraphs in your notebook.

1. It's the year 2025. The Governor General awards you the Order of Canada, one of the country's most distinguished awards. For what important contribution to Canada have you been honoured?

2. What qualities make you a reliable person?

3. What would you do if you had to spend the rest of your life in a wheel chair?

4. If you could be an animal, what would you be?

5. What do you like best about yourself?

6. You are a successful writer. What was the subject of your latest article or book?

7. What would you be willing to risk your life for? Why?

8. What well-known person are you like? In what ways?

9. You have one year to live. Someone gives you unlimited funds for a one-month vacation. Your health is still good. Where would you go?

10. Two of your best friends aren't speaking to each other because they've had a disagreement. Each wants you to take his or her side in the dispute. What do you do?

6. DARK SIDE/LIGHT SIDE

Everyone is a mixture of things. Everyone is unique. Everyone has both strengths and weaknesses. In your notebook:

1. List at least five qualities that you *like* about yourself.

2. List at least five qualities that you *dislike* about yourself.

3. Then list which of these qualities apply to each of the following categories.

a) A friend would like.

b) A friend would dislike.

c) Would help you to live with others.

d) Would make it hard to live with others.

e) Would make you a good co-worker.

f) Would make you a difficult co-worker.

g) Would make you a good leader.

h) Would make you a poor leader.

i) Would make you a good employee.

j) Would make you a difficult employee.

7. WHAT IF?

1. You've moved to a distant, strange city that has a different custom to enable newcomers to meet new friends: by law you are required to make a poster that describes you and post this on a special bulletin board in a public place. Prepare such a poster.

2. You have a new pen pal, the same gender as you, who lives in another part of Canada. Write your first letter to him or her, describing yourself.

3. You attend university in a distant city. You have a large apartment and need someone to share the expenses. Make a list of characteristics you'd want in a room-mate. Then make a list of ten questions that you would ask a potential candidate to determine if she or he had the characteristics you'd like in a room-mate.

4. You need someone to look after your teenage children this summer while you and your spouse are on vacation. What would the person you chose be like? Write a letter of application from the successful candidate in which the person describes herself or himself.

8. PEOPLE WHO WORK

1. In your notebook, write down the letters of the following items and then supply the names of three occupations that each of the descriptions fits.

   a) People who sometimes work at night.
   b) People who work with numbers.
   c) People who work with textual information.
   d) People who design.
   e) People who work alone.
   f) People who work on the street.
   g) People who evaluate.
   h) People who work on the telephone.
   i) People who work at home.
   j) People with seasonal employment.
   k) People who organize events.
   l) People who operate machines.
   m) People who work toward deadlines.
   n) People who work outdoors.
   o) People who do repetitive tasks.
   p) People who work with nature.
   q) People who work on teams.
   r) People who repair items.
   s) People who work on computers.

2. Pick five of the jobs you listed that you would like to do.

3. Pick five of the jobs you listed that you would not like to do.

9. YOUR WORK PREFERENCES

In your notebook, indicate your work preferences by putting the applicable letter next to the number of each of the following items, using the key provided. When you've finished, look at your "Yes" answers and name three occupations that you think would suit these preferences. Then take into account your "Maybe" answers and add three more possible occupations.

Y = Yes   M = Maybe   N = No

1. Work with numbers.
2. Work with computers.
3. Perform a variety of duties.
4. Work with nature.
5. Work on a team.
6. Perform repetitive, easy tasks.
7. Travel frequently.
8. Make presentations.
9. Work outdoors.
10. Use initiative.
11. Have to meet deadlines.
12. Attend to details.
13. Respond to emergencies.
14. Organize events.
15. Frequently work on the telephone.
16. Work with information.
17. Operate machinery.
18. Look after customers.
19. Have to dress up.
20. Work at night.
21. Communicate in writing.
22. Repair equipment or machinery.
23. Deal with people in a crisis.
24. Be exposed to danger.
25. Solve problems.
26. Supervise other workers.
27. Attend university.
28. Provide a service.
29. Work for a large organization.
30. Work part-time.
31. Work with ideas.
32. Set my own priorities.
33. Work with different age groups.
34. Be required to use many skills.
35. Have prestige.
36. Work hard physically.
37. Design a product.
38. Work alone.
39. Be required to do light physical work.
40. Be closely supervised.

10. APPEALING JOBS

Name four jobs that appeal to you and write a paragraph explaining the appeal of each.

CHAPTER SUMMARY EXERCISES

1. Write the following statements in your notebook, inserting the missing words that are indicated by the blanks.

a) I feel angry when ___.

b) The most important thing I've learned from my family is ___.

c) The nicest thing I ever did for someone was when ___.

d) The biggest project I ever undertook was ___.

e) I can't wait until I ___.

f) I'd like to be able to ___.

g) I like my friend ___ because ___.

h) My friends think I'm special because I make a great effort to ___.

i) I want to learn about ___.

j) I feel competitive when ___.

k) If I had a million dollars to give to charity, I'd give it to ___.

l) If I could change my name I'd call myself ___ because then I ___.

m) I feel optimistic about ___.

n) My biggest hero/heroine is ___ because ___.

o) I sometimes find it hard to decide ___.

p) I'd like to change the way I always ___.

q) A perfect day for me would be ___.

r) I almost never ___.

s) I feel most independent when ___.

t) I'd like to try to ___ again.

u) I dream of the day when ___.

v) ___ has/have always fascinated me because ___.

w) I often get impatient with ___ because ___.

x) I'm happiest when ___.

2. Choose an occupation that you think you would enjoy and write a 500-word essay about the characteristics you possess that would enable you to succeed at such a job. Educational and experience factors do not have to be considered in this exercise.

3. In a 250-word essay, explain why you are (or are not) a good friend to have.

2

Values

O B J E C T I V E S
▼▼▼▼▼▼▼▼▼▼▼▼▼▼▼▼▼

After completing this chapter you should be able to:

- Define the meaning and importance of values.
- Explain the relationship between values and decision making.
- Understand that values can change.
- Analyse your own values and those of people who are important to you.
- Realize how values apply to work situations.

I N T R O D U C T I O N
▼▼▼▼▼▼▼▼▼▼▼▼▼▼▼▼▼▼▼▼▼

Your values are your private, personal beliefs about what is most important to you, and about what is right or wrong, good or bad. Values are basic to decision making. Every day we make choices and decisions, choosing certain courses of action rather than others, using values as our guides. If a person achieves a goal but, in order to do so, violates his or her own belief about what is right or wrong, unhappiness results.

People have different values because every one of us experiences the world in a unique way. Your values might be right for you but completely wrong for someone else. Everyone has different concerns.

By understanding what your own values are and where they come from, you are better able to make decisions that are right for you. You get the most you can from life when you are careful about the choices you make.

To truly grow, change, and prosper, you need to become consciously aware of the rules you have for yourself and for others. When choosing a career, you really need to know what is important to you. Otherwise, how will you be able to measure your success or failure?

Values change when you change goals or your self-image. Different things become important when you have different goals. By understanding what your values are and where they come from, you're better able to make decisions that are right for you. The following exercises will help you to do this.

1. WHERE ARE VALUES LEARNED?

Values are learned. How you perceive what is good and bad, worthy and unworthy, is based on your own experiences. Some things that seem right to you might seem wrong to others. In your notebook, make a list of where you think values are learned and explain how they are learned in each case.

2. PREFERRED OPTIONS

Rate from 1 to 4 your choices of answers for the following statements, with 4 indicating your first choice. If there's a choice you wouldn't make, indicate this with a zero.

1. I like to use my leisure time to:
   a) Complete personal projects.
   b) Visit friends.
   c) Do extra work.
   d) (Add another.)

2. If I had a party, I would:
   a) Invite as many people as I could.
   b) Just invite close friends.
   c) Plan every detail.
   d) Have high expectations.

3. If I could choose where I lived, it would be:
   a) In the country.
   b) In a downtown condominium.
   c) In a small town.
   d) In the suburbs.

4. After I turn sixty-five I want to:
   a) Travel.
   b) Do volunteer work.
   c) Continue at whatever job I've been doing.
   d) (Add another.)

5. If I had a house, it would have:
   a) Lots of private spaces.
   b) A large kitchen.
   c) Lots of furniture and keepsakes.
   d) Easy-maintenance features.

6. My favourite things are:
   a) Items that help me to do things.
   b) Books.
   c) Clothes.
   d) Animals.

7. I'd like to have:
   a) A group to hang around with.
   b) Several close friends.
   c) Many acquaintances.
   d) A best friend.

8. If a co-worker was abrupt with me, I'd:
   a) Choose to ignore her or him.
   b) Ask her or him if I've caused a problem.
   c) Ask if I could help.
   d) Ask other workers for advice on how to deal with the problem.

3. VALUE STATEMENTS

Write the following statements in your notebook, inserting the word or phrase that best expresses your values.

1. I'd like to participate on a team that ___.
2. I'd like to support ___.
3. I'd like to produce ___.
4. Children are really ___.
5. I think pets are ___.
6. I'd like to sell ___.
7. If I could change what school was like, I'd ___.
8. If I could meet one famous person, I'd choose ___.
9. My favourite season is ___.
10. I feel blue when ___.
11. I want to become skilled at ___.
12. I think I'm the best ___.
13. My favourite time of day is ___.
14. I get my best ideas ___.
15. I'd like to start ___.
16. I'd like to stop ___.
17. I'd like to tell the leaders of this country to stop ___.
18. I think children should ___.
19. The most important thing I learned in school was ___.
20. If I had unlimited funds, I'd go on a trip to ___.
21. ___ really makes me laugh.
22. My family likes to ___.
23. I feel really alive when I ___.
24. I feel confident about my ___.
25. I become angry when my friend ___.

4. VALUES CHART

How important are the following things to you? to your family? to your friends? Use a copy of the following chart provided by your teacher and check the appropriate boxes for each group. You'll then see at a glance if you think your values are different than those of the other important people in your life.

Values Chart

Value	Person	Very Important	Somewhat Important	Less Important	Not Important
Ambition: Desire for success	Me				
	Parent or Guardian				
	Best Friend				
Beauty in both art and nature	Me				
	Parent or Guardian				
	Best Friend				
Benevolence: Humanitarianism, generosity	Me				
	Parent or Guardian				
	Best Friend				
Compassion: Kindliness, sympathy, concern for others	Me				
	Parent or Guardian				
	Best Friend				
Competence: Skilfulness, capability, efficiency	Me				
	Parent or Guardian				
	Best Friend				
Creativity: Ingeniousness, innovation, originality	Me				
	Parent or Guardian				
	Best Friend				
Emotional Health: Mental well-being	Me				
	Parent or Guardian				
	Best Friend				

Value	Person	Very Important	Somewhat Important	Less Important	Not Important
Ethics: Principles, moral standards	Me				
	Parent or Guardian				
	Best Friend				
Equality: Belief in equal opportunity for others	Me				
	Parent or Guardian				
	Best Friend				
Honesty: Truthfulness, frankness	Me				
	Parent or Guardian				
	Best Friend				
Honour: Integrity, having a good name	Me				
	Parent or Guardian				
	Best Friend				
Influence: Control or power over events or people	Me				
	Parent or Guardian				
	Best Friend				
Knowledge: Information, learning, instruction	Me				
	Parent or Guardian				
	Best Friend				
Leisure: Free or spare time	Me				
	Parent or Guardian				
	Best Friend				

Value	Person	Very Important	Somewhat Important	Less Important	Not Important
Love: Affection, devotion, attachment to others	Me				
	Parent or Guardian				
	Best Friend				
Peace: Absence of conflict or hostilities	Me				
	Parent or Guardian				
	Best Friend				
Physical Health: Physical well-being	Me				
	Parent or Guardian				
	Best Friend				
Popularity: Acclaim, regard, well-liked	Me				
	Parent or Guardian				
	Best Friend				
Prestige: Good reputation, influence, social status	Me				
	Parent or Guardian				
	Best Friend				
Religious Faith: Belief, conviction	Me				
	Parent or Guardian				
	Best Friend				
Security: Safety, stability, confidence	Me				
	Parent or Guardian				
	Best Friend				

Value	Person	Very Important	Somewhat Important	Less Important	Not Important
Self-Sufficiency: Self-reliance, independence	Me				
	Parent or Guardian				
	Best Friend				
Sincerity: Earnest, honest, truthful	Me				
	Parent or Guardian				
	Best Friend				
Success: Attainment, accomplishment	Me				
	Parent or Guardian				
	Best Friend				
Tolerance: Open-mindedness, patience, acceptance	Me				
	Parent or Guardian				
	Best Friend				

In your notebook, answer the following questions.

1. Look at the check marks you inserted in the values chart. If the values were different for each group, why do you think they were different? Which values would you like to share with more people in your life?

2. Do you think that you can have seemingly conflicting values at the same time? For example, equality and prestige? Explain your answer.

3. If you had your dream career, which values of those listed in the chart would become more important to you?

4. How does the general population tell the government what they think is important? What are some of the policies of the government that demonstrate to us what politicians think is important?

5. Which of the values listed in the chart do you think might be important to people in the following occupations?

   a) Department store buyer   e) Social worker
   b) Newspaper editor   f) Architect
   c) Personnel officer   g) Banker
   d) Nurse   h) Farmer

CHAPTER SUMMARY EXERCISES

1. Which values do you think are most important to you in a work situation? In your notebook, rank your answers to the following questions, using the letters in the key.

    Y = Yes   M = Maybe   No = No   N = Neutral

    a) Is a pleasing physical environment important to you?

    b) Do you want a job that has opportunity for advancement?

    c) Would you mind getting dirty on the job?

    d) Would you like to dress up every day?

    e) Do you want to be able to use a skill that you have developed?

    f) Do you want to be able to use your creative abilities?

    g) Would you like to have a job that you could forget about at the end of the day?

    h) Would it bother you if you disagreed with the moral conduct of the company for which you were working?

    i) Would you mind having less money but more leisure time?

    j) Do you want prestige from your job?

    k) Would you be willing to risk your physical health at your workplace?

    l) Would working with a team be important to you?

    m) Would you like to work alone?

    n) Would you be willing to sacrifice change for security?

    o) Would you like to influence decisions in your workplace?

2. In a 500-word essay, describe five jobs that would suit you, based on the values you hold. Name the values as these apply to each job.

Goals

OBJECTIVES
▼▼▼▼▼▼▼▼▼▼▼▼ ▼▼▼

After completing this chapter you should be able to:

- Explain the importance of setting short- and long-term goals.
- Discuss the importance of having career goals.
- Identify possible career goals.
- Describe various methods of improving employability.
- Set goals that are realistic and that fit with your values.

INTRODUCTION
▼▼▼▼▼▼▼▼▼▼▼▼▼▼▼▼▼▼▼

Goals are the aims, purposes, intentions, aspirations, ambitions, ideals, and destinations that give direction and meaning to our lives. In your life you will set many goals for yourself and spend much of your time trying to attain them.

Perhaps you know people who'd like to tell you how to run your life. Their experience, knowledge, and ideas might be useful, but ultimately it is you who must decide which goals are important for you to pursue. The goals you choose should be reflective of who you are, your strengths, your weaknesses, and your values. As you change, your goals will change.

Becoming committed to achieving your goals involves thinking about what you want your future to be like and what type of person you want to be. We can't predict the future, but we can set goals and then work toward achieving them. Setting goals might sound like a big step, like a win or lose situation, like it requires too much commitment. But treat the future as your friend; be prepared for its arrival. Opportunities open up for those who are prepared.

Don't wait around for life to happen to you. If you see yourself as a passive participant in your life, a victim at the mercy of "the system," you're ducking responsibility for your life. Remember, we're all disadvantaged in some way and have to overcome obstacles.

People who achieve their goals start out by believing that they *can* achieve those goals. Take charge of the part of your life that you can control. Decide what you want. Remember, if you think you can or if you think you can't, you're always right. Think your goals through, obtain as much information as you can, and have faith in your belief that you can achieve your goals.

This section will help you to learn how to set short- and long-term goals and how to take steps toward reaching these goals.

1. IDENTIFYING GOALS

1. In your notebook, write the following statements, supplying the word or phrase that best completes each statement.

   a) When I was in elementary school, I wanted to be a ___ .

   b) When I started high school I wanted to be a ___ .

   c) Now I'd like to be a ___ .

   d) My family has always wanted me to be a ___ .

   e) I've always wanted to learn ___ .

   f) I've always wanted to be ___ .

   g) I've always wanted to have ___ .

2. List five of the most important changes that you want to make in yourself and your behaviour.

3. List five key reasons why you've not yet changed the attitudes/beliefs/behaviours you listed in question 2.

4. Write a positive statement of how you can accomplish some of your desired changes. List positive beliefs and behaviours that you feel will support you in achieving your goals.

5. List five of the things you're most afraid might happen to you in the working world.

6. Change each item in question 5 to its positive opposite. For example, "I'm afraid I won't get a job this summer" would be changed to "I *will* get a job this summer."

SETTING GOALS
▼ ▼

Before you begin to think about long-term goals, you should start by setting goals that you can reach soon. It's important to have a specific objective that can be reached in a short time. That way you'll learn what it's like to plan the steps you should take, follow through and take these steps, and succeed.

SHORT-TERM GOALS

Five steps must be followed for goal achievement:

1. *Identify a specific goal* you want to reach and set yourself a time limit in which to achieve it.

2. *Plan ways of achieving your goal* by listing the steps that must be taken.

3. *Identify any obstacles or barriers* that might get in the way of achieving your goal.

4. *List ways of overcoming those obstacles or barriers*, or of planning around them.

5. *Evaluate your progress.* If you haven't succeeded, ask yourself why.

C A S E   S T U D Y

You want to get a job in an office this summer, but you feel that you need faster and more accurate inputting skills. You have three months before it's time to start applying for jobs. You map out the following plan.

Step 1 Identify your goal: Your goal is to improve the speed and accuracy of your inputting skills.

Step 2 Make a list of how you're going to go about reaching your goal (be specific):

    a) I'll get the necessary supplies for the typewriter or word processor (new ribbon, etc.).

    b) I'll key all my homework assignments until the end of the school year.

    c) I'll key letters to my friends and relatives that I usually write longhand.

    d) I'll use an inputting textbook to help me practise.

    e) I'll key some of the notes that I make in class (perhaps my history and geography notes).

Step 3 Identify any obstacles or barriers: I might wake up my sisters and brothers if I practise after they've gone to bed.

Step 4 Make a list of ways to overcome your obstacles or plan around them: I'll ask my parents if there is another place where I could work and not disturb my family, perhaps a corner of the spare bedroom in the basement. Dad would help me to find an old desk or to make one with sawhorses.

Step 5 Evaluate your progress: After three weeks of keying my homework and letters and doing four lessons from the inputting textbook, my confidence and speed have increased. I'll be ready to apply for jobs soon.

2. SPECIFIC GOALS

1. Now it's your turn. In your notebook, list two specific goals on which you have decided to take action within the next week.

2. List the ways in which you plan to achieve these goals.

3. Are there any obstacles or barriers in your way? If so, list them.

4. List ways in which you can overcome these obstacles.

3. GOAL ATTAINMENT WORKSHEET

Prepare a worksheet for yourself that resembles the one at the top of the next page, with a separate section for each goal. During this course, use your worksheet to track your progress in attaining goals that you set for yourself. If you fail to achieve a goal, examine carefully the reasons why: Did you become lazy? discouraged? Were the obstacles or barriers too difficult to overcome? Were your goals unrealistic? These problems must be taken into consideration before you set other goals.

Goal	Attained	Not Attained

Reason goal not attained: _____

_____

LONG-TERM GOALS

Long-term goals are much like short-term goals, but much more planning is involved and sometimes there's much more uncertainty about whether or not you'll ever reach your goals. For this reason, it's better if you think of long-term goals as many short-term goals put together, leading to a larger goal.

When you think about what you eventually want to do with your life, you must consider many things about yourself and identify what things are most important to you. The following exercise will help you to do this.

4. EXAMINING YOUR BROAD LIFE GOALS

Clarify your own priorities by examining your broad life goals. In your notebook, write down the numbers of the following items and use a letter from the key to rank each in relation to your own values. Think carefully about your choices.

A = Highly Important   B = Important   C = Somewhat Important
D = Least Important

Affection: To obtain and share companionship and affection.
Duty: To dedicate myself to what I call duty.
Expertness: To become an expert in a particular field.
Health: To work toward soundness of body and mind.
Independence: To have freedom of thought and action.
Leadership: To develop leadership skills.
Parenthood: To raise a fine family.
Pleasure: To enjoy life, to be happy and content.
Power: To have control over others.
Prestige: To become well-known.
Security: To have a secure and stable position.
Self-realization: To maximize my personal development.
Service: To contribute to the satisfaction of others.
Wealth: To earn a lot of money.

DEVELOPING YOUR CAREER GOALS
▼▼▼▼▼▼▼▼▼▼▼▼▼▼▼▼▼▼▼▼▼▼▼▼▼▼▼▼

What do you have to do to prepare for your future? Are there any things that you should be planning now? Do you know how much money you'd have to earn to have the type of lifestyle you want?

Think about money for a minute. Many people who don't develop special skills for the job market end up holding lower-paid jobs for the rest of their lives.

Money might not be the most important thing in this world but it makes possible the things that *are* important. Many of the goals in the "Examining Your Broad Life Goals" exercise directly or indirectly involve money.

What most people want is the ability to make choices. Having few skills and little earning power limits the jobs available to you and the money you'll have to spend. With less money there are fewer things you can buy, fewer places you can go, and less time to do the things that are important to you. Find out the current minimum wage and then think about the following problem. In your notebook, write the dollar amounts that fit in the blanks.

A job at minimum wage, for a forty-hour week, would mean a before-deductions, take-home wage each week of $___. Let's take 10% off for deductions each week. Now you have a weekly take-home wage of $___ or a yearly income of $___.

How much does shelter cost? How much do groceries cost per week? Do you think you could afford a new car? a used car? running your car? fixing your car? Could you afford a vacation?

Do you have enough information about possible careers? Do you know the range of income you could expect? Do you know what skills, aptitudes, and training these careers require?

If you're still trying to decide on the type of job you want, you need information and assistance. Your school guidance counsellor will be a good source of both. Many schools can arrange for you to use **CHOICES**, a computerized career counselling and information system, to help you select a career. Also, check the library for career information materials and talk to people who are in the career in which you are interested.

If you feel confident about setting a career goal for yourself now, how are you going to go about attaining it? Do you need more education (academic or technical)? Could you improve any of your skills? Do you know where the job opportunities are? The following sections will help you to answer these questions.

IDENTIFYING YOUR PRESENT INTERESTS AND SKILLS

If you're not sure what type of career you should be considering, taking the time to identify your present interests and skills can help. One way is to use the information or ideas, people or animals, and things or ideas concept.

- *Information or ideas* includes statistics, facts, goals, and policies.
- *People or animals* mean people of all ages, both genders, and of all ethnic and social groups, and all types of animals.
- *Things or ideas* includes work related to tools, machines, equipment, and materials.

All jobs involve all three categories, but most jobs emphasize one category more than the others. For example, a nurse works mostly with people, a researcher deals more with information or ideas, and an engineer works mainly with things.

5. IDENTIFYING YOUR INTERESTS AND SKILLS

Before each question is a detailed list of the types of information or ideas, people or animals, and things or ideas with which you might work. Read through the list in each case and then answer each question in a table set up like the following one.

Skill Category	Appealing Skills	Skills I've Already Used
Information or Ideas	_____	_____
	_____	_____
	_____	_____
	_____	_____

Information or Ideas:

• words • symbols • knowledge • facts • information • numbers • ideas • charts • graphs • designs • blueprints • statistics • opinions • theories • techniques • budgets • evaluation measures • tests • drawings • flow charts • surveys • costs • work assignments • objectives • goals • policies • procedures • recommendations • memorandums • curriculums • monitor systems • stock figures • handbooks • guidelines • literature • historical documents • catalogues • reports • regulations • future plans

---

1. What skills can you use in working with information or ideas? From the following list, choose five that most appeal to you and enter them in your table. Then use your table to list five of the skills that you've already used.

   • examining • comparing • calculating • computing • gathering • compiling • classifying • filing • analysing • collating • observing • investigating • composing • reporting • presenting • organizing • writing • reading • copying • creating • transcribing • co-ordinating • combining • synthesizing • interpreting

---

People or Animals:

• children • young adults • older • all races • men • women • highly educated • deprived • retarded • handicapped • gifted • students • professional • trades• emotionally disturbed • powerful • influential • sociable • extroverted • introverted • sick • middle-aged • ex-prisoners • abused • religious • residents of underdeveloped nations • people of different cultures • political • alcoholics • drug abusers • normal • wealthy • middle-class • poor • deviants • rigid • flexible • free spirits • conformists • high achievers • ambitious • laid-back • high-pressured • risk-takers • carefree • task-oriented • all types of animals

---

2. What skills can you use in working with people or animals? List in your table the five most appealing ones from the following list, and then five of the skills that you've already used.

- attending to • serving • taking instruction from • supervising
- communicating • instructing • caring for • persuading
- managing • training • teaching • entertaining • motivating
- coaching • consulting • co-ordinating • treating • leading
- facilitating • criticizing • counselling • advising • negotiating
- confronting • informing • empathizing • problem solving
- supporting

Things:

- electrical sockets • lamps • word processors • photocopy machines • computers • stoves • brooms • vacuum cleaners
- ovens • pots • paper • chain saws • pliers • screwdrivers • lawn mowers • power tools • heavy equipment • fork-lifts • cars
- bicycles • motorcycles • telephones • gauges • controls • hair dryers • laser equipment • microwave ovens • furnaces • air conditioners • nuclear reactors • gasoline motors • electric motors
- transformers • gas turbines • cleaning equipment • cameras
- showers • spinning wheels • building supplies • dental equipment
- airplanes

---

3. What skills can you use in working with things or ideas? List in your table the five most appealing ones from the following list, and then five that you've already used.

- moving • pushing • carrying • loading • running • emptying
- stacking • flying • starting • delivering • adjusting • monitoring
- manipulating • cutting • guiding • assembling • operating
- controlling • regulating • setting • overseeing • adapting
- designing • demonstrating • repairing • inputting • painting
- calibrating • selling

Adapted from Dr. Darryl Laramore (co-author). *Joyce Laine Kennedy's Career Book*. Chicago: National Textbook Co., 1988, pp. 119-120.

WORKING WITH INFORMATION OR IDEAS, PEOPLE OR ANIMALS, AND THINGS OR IDEAS

Figure 3.1 on the next page will give you a general idea of how many occupations interrelate when you use the information or ideas, people or animals, and things or ideas concept. The position of each circled number in the diagram indicates the extent to which each occupation involves a particular category. For example, occupation category 13,"Service Occupations" (see the key beside the diagram) involves mainly people, so the number is located well into the circle labelled *People or Animals*. The number 9, "Writers, Artists, and Entertainers," however, is in the area where *People or Animals* and *Information or Ideas* overlap, because while people are involved as the audience, information and ideas are the vital elements of these occupations. For full details of the occupations indicated by the numbered labels, see the table in the next section, entitled ''Matching Yourself with the World of Work.''

Figure 3.1

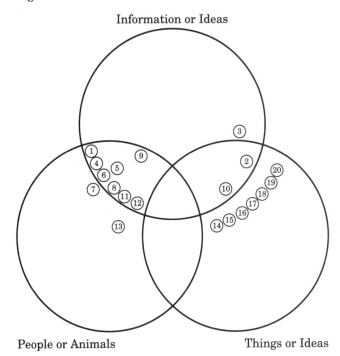

Information or Ideas

People or Animals   Things or Ideas

1 Executive, Administrative, and Managerial
   Occupations
2 Engineers, Surveyors, and Architects
3 Natural Scientists and Mathematicians
4 Social Scientists, Social Workers, Religious Workers,
   and Lawyers
5 Teachers, Counsellors, Librarians, and Archivists
6 Health Diagnosing and Treating Practitioners
7 Registered Nurses, Pharmacists, Dietitians,
   Therapists, and Physician Assistants
8 Health Technologists and Technicians
9 Writers, Artists, and Entertainers
10 Technologists and Technicians Except Health
11 Marketing and Sales Occupations
12 Administrative Support Occupations
13 Service Occupations
14 Agricultural, Forestry, and Fishing Occupations
15 Mechanics and Repairers
16 Electrical and Electronic Equipment Repairers
17 Construction and Extractive Occupations
18 Production Occupations
19 Machine Operators, Tenders, and Set-Up Movers
20 Transportation and Material-Moving Occupations

M A T C H I N G   Y O U R S E L F   W I T H   T H E   W O R L D   O F   W O R K *

▼▼

The following guide was designed to help you compare job characteristics with your interests and skills. Listed and defined are 11 occupational characteristics and requirements that are matched with 200 occupations.

The table can be used in at least three ways. First, if you already have some idea of which occupation you wish to enter, you can use the table to find out the general characteristics of that occupation. Second, if you've decided on a general field of work—such as health or sales—but not on a particular occupation, the table can help you learn about the different jobs in that field. Third, if you haven't thought much about occupations but you do know what skills you have, the table can introduce you to several occupations you might be good at.

One note of caution: The chart can be helpful in organizing occupational information, but it is intended only as a general exploratory tool. Before you eliminate an occupation from consideration because of a single characteristic, you should realize that the job characteristics presented in the table refer only to a typical job in the occupation.

All jobs in an occupation are not alike. Most accountants, for example, work alone, but accountants who are auditors or investigators may work with others. Therefore, if you have an interest in an occupation, you should not disregard that career simply because one or two of its characteristics do not appeal to you. You should check further into the occupation—either through reading or by talking to your counsellor—to find out how particular jobs in the occupation or occupational cluster might match up with your personality, interests, and abilities.

*Melvin Fountain. *Occupational Outlook Quarterly*. Fall 1986. U.S. Department of Labour, Bureau of Statistics.

	1. Leadership/persuasion	2. Helping/instructing others	3. Problem solving/creativity	4. Initiative	5. Work as part of a team	6. Frequent public contact	7. Manual dexterity	8. Physical stamina	9. Hazardous	10. Outdoors	11. Confined
1. Executive, Administrative, and Managerial Occupations											
Managers and Administrators											
Bank officers and managers	•	•	•	•	•	•					•
Health services managers	•	•	•	•	•	•					
Hotel managers and assistants	•	•	•	•	•	•					
School principals and assistant principals	•	•	•	•	•	•					
Management Support Occupations											
Accountants and auditors		•	•		•	•					•
Construction and building inspectors		•	•	•	•		•			•	
Inspectors and compliance officers, except construction		•	•	•	•		•			•	
Personnel, training, and labour relations specialists	•	•	•	•	•	•					
Purchasing agents	•		•		•	•					
Underwriters			•								
Wholesale and retail buyers	•	•	•	•	•						
2. Engineers, Surveyors, and Architects											
Architects			•	•	•	•	•				
Surveyors	•				•		•	•		•	
Engineers											
Aerospace engineers			•	•	•						
Chemical engineers			•	•	•						
Civil engineers			•	•	•						
Electrical and electronics engineers			•	•	•						
Industrial engineers			•	•	•						
Mechanical engineers			•	•	•						
Metallurgical, ceramics, and materials engineers			•	•	•						
Mining engineers			•	•	•						
Nuclear engineers			•	•	•						
Petroleum engineers			•	•	•						

	Job requirements								Work environment		
	1. Leadership/persuasion	2. Helping/instructing others	3. Problem solving/creativity	4. Initiative	5. Work as part of a team	6. Frequent public contact	7. Manual dexterity	8. Physical stamina	9. Hazardous	10. Outdoors	11. Confined
3. Natural Scientists and Mathematicians											
Computer and Mathematical Occupations											
Actuaries			•	•							•
Computer systems analysts	•	•	•	•	•						•
Mathematicians			•	•							
Statisticians			•	•							
Physical Scientists			•	•							
Chemists			•	•							
Geologists and geophysicists			•	•	•					•	
Meteorologists			•	•	•						
Physicists and astronomers			•	•							
Life Scientists											
Agricultural scientists			•	•							
Biological scientists			•	•							
Foresters and conservation scientists		•	•	•	•			•	•	•	
4. Social Scientists, Social Workers, Religious Workers, and Lawyers											
Lawyers	•	•	•	•	•	•					
Social Scientists and Urban Planners											
Economists			•	•							
Psychologists		•	•	•		•					
Sociologists			•	•		•					
Urban and regional planners	•		•	•	•	•					
Social and Recreation Workers											
Social workers	•	•	•	•	•	•					
Recreation workers	•	•	•	•	•	•	•	•		•	
Religious Workers	•	•	•	•	•	•					

	Job requirements								Work environment		
	1. Leadership/persuasion	2. Helping/instructing others	3. Problem solving/creativity	4. Initiative	5. Work as part of a team	6. Frequent public contact	7. Manual dexterity	8. Physical stamina	9. Hazardous	10. Outdoors	11. Confined
5. Teachers, Counsellors, Librarians, and Archivists											
Kindergarten and elementary school teachers	•	•	•	•	•	•	•	•			
Secondary school teachers	•	•	•	•	•	•		•			
Adult and vocational education teachers	•	•	•	•	•	•	•	•			
College and university faculty	•	•	•	•	•	•		•			
Counsellors	•	•	•	•	•	•					
Librarians	•	•	•	•	•	•		•			
Archivists and curators			•	•	•						
6. Health Diagnosing and Treating Practitioners											
Chiropractors	•	•	•	•	•	•	•				
Dentists	•	•	•	•	•	•	•				
Optometrists	•	•	•	•	•	•	•				
Physicians	•	•	•	•	•	•	•				
Podiatrists	•	•	•	•	•	•	•				
Veterinarians	•	•	•	•	•	•	•	•	•		
7. Registered Nurses, Pharmacists, Dietitians, Therapists, and Physician Assistants											
Dietitians and nutritionists	•	•	•	•	•	•					
Occupational therapists	•	•	•	•	•	•	•	•			
Pharmacists	•	•	•	•	•	•					•
Physical therapists	•	•	•	•	•	•	•	•			
Physician assistants	•	•	•	•	•	•	•				
Recreational therapists	•	•	•	•	•	•	•	•		•	
Registered nurses	•	•	•	•	•	•	•	•	•		
Respiratory therapists	•	•	•	•	•	•	•				
Speech pathologists and audiologists	•	•	•	•	•	•					
8. Health Technologists and Technicians											
Clinical laboratory technologists and technicians			•		•		•				•
Dental hygienists		•			•	•	•	•			

	Job requirements								Work environment		
	1. Leadership/persuasion	2. Helping/instructing others	3. Problem solving/creativity	4. Initiative	5. Work as part of a team	6. Frequent public contact	7. Manual dexterity	8. Physical stamina	9. Hazardous	10. Outdoors	11. Confined
Dispensing opticians		•	•	•	•	•	•				
Electrocardiograph technicians		•	•		•	•	•				
Electroencephalographic technologists and technicians		•	•		•	•	•				
Emergency medical technicians	•	•	•	•	•	•	•	•	•	•	
Licensed practical nurses		•			•	•	•	•	•		
Medical record technicians					•						•
Radiologic technologists		•			•	•	•		•		
Surgical technicians		•			•	•	•				
9. Writers, Artists, and Entertainers											
Communications Occupations											
Public relations specialists	•		•	•	•	•					
Radio and television announcers and newscasters	•	•		•	•	•					
Reporters and correspondents	•		•	•	•	•					
Writers and editors	•		•	•	•						
Visual Arts Occupations											
Designers			•	•	•	•	•				
Graphic and fine artists			•	•			•				
Photographers and camera operators			•	•		•	•				
Performing Arts Occupations											
Actors, directors, and producers			•	•	•	•	•	•			
Dancers and choreographers			•	•	•	•	•	•			
Musicians			•	•	•	•	•	•			
10. Technologists and Technicians, Except Health											
Engineering and Science Technicians											
Drafters					•		•				•
Electrical and electronics technicians			•		•		•				
Engineering technicians			•		•		•				

		Job requirements								Work environment		
	1. Leadership/persuasion	2. Helping/instructing others	3. Problem solving/creativity	4. Initiative	5. Work as part of a team	6. Frequent public contact	7. Manual dexterity	8. Physical stamina	9. Hazardous	10. Outdoors	11. Confined
Science technicians			•		•		•				
Other Technicians											
Air traffic controllers		•	•	•	•		•				•
Broadcast technicians			•		•		•				•
Computer programmers			•		•						•
Legal assistants					•						
Library technicians		•			•	•	•				
Tool programmers, numerical control			•				•		•		
11. Marketing and Sales Occupations											
Cashiers		•				•	•				•
Insurance sales representatives	•	•	•	•		•					
Manufacturers' sales representatives	•	•	•	•		•					
Real estate agents and brokers	•	•	•	•		•				•	
Sales representatives	•	•		•		•					
Securities and financial services sales representatives	•	•	•	•		•					
Travel agents	•	•	•	•		•					
Wholesale trade sales representatives	•	•	•	•		•					
12. Administrative Support Occupations, Including Clerical											
Bank tellers						•	•				•
Bookkeepers and accounting clerks						•					•
Computer and peripheral equipment operators			•			•	•				•
Data entry keyers						•	•				•
Mail carriers						•	•	•		•	
Postal clerks						•	•	•			•
Receptionists and information clerks		•				•	•				•
Reservation and transportation ticket agents and travel clerks		•	•			•	•				•
Secretaries, administrative assistants				•		•	•	•			
Statistical clerks						•					•

	1. Leadership/persuasion	2. Helping/instructing others	3. Problem solving/creativity	4. Initiative	5. Work as part of a team	6. Frequent public contact	7. Manual dexterity	8. Physical stamina	9. Hazardous	10. Outdoors	11. Confined
Teacher aides	•	•			•	•	•	•			
Telephone operators		•				•					•
Traffic, shipping, and receiving clerks			•	•	•						
Word processors							•				•
13. Service Occupations											
Protective Service Occupations											
Correction officers	•	•			•			•	•		•
Firefighting occupations		•	•		•	•	•	•	•	•	
Guards						•	•	•	•		•
Police and detectives	•	•	•	•	•	•	•	•	•	•	
Food and Beverage Preparation and Service Occupations											
Bartenders			•			•	•	•			•
Chefs and cooks except short order			•				•	•			•
Waiters and waitresses			•			•	•	•			
Health Service Occupations											
Dental assistants		•			•	•	•	•			
Medical assistants		•			•	•	•		•		
Nursing aides		•			•	•	•	•	•		
Psychiatric aides		•			•	•		•	•		
Cleaning Service Occupations											
Janitors and cleaners								•			
Personal Service Occupations											
Barbers						•	•	•			•
Child care workers	•	•		•		•		•			
Cosmetologists and related workers					•	•	•	•			•
Flight attendants		•			•	•	•	•			
14. Agricultural, Forestry, and Fishing Occupations											
Farm operators and managers	•	•	•	•	•		•	•		•	

			Job requirements							Work environment		
	1. Leadership/persuasion	2. Helping/instructing others	3. Problem solving/creativity	4. Initiative	5. Work as part of a team	6. Frequent public contact	7. Manual dexterity	8. Physical stamina	9. Hazardous	10. Outdoors	11. Confined
15. Mechanics and Repairers											
Vehicle and Mobile Equipment Mechanics and Repairers											
Aircraft mechanics and engine specialists			•		•		•	•	•		
Automotive and motorcycle mechanics			•			•	•	•	•		•
Automotive body repairers			•				•	•	•		•
Diesel mechanics			•			•	•	•	•		•
Farm equipment mechanics			•				•	•	•	•	
Mobile heavy equipment mechanics			•				•	•	•		•
16. Electrical and Electronic Equipment Repairers											
Commercial and electronic equipment repairers			•	•		•	•				
Communications equipment mechanics			•	•		•	•				
Computer service technicians			•	•		•	•				
Electronic home entertainment equipment repairers			•	•		•	•		•		
Home appliance and power tool repairers			•	•		•	•				
Line installers and cable splicers			•		•		•	•	•	•	
Telephone installers and repairers			•		•	•	•	•	•		
Other Mechanics and Repairers											
General maintenance mechanics			•				•		•		
Heating, air-conditioning, and refrigeration mechanics			•				•		•		
Industrial machinery repairers			•				•	•	•		
Millwrights			•				•		•		
Musical instrument repairers and tuners							•				
Office machine and cash register servicers			•	•	•		•				
Vending machine servicers and repairers			•	•			•				
17. Construction and Extractive Occupations											
Construction Occupations											
Bricklayers and stonemasons			•		•		•	•	•	•	

	1. Leadership/persuasion	2. Helping/instructing others	3. Problem solving/creativity	4. Initiative	5. Work as part of a team	6. Frequent public contact	7. Manual dexterity	8. Physical stamina	9. Hazardous	10. Outdoors	11. Confined
	Job requirements								**Work environment**		
Carpenters			•		•		•	•	•	•	
Carpet installers			•		•	•	•	•	•		
Concrete masons and terrazzo workers			•		•		•	•	•	•	
Drywall workers and lathers			•		•		•	•	•		
Electricians			•		•		•	•	•	•	
Glaziers			•		•		•	•	•	•	
Insulation workers			•		•		•	•	•		
Painters and paperhangers			•		•	•	•	•	•	•	
Plasterers			•		•		•	•	•		
Plumbers and pipefitters			•		•	•	•	•	•	•	
Roofers			•		•		•	•	•	•	
Sheet-metal workers			•		•		•	•	•		
Structural and reinforcing metal workers			•		•		•	•	•	•	
Tilesetters			•		•		•	•			
Extractive Occupations											
Roustabouts					•		•	•	•	•	
18. Production Occupations											
Blue-collar worker supervisors	•	•	•	•	•		•		•		
Precision Production Occupations											
Boilermakers			•				•		•		
Bookbinding workers		•			•		•	•	•		•
Butchers and meat-cutters						•	•	•	•		•
Compositors and typesetters							•	•	•		•
Dental laboratory technicians								•			•
Jewellers	•	•	•	•	•	•	•				•
Lithographic and photo-engraving workers		•	•		•		•	•			•
Machinists			•				•	•	•		•
Photographic process workers							•				•

	1. Leadership/persuasion	2. Helping/instructing others	3. Problem solving/creativity	4. Initiative	5. Work as part of a team	6. Frequent public contact	7. Manual dexterity	8. Physical stamina	9. Hazardous	10. Outdoors	11. Confined
									Work environment		
Shoe and leather workers and repairers		•			•	•	•				
Tool-and-die makers			•				•	•	•		•
Upholsterers							•	•			•
Plant and System Operators											
Stationary engineers			•				•	•	•		
Water and sewage treatment plant operators			•	•			•		•	•	
19. Machine Operators, Tenders, and Set-up Workers											
Metal-working and plastic-working machine operators							•	•	•		•
Numerical-control machine-tool operators			•				•	•	•		•
Printing press operators	•		•		•		•	•	•		•
Fabricators, Assemblers, and Handworking Occupations											
Precision assemblers					•		•	•			•
Transportation equipment painters							•	•	•		•
Welders and cutters							•	•	•	•	
20. Transportation and Material-Moving Occupations											
Aircraft pilots			•	•	•		•				•
Bus drivers			•			•	•	•			•
Construction machinery operators			•				•	•	•	•	•
Industrial truck and tractor operators			•				•	•			•
Truck drivers			•				•	•			•
Handlers, Equipment Cleaners, Helpers, and Labourers											
Construction trades helpers					•		•	•	•	•	

As technology brings changes to the workplace, society has an increasing need for a skilled work force. Old jobs become obsolete, and workers must learn new skills and techniques to maintain their employability—the ability to stay employed.

People who leave school early often discover that, once they're out on the job market, they need to expand or strengthen their skills, such as those in mathematics and language, which are very important in today's workplace. Some people discover the need to develop a specific skill or acquire some type of certification if they're to reach their career goals. Other people find that learning to speak a second language can provide them with new opportunities.

Many options exist for people who'd like to obtain further training after they've entered the labour force. Going back to school full-time is the best choice for some people. Others take part-time courses at night or by correspondence. Sources of financial assistance are often available to help pay for further training. Some employers help to cover the cost of training that will enhance an employee's job performance.

Canada Employment Centre counsellors can be of assistance in relation to training and retraining. They also can provide current data about which parts of the labour market need more workers and what type of training is required.

These Employment Centres can also supply information on a full range of the full- and part-time training programs sponsored by the Canadian government. Special programs are in effect for the long-term unemployed, for people facing difficulties re-entering the job market, for people new to the job market, and for people affected by layoffs.

APPRENTICESHIP

Gone are the days when an unskilled person could walk onto a construction site or into a factory and get a decent job. Employers need *skilled* workers, often people with some familiarity with computerized equipment or other high-tech expertise.

The traditional way to learn a skilled trade is apprenticeship. An apprentice is a person who learns a trade or a craft by actually working at it under skilled supervision for a certain length of time.

Every province and territory in Canada offers apprenticeship programs, usually through provincial education, employment, labour, trade, or industry departments. In some provinces, applicants for apprenticeship programs must be 16 and have completed Grade 10. Math is a definite requirement. To find out the entrance requirements and program details in your province, look in the telephone book for the number of your local provincial government information source and call to ask which department administers apprenticeship programs.

To become a skilled worker in a particular occupation often requires an apprenticeship that involves a combination of on-the-job experience and in-school training. Such a program usually takes anywhere from two to five years, but apprentices are paid for both their hours on the job and, if they qualify, for the time spent in school.

The first step to becoming an apprentice is deciding which occupation best matches your interests and goals. Once you've decided this, the next step is to find an employer or union to train you as an apprentice. If you're lucky, you already know someone who could help but, if not, the best idea is to contact your provincial government, as mentioned above.

Once you've connected with the right department, you'll find that counsellors are available who can advise you on apprenticeship opportunities in your area and answer any questions you might have about apprenticeship.

After you've found an employer and completed a copy of the apprenticeship application form, these counsellors are usually able to give you yet more help. For example, they can help you to confirm that you meet the age and educational requirements and whether your schooling and previous work experience entitle you to a shortening of your apprenticeship period or a decreasing of your apprenticeship requirements. They also can help with the administrative work so that you and your employer can sign a formal contract of apprenticeship.

A contract of apprenticeship specifies the hours, terms, and sometimes the wages that apply to your apprenticeship training. It could specify that, over the course of a set period, you're to go to school full-time for a certain length of time and then receive a specified amount of on-the-job training. Or it could outline a "day-release" arrangement, under which you're off the job a certain amount of time each week to attend courses. Another alternative might involve night school or correspondence courses.

Apprenticeship training is divided into periods of time that are measured by the total number of hours the apprentice spends at school and at work. When each period is successfully completed, apprentices usually receive pay increases that reflect their increased knowledge and experience. At the end of the apprenticeship program, after completion of all requirements, the successful apprentice is presented with a Certificate of Apprenticeship that is proof of his or her achievement. This certificate indicates a certain level of skill to prospective employers, and some employers and unions actually require such a certificate before hiring a job applicant. For some trades, you will also be required to write a Certificate of Qualification examination.

Completion of an apprenticeship program is a major step in ensuring employability. Being a member of a skilled, needed profession and knowing that you're fully capable of doing a complex, demanding job also brings great satisfaction. Possessing such skills and capability can lead to other opportunities, such as going into management or setting up your own business. Options in employment are extremely important, and apprenticeship can increase such options.

Based on Ontario Ministry of Skills Development. *Apprenticeship: For careers with a future.*

OTHER EMPLOYMENT OPTIONS

Another way to earn and learn is to join the Canadian Armed Forces. Members of the armed forces learn skills that can be of great value in the civilian job market. Information is available at recruiting offices across Canada.

Many companies have very specific needs and train their own employees or pay the expenses of courses their employees take. Companies sometimes prefer to promote people inside their organization and so are willing to pay these additional expenses.

Some professions have their own educational programs, which guarantee a level of competency in the profession. These professions include accounting, banking, insurance sales and services, nursing, police work, and firefighting. Many professional associations encourage their members to upgrade their skills by providing courses for them.

A current and future trend is based on the concept that learning must be a lifelong concern. Some of the personal pride and financial satisfaction that employees receive from their jobs result from the use of skills they have acquired in training they've received after they entered the workplace.

DEVELOPING AN EDUCATION PLAN

Different jobs require different levels of education and training, as well as different personal characteristics. So, to attain your career goal you must develop an appropriate education plan.

The selection of your education path should be based on your strong points, on the things you do best and the things that interest you most. If you pick an unrealistic education goal you might fail, not because you're inferior but because that goal did not fit with your capabilities and interests. You could then become discouraged and give up, and the work force might lose a valuable worker who was not able to identify where she or he would do the best work. And your hope of a happy, satisfying, and rewarding work life would suffer a severe setback.

Development of a successful education plan begins with taking a good look at yourself—your values, abilities, aptitudes, academic intelligence, interests, and temperament and health.

- **Values**: Your personal beliefs about what is most important to you.
- **Abilities**: Your ease in performing certain tasks.
- **Aptitudes**: Your natural ability in certain areas, such as a mechanical ability, musical talent, etc.
- **Academic intelligence**: Your capacity to handle academic subjects, to solve quickly and accurately problems involving words or figures.
- **Interests**: Your likes and dislikes; the things you enjoy doing and the things you'd like to avoid.
- **Temperament and health**: Your emotional characteristics and state of health could restrict attainment of some goals.

Added to these should be an analysis of other traits that are valuable both at school and at work: ambition, drive, initiative, dependability, endurance, persistence, courtesy, punctuality, tolerance, and the amount of energy you are willing to expend to attain a goal.

6. CAREER FLOW CHART

Prepare a career flow chart by listing the required information under the following headings. Put your name at the top of the chart.

- Three main interests
- Three things I do well
- Three points that describe the way I want to live my life

- Three careers I'm considering
- Three important things I want from a career

CHAPTER SUMMARY EXERCISES

▼▼▼

1. In your notebook write the following statements, supplying the word or phrase that best completes each sentence.

   a) The skills that I want to continue to develop are ___.

   b) The new skills that I want to acquire are ___.

   c) In my first year on the job, I hope to ___.

   d) To ensure that I remain technically competent, I plan to ___.

   e) To ensure that I remain physically fit and in good health, I plan to ___.

   f) My immediate career goal is ___.

   g) An alternative career goal is ___.

2. Select a career that appeals to you but appears to be beyond your reach for educational, financial, physical, or any other reasons. Research in depth the requirements for this career and then write a 500-word essay detailing the requirements. In a summary at the end, state whether this career still seems unattainable or whether you think you could perhaps pursue it. Give your reasons in either case. If you think that you *could* aim for this career after all, list the goals that you would have to set to attain it.

4

Why Work?

O B J E C T I V E S
▼▼▼▼▼▼▼▼▼▼▼▼▼▼▼▼

After completing this chapter you should be able to:

- Explain how work can yield rewards other than money.
- Describe some of the employee characteristics that are valued by employers.
- Discuss which job expectations are the most important to you.
- Define some of the reasons why people work.

I N T R O D U C T I O N
▼▼▼▼▼▼▼▼▼▼▼▼▼▼▼▼▼▼▼▼

You know quite a bit about yourself right now. You know what you like to do and what you don't like to do. You know the tasks that you're good at and those you can't do very well. What do you do with all of this information? You put it to work.

Work is a way to use your abilities in order to learn and produce something of value to the world. Work is also the way to fulfil your needs—from self-satisfaction to a new car. In this chapter you'll investigate why people work, what motivates them, and what satisfies them.

C A S E S T U D Y

They could hardly believe it had been twenty years since high school graduation. There they were, having the type of intense discussion that sometimes occurs between friends, even though they'd lost track of one another over the years.

"There were only three things that I wanted," John was saying. "To get out of school, to get a job, and to get a car. I couldn't have cared less what type of job it was, as long as it paid. I thought I had other things to live for, besides work. I thought if I had a little money, I'd know how to enjoy myself."

"I never saw it that way at all," Keetah replied. "I decided that when I finished high school I was going to look for something useful and interesting to do, something worthwhile. I wasn't going to work just for the sake of working, just to get a pay cheque."

"Are you still into that 'leading a meaningful life' stuff? You must have discovered reality by now!"

"I found a job that gives me some real purpose and is fulfilling. I really feel like I'm accomplishing something important. I feel like I make a difference. I really enjoy using my skills. When I was growing up I never thought work was going to be as enjoyable as it is."

"I've always had an excellent reason to work—I don't like being hungry!"

"A job is a job, no matter how you look at it," said Anne, entering the conversation. "Most people work because they've got to make a living; they've got to earn money."

"But there are other reasons for working," John put in.

"Like what?" challenged Marco.

"Like being with people, or having a chance to be recognized, or accomplishing something, maybe. If you've got the ability to do something, naturally you'll want to do it. I found that out. I guess I'm still not that anxious to talk about it, but three months ago I won a nice chunk of the green stuff in a lottery. I'd always thought I'd quit my job if something like that ever happened. My wife works, we don't have a big mortgage, the kids will be gone in five years . . . "

"So what did you do? Did you quit your job?"

"I quit my job and three weeks later I got it back. I quit during a slow time; I'd been getting bored. But I really missed the people at work. I've been working there for ten years. Now we've made an agreement. I'll get laid off in the slow periods and have more leisure time. We'll see how it works out."

"If you'd said that people work to gain independence, privacy, and respect, I'd agree with you," Akiko added. "A year after I started my first job, I decided to leave my husband. I'd found that I had important skills and talents. The people at work respected my abilities. At first the job was a way to get out of a bad marriage. Then I realized I enjoy having a world that's separate from my private life. I like people not knowing my past. I feel confident and competent when I'm at work."

"In the end, it probably determines how you see yourself and how others see you," said John. "You come to have a very special concept of yourself as a result. If you liked to work for the good of others, you'd think of yourself as a 'people helper.' Or if you were a first-class plumber, you'd see yourself as someone skilled at working with tools and objects and equipment. A situation where you had to fix things would never throw you—but it might throw the 'people-helper' person."

"That's a little too philosophical for me," said Marco. "Really, working is simply a way to keep busy."

"Keeping busy? That's not work," countered Keetah.

"Look," Michel's entry into the conversation was abrupt. "Work is just for one thing: financial security. Period."

"But people work for other reasons," said John. "Jobs can satisfy other needs besides that. For example, our next-door neighbour is an accountant. He was offered a job at much better pay as chief accountant with a larger company, supervising an entire section. He turned it down cold because he preferred the job he was doing and the employer he was with. It's not just a matter of economics."

"And think of all the people who win huge money prizes, yet still keep their jobs. Look at John here," added Keetah.

"They're in a rut," Michel retorted.

"Or the people who've got all the money they need already, but keep working because they enjoy it. Or people who prefer working with their hands even though they could get better pay doing something else."

"Or painters, writers—people who like to create something beautiful."

"But that's not work."

"You know," said Marco, "in a way it's like any game you play as kids. You want to exercise your muscles and your mind—just for the fun of it."

"But that's not work either."

"Well, then, just what do you mean by 'work'?"

Adapted from Ontario Ministry of Education. *Work and Employability Skills Program,* 1982, pp. 11-12.

QUESTIONS

1. List five different reasons the former classmates gave for working.

2. What is your definition of work?

1. WORK ATTITUDES

In your notebook, answer "Yes" or "No" to each of the following questions.

1. Do you have a willingness and desire to learn new skills and new ways of doing things?

2. Are you neat in your personal appearance and work habits?

3. Are you punctual?

4. Can you apply yourself to a job without being easily bored or distracted?

5. Can you adapt to new and unexpected situations easily?

6. Can you work under pressure without becoming overly nervous and upset?

7. Are you aware of your strengths and weaknesses?

8. Are you emotionally stable, capable of taking things in stride?

9. Have you enough initiative to be able to work on your own?

10. Are your job plans in keeping with your own capacities and with the job market?

11. Do you have a sense of duty and responsibility?

12. Are you reliable? Can you be depended on to do a satisfactory job?

13. Can you gain the friendship and respect of co-workers?

14. Can you co-operate with co-workers?

15. Can you co-operate with supervisors and managers?

16. Can you follow directions willingly, asking questions when necessary?

17. Can you understand instructions and carry them out properly?

18. Do you ask questions when instructions are unclear?

19. Can you accept criticism without feeling hurt?

20. Can you work without constant supervision?

21. Can you complete a job once you start it?

22. Are you pleasant, friendly, and congenial? Do you like people?

THE RIGHT MENTAL ATTITUDE

By now you must realize that it's important to have the right mental attitude if you're going to attain your goal of finding a satisfying job. You have to be positive about yourself and your choice.

Many of us want to learn from our jobs. We strive to improve ourselves; otherwise we would come to a standstill. To learn, you have to be eager and you have to demonstrate this eagerness to others. If others know that you want to learn and that you do the best you can, they'll be co-operative. Soon you'll not only feel good about your job, but also about the people with whom you're involved. Work will provide you with many benefits if you have the right mental attitude.

FREQUENT COMMENTS FROM DISSATISFIED EMPLOYERS

1. Applicants not really interested in working—applying only to ensure that unemployment benefits are not cut off.

2. Frequently late.

3. Feel they should be able to work when they want, not the hours the business needs them.

4. Negative attitude about working in general.

5. Feel they're worth more than they are.

6. Expect too much from the employer.

7. Can't fill in application forms.

8. Can't sell self to employer.

9. Unreliable—can't depend on them.

10. Immature attitude.

11. Expect too-high salaries.

12. Can't take criticism or supervision.

13. Poor academic basics—particularly math and spelling.

14. Sloppy in appearance and work habits.

15. Can't accept responsibility.

16. Lack initiative.

17. Feel they're always overworked—want a job but don't want to work.

18. Transient—finish training then leave.

19. View job as a resting place—better than having no job—and then move to something else.

Adapted from a survey done by the Mirror Unemployment Youth Centre, London, Ontario, 1977. Five hundred London employers participated.

2. "FREQUENT COMMENTS FROM DISSATISFIED EMPLOYERS" QUESTIONS

1. What might result if an employee can't take criticism or accept supervision?

2. What do you think it means to say that some employees feel they're worth more than they are?

3. How would a mature attitude be valuable on the job?

4. Why might employers be dissatisfied with employees who can't accept responsibility?

5. Why do you think employers appreciate employees with initiative?

BASIC CHARACTERISTICS OF A GOOD EMPLOYEE

The following is a list of the basic characteristics of a good employee.

1. *Consistency:* To behave and make decisions in ways that are reasonably consistent with your values and goals.

2. *Commitment:* To demonstrate to your co-workers a sense of duty, commitment, and respect for the area of endeavour you've chosen.

3. *Competence:* To demonstrate a level of competency within your chosen area of study or work.

4. *Creativity:* To go beyond consistency, commitment, and competence and use your imagination.

5. *Self-Control:* To experience emotions such as joy, fear, and anger at a reasonable level of intensity, proportional to the situation.

3. EXAMPLE OF A GOOD EMPLOYEE

Choose an occupation that interests you and write a description of what you think would be the characteristics of a good employee in this occupation.

4. CAREER ASSIGNMENT

Interview a friend, relative, or someone whose career or job is closely related to your choice of career and prepare a report on the responses you receive. Try to choose someone with more than two years' experience.

Ask him or her for advice and opinions on matters that are of interest to you. The following questions are merely suggestions; it's not necessary that you ask these exact questions.

1. What schooling do you have?

2. Do you feel that this education is adequate for your present job? If not, what additional training is desirable?

3. How long have you been in your present job?

4. What additional training, other than high school, did you acquire for this position?

5. What was your starting salary on your very first job?

6. Since you first started working in this field, by what percentage has your salary increased?

7. What personal attributes do you feel are necessary for your type of work?

8. What are some of the disagreeable aspects of your job?

9. How would you rate the following personal characteristics in order of importance for success at your job?
    a) attitude   c) appearance   e) co-operation
    b) skill   d) punctuality   f) dependability

10. What are your specific duties or areas of responsibility?

11. What particular aspect of your work gives you the most pleasure?

12. To what do you attribute your success?

13. What other careers or fields of work can you branch out into with this work background?

14. What advice can you offer about obtaining employment in this field?

15. Can you provide me with any additional information?

Based on Ontario Ministry of Education. *Work and Employability Skills Program*, 1982, pp. 24-26.

CHAPTER SUMMARY EXERCISES
▼▼▼

1. What will a job do for you? If you make the wrong choice, a job might not do much for you—in fact, it might make you very unhappy. That's why, when making job choices, it's very important to take into consideration the things you've learned about yourself.

    Your job should make you feel like "somebody." For many people a job gives a sense of identity; it makes them feel as though they have something to offer. At the same time, a job should provide you with something interesting to do and with the money to buy things you need and want.

Below is a list of expectations that many people have about jobs. Decide the importance of each to you and rank them in your notebook, using the following key.

A = Most Important   B = Very Important   C = Somewhat Important
D = Least Important

a) Good pay
b) Job security
c) Promotion possibilities
d) Good working conditions
e) Interesting work
f) Company loyalty to employees

g) Feedback from supervisor
h) Full appreciation for efforts
i) Sympathetic help with personal problems
j) Feeling of being "in" on things

2. Obtain their definitions of work from ten of your classmates. Then prepare a report summarizing the results of your interviews. Do most of them have the same attitude or did each give a different definition? How does the definition given by the majority of your classmates compare with your definition of work?

Occupational Trends

O B J E C T I V E S
▼▼▼▼▼▼▼▼▼▼▼▼▼▼▼▼

After completing this chapter you should be able to:

- Discuss the employment factors in Canada that are changing the job market.

- Explain why people should be prepared to change careers.

- Understand why it is important to obtain as much education as possible.

- List some jobs and skills that are predicted to be in demand in the future.

I N T R O D U C T I O N
▼▼▼▼▼▼▼▼▼▼▼▼▼▼▼▼▼▼

The numbers and types of jobs and careers available to job seekers of the 1990s and beyond will be the result of many forces of change in Canadian society. Changes in employment factors are difficult to predict, but some indications can be identified by looking at the past.

A C H A N G I N G P O P U L A T I O N
▼▼▼▼▼▼▼▼▼▼▼▼▼▼▼▼▼▼▼▼▼▼▼▼▼▼▼▼

After World War II, there was a dramatic increase in the number of children born—a "baby boom." This was followed by a period of fewer births in the late 1960s and 1970s, but in the 1980s the baby boomers started having babies themselves and the birth rate began to increase again.

What do these population changes mean for job seekers in the future? One implication is that job opportunities should be greater for people born in the late 1960s and 1970s because of their fewer numbers. On the other hand, the generation of baby boomers faced, and are still facing, much more job competition because of their greater numbers. Because these baby boomers make up such a large proportion of Canada's population, the country is experiencing an "aging" phenomenon—there are more older people than young people. And, due to improved health and medical provisions, these baby boomers are expected to live longer than their parents, which will result eventually in a population in which seniors will outnumber younger people. And, as mandatory retirement policies are relaxed, more of these seniors will choose to work until a later age—another factor that increases competition in the workplace.

TECHNOLOGICAL CHANGE
▼▼▼▼▼▼▼▼▼▼▼▼▼▼▼▼▼▼▼▼▼▼▼▼▼▼▼▼▼▼▼▼▼▼▼▼

Another factor that affects occupational trends is technology, which changes the way society is structured and functions. What would life be like if no one had a car or a telephone? Technological advances have made tasks that were previously impossible a reality and have created easier, safer, and more efficient ways of accomplishing many other tasks. For example, technology has eliminated many jobs that were routine, dangerous, or damaging to people's mental or physical health.

Yet some people are afraid of technology and the changes it brings. They hear of jobs being eliminated or restructured because of automation and are afraid that this will happen to them. For others, who are ready and willing to change with the times, technology has meant new opportunities, because every advance is accompanied by a demand for people to work with it, or to sell, repair, maintain, build, or improve the equipment involved.

Also, at one time, almost all business had to have certain types of locations to guarantee success. Now, computer links and related technological advances have made it possible for many businesses to be located in remote, less expensive areas and still maintain the necessary communications contacts. And for people living in those areas, where perhaps employment opportunities were previously limited, new jobs are made available, particularly for people who have kept in step with the times.

We're living in a time when information is a major product and, unlike in the production of hard goods, people who are information workers don't always have to go to a particular building to do their jobs. With the aid of telecommunications technology, almost anyone with a computer and telephone can work at home. This is called *telecommuting* and many people like the advantages it provides: avoiding the stress and cost of commuting to work; being at home to care for the family; reducing the cost of a wardrobe; and working at one's own pace and at times of the day that best suit the person. For parents and handicapped people in particular, telecommuting is a valuable option.

To keep pace with technology, you must be prepared to continue to learn new skills throughout your work life. Only in this way will you remain employable in our rapidly changing times.

ECONOMIC IMPACTS
▼▼▼▼▼▼▼▼▼▼▼▼▼▼▼▼▼▼▼▼▼▼▼▼▼▼▼▼▼▼▼▼▼

Better and cheaper communications technology continue to make the world a smaller place, and there are strong indications that businesses will be smaller also. Predictions are that much of the employment in the next decade will be generated by small and medium-sized businesses instead of multinational corporations.

Employment opportunities in small businesses usually require people to be flexible and have a broad base of skills to handle a wider range of responsibilities. Good communication and interpersonal skills are always important, and speaking more than one language is often an advantage.

FIVE GUIDELINES
FOR JOB SUCCESS
▼▼▼▼▼▼▼▼▼▼▼▼▼▼▼▼▼▼▼▼▼▼▼▼▼▼

1. **Take advantage of your educational opportunities**: According to 1987 statistics, young people who didn't finish high school were twice as likely to be unemployed as those who had finished twelve or thirteen years of schooling. Twenty percent of young people who didn't finish high school were unemployed. Those with post-secondary education were most likely to be employed.

   The number of job openings for people with lower levels of education is declining every year, while the demand for highly skilled workers is rising. It is estimated that, in the 1990s, almost two-thirds of all new jobs will require more than twelve years of education and training.

   Statistics source: Public Affairs and Youth Affairs, Employment and Immigration Canada. *A National Stay-In-School Initiative,* 1990.

2. **Take as many math courses as possible**: Having a comprehensive math background increases your choices of further training, because math is a prerequisite for many fields of study. Although machines can be used for calculations, it's people who input the required formulas and who must possess the logical thought patterns that result from math studies.

3. **Maintain a balance between general and career education**: Specializing in one area does not mean neglecting everything else. It is estimated that, out of the estimated five jobs today's graduate will hold throughout his or her career, four have not yet been invented. A general academic background will assure an employer that the person has an alert mind and good written and oral skills.

   The job market of the 1990s will require versatility, constant retraining, and even the ability to switch from one profession to another as some jobs disappear and new ones are created. These qualities are possible only with a solid educational base.

4. **Aim for the top**: More than ever, those with outstanding qualities will be on top. Where there are many job openings, there will also be numerous candidates. Employers will be very selective and, after screening, will make their choices based on the experience each candidate has gained throughout her or his education, indicating the person's resourcefulness and maturity.

5. **Be prepared to relocate:** For the sake of your future, you must be prepared to change your geographic location if necessary, to go where the jobs are. In some cases this might necessitate a move to a larger metropolitan area, but in others a smaller community might be indicated. In some fields, the lack of services available in isolated communities might ensure better job opportunities than are available in major centres, which might be oversaturated with specialists. Also, because of the flexibility afforded by sophisticated telecommunications link-ups, many businesses are setting up operations in outlying areas, taking advantage of less expensive real estate. For the same reason, workers in information

fields might choose less populated areas in which to live and then telecommute via computer.

Adapted from Quebec Ministry of Education. *Canal-ISEP*. "The Jobs of 1990."

T E N   W I N N I N G   J O B   O P T I O N S

▼▼▼▼▼▼▼▼▼▼▼▼▼▼▼▼▼▼▼▼▼▼▼▼▼▼▼▼▼▼▼▼▼▼▼▼

What should you study to better your chances of getting a good job? Where are the best jobs going to be? What are the most promising careers?

Current indications are that the most promising employment fields are in high-technology sectors, such as aerospace and aeronautics, agriculture and food sciences, biotechnology, business and office administration, engineering and physics, environmental science, health sciences, micro-electronics and computer science, telecommunications, and transportation. And, of course, in addition to the specialized occupations that exist in the technical fields, many sales and office support jobs are also available.

AEROSPACE AND AERONAUTICS

AEROSPACE

The aerospace industry includes the design of structures and systems for use in space, including telecommunications, robotics, and remote sensing. Canada is a leader in the field of remote sensing, in particular in the engineering of satellites that orbit the earth in a matter of minutes, sending back information on many subjects including new sources of pollution, soil conditions, icebergs in shipping lanes, military installations, etc. This field is presently experiencing a drastic shortage of systems (software) engineers, the people who evolve the overall design of the system and analyse how the components of the system relate to each other, at which point programmers take over. Good prospects are indicated for this field for many years to come.

Educational Information

University Level:
Mechanical or electrical engineering; some universities offer programs or courses specifically designed for systems (software) engineers.

College Level:
Electronic technology.

AERONAUTICS

In the aeronautics industry, aeronautical engineers are much in demand in the areas of design, testing, production, and development of new products related to aircraft.

Educational Requirements

University Level:
An option in aeronautics is offered in mechanical engineering programs.

College Level:
Aeronautical technicians are involved in the testing of prototypes, development of production methods, and servicing, operation, and maintenance of the finished products. College courses that are applicable are mechancial and electrical technology.

AGRICULTURE AND FOOD SCIENCES

The packaged food used by astronauts might be an indication of the diet of the future. One thing is certain: by the twenty-first century the world will be faced with a serious food shortage due to the limited supply of arable land. Will we have the resources to feed a population of more than seven billion?

Maximum exploitation of land becomes all the more imperative as arable land becomes increasingly scarce. More research is required. It will be up to agronomists (people skilled in the science of farm land management and crop production) to find solutions to this problem, and in order to do so they will need some knowledge of biotechnology.

The production of food without the application of harmful chemicals and pesticides, in a way that is environmentally safe, is a priority with consumers and producers.

Educational Information

University Level:
Courses in agriculture and food sciences include agricultural engineering, agricultural economics, bioagronomy, food science and consumer services.

College Level: (Some courses also offered at university level)

Agricultural hydrology relates to water control (drainage and irrigation), soil development, and building construction, with a view to obtaining maximum crop yield.

Agricultural mechanics involves the installation, repair, operation, and maintenance of agricultural equipment.

Dairy technology is the analysis of dairy products and their by-products for quality control, ensuring the hygiene of the production facility.

Farm management trains qualified farm workers, specialized farmers, and managers of agricultural enterprises.

Food management technology includes the analysis, control, processing, preservation, and marketing of all food products except milk.

Horticulture is the cultivation of fruits and vegetables.

Industrial food science engineering involves ensuring that instructions from industrial engineers or agronomists specialized in food supplies are properly carried out, and supervision of personnel in food preparation and equipment maintenance.

Ornamental horticulture includes landscaping and development (planning, design modification, creation), production (planting, protection, fertilization, maintenance), floral design, and marketing.

Public health technology focusses on the protection of human health, including occupational health, the prevention and control of contagious diseases, etc. The public health technologist inspects primary products as well as factories and businesses that produce food for humans.

Zootechny (animal husbandry) is the management, breeding, feeding, and reproduction of farm animals.

BIOTECHNOLOGY

Recent progress in the study of cellular and molecular biology, combined with a better understanding of the particular characteristics of micro-organisms, has brought us to the threshold of a technological revolution. Biotechnology will have a strong impact on a number of fields, particularly agriculture, energy, environment, food, industrial chemistry, and mining.

Biotechnology is the use of a biological process in order to produce goods and services. Biotechnology involves the use of micro-organisms and their components. It is used in a large number of fields: the agricultural, forestry, pharmaceutical, and pulp and paper industries all depend directly on biotechnology on a short-term basis.

Agricultural applications include inexpensive diagnostic tests to spot diseases that are potentially dangerous to humans and animals; genetically engineered vaccines that are safe and effective; growth hormones to increase milk yield, reduce fat in meat, and bring poultry to market more quickly; and fertility hormones and other techniques that will lead to more births of higher-quality livestock.

Cellular fusion technology helps develop new plants or ones that are more resistant to disease or unfavourable growth conditions. Developments in this field will greatly influence the future of agriculture and forestry.

Enzyme technology makes it possible to accelerate industrial chemical reactions while saving time and energy, thereby increasing productivity.

Genetic technology permits the manufacturing of drugs (e.g., interferon, insulin, growth hormones), the conversion of sugars, and the use of substances such as yeasts.

Recycling and reprocessing waste materials is another area in which biotechnology is used. Techniques to make material soluble through the use of bacteria are absolutely necessary to deal with mountains of mining refuse. Waste disposal techniques will be altered through the work of biotechnologists.

Biotechnology is an interdisciplinary science and a need is indicated for all types of engineers, especially those in mechanical, electronic, and chemical engineering.

Educational Information

Biotechnologists need a basic background in organic chemistry, biochemistry, biology, and microbiology, normally acquired through a university or college bioscience program. Additional training is currently acquired on the job.

Technical support staff are often community college graduates in biochemical technology or university science graduates. Professional support staff generally have a Ph.D. degree with a biotechnological orientation.

University Level:
Engineering disciplines, chemistry, biochemistry, biology, microbiology.

College Level:
Industrial chemical technology, data processing, pulp and paper technology, natural science technology, mineral technology.

BUSINESS AND OFFICE ADMINISTRATION

Today's highly automated offices require skilled information workers at all levels, for administration and support services. Computer applications have eliminated many low-end clerical jobs, and the remaining jobs generally demand a higher level of education, good interpersonal skills, and a level of computer literacy. As Canada's aging population increases, a greater demand for financial and insurance services in particular is predicted.

Educational Information

University Level:
Courses include accounting, actuarial science, business administration, business management, computer science, finance, human resource management, marketing.

College Level:
College-level courses include accounting, basic finance programs, basic human resource management, computer programs, documentation technology, general business administration, industrial management, insurance, marketing, records management, office administration, and real estate appraisal (also requires completion of some university courses).

ENGINEERING AND PHYSICS

The role of professional engineers, who are specialists in applied science, is to transform scientific discoveries into practical applications. Engineering is divided into the following main disciplines: civil, mining, metallurgical, chemical, electrical, mechanical, industrial, geological, and engineering physics.

Educational Information

University Level:
To enter an engineering school, students need to have a background in mathematics, physics, and chemistry, up to the Grade 13 level.

College Level:
College-level technical programs are also available for those who want to become technologists or technicians in engineering fields.

ENVIRONMENTAL SCIENCE

With the growing concern for our environment and tougher environmental protection legislation being enacted, more products and services will be needed by industry and municipalities to recycle waste material, control pollution in waterways, and restore damaged ecosystems.

Educational Information

University Level:
Courses available include agrology, agronomy, biochemistry, biology, chemistry, engineering (many types), forestry, microbiology, and urban planning.

College Level:
Courses include data processing, forestry technology, industrial chemical technology, land survey, mineral technology, natural resource technology, natural science technology, pulp and paper technology, and water and air purification technology.

HEALTH SCIENCES

The baby boom that occurred in Canada after World War II has resulted in a population that has more older people than younger ones. In addition, Canadians are living longer. Since the need for medical and rehabilitation services increases with age, job opportunities are excellent in the field of health sciences.

Educational Information

University Level:
University-level training is required for audiologists, chiropractors, dentists, dietitians, doctors, naturopaths, nurses (college-level diploma also available), occupational therapists, pharmacists, physiotherapists, podiatrists, speech therapists, and veterinarians (much in demand due to the popularity of domestic animals).

College Level:
College courses are available for cytogenetic technologists, dental assistants, dental hygienists, dental technicians, dental therapists, dispensing opticians, health record technicians, medical laboratory technologists, nuclear medicine technologists, nursing assistants, prosthetic/orthotic technicians, radiotherapy technicians, and respiratory technologists.

This is by no means a complete list of health-care professions. Medical technology is becoming increasingly more complex and new occupations are frequently created. Most courses for health-care professions require high school science and mathematics courses.

MICRO-ELECTRONICS AND COMPUTER SCIENCE

The increasing application of computer technology to all fields has led to the importance of the creation, production, and processing of information being at least as great as that of raw materials. Most companies are or will become computerized. Almost every job has in one way or another been influenced by computer science, whether the field is researching, teaching, manufacturing, management, or marketing. Office automation, telecommunications, and computer-assisted design (CAD) have become commonplace, and robotics have changed manufacturing systems.

Electronic engineers are needed to design new equipment (hardware), and *computer hardware specialists* to install, maintain, and repair computers.

Computer programmers write the instructions (programs) that operate the computer to perform a specific task.

Applications programmers write, test, and evaluate computer programs.

Systems analysts design the data processing systems for specific companies or institutions.

Technical writers write the manuals that assist computer users.

Educational Information

University Level:
University courses include computer science, applied computer science engineering, and electronics engineering.

College Level:
College-level courses include two- and three-year programs for the following careers: computer applications programmers, computer graphics specialists, computer hardware specialists, computer programmers, data processors, systems analysts, and telecommunications specialists.

TELECOMMUNICATIONS

The nerve centre of the modern world, the science of telecommunications is an extension of micro-electronics and computer science and is expected to develop considerably up to the end of this century. Canada has been a leader in telecommunications. Our society, like most other societies, gravitates around an electronic network consisting of cables and communications satellites that link homes, offices, and factories.

Educational Information

University Level:
Much of communications engineering is related to the fields of micro-electronics and computer technology. Communications engineering is usually offered only at the Master's level.

College Level:
College-level courses are available in computer telecommunications. Many telecommunications companies train their own employees.

TRANSPORTATION

This field is vast and complex: passenger, merchandise, urban, rural, air, rail, on wheels or water. It includes the design, manufacture, and management of transportation systems. Ways of improving all forms of transportation are constantly being researched, to reduce noise, use less energy, and increase efficiency.

Educational Information

University Level:
Programs include transportation engineering, a program often integrated with civil engineering, and physical, mechanical, aeronautical, and electronical engineering. Universities also offer systems and instrumentation engineering.

College Level:
Several college courses are related to transportation, such as aeronautics, data processing, mechanical technology, cartographic and geodesic technologies, and transportation technology.

Adapted from Quebec Ministry of Education. *Canal-ISEP*. "The Jobs of 1990."

FIVE PRACTICAL SUGGESTIONS

1. **Ensure your employability**. Develop broad, transferable skills such as interpersonal skills (being able to interact well with clients and co-workers, both orally and in writing); knowledge of computers and their applications; decision-making, problem-solving, and interpretation skills; and use of common sense and good judgment.

2. **Take the time to prepare for your career**. Get as much education as you can, and become as diversified as possible. Try to include mathematics, computer science, economics, and humanities courses in your regular program.

3. **Be practical**. The era of free choice is over and it's now a matter of striking a balance between your main interests and your need to make a living. If the job prospects are not good for your preferred occupation, review related fields carefully. You should be able to identify some occupation that will give you a satisfying career and then, in your free time, you could pursue your main interests. Examine a specific career from all angles before you make a decision, particularly job prospects, working conditions, salary, and opportunities for advancement.

4. **Avoid gender stereotypes.** Women should not be afraid to pursue a traditionally male-oriented career, such as electrotechnology, engineering, or police technology.

5. **Learn a second language.** Being able to read and write a second language gives you an extra edge on the job market.

Based on Quebec Ministry of Education. *Canal-ISEP*. "The Jobs of 1990."

C H A P T E R   S U M M A R Y   E X E R C I S E S

▼▼

1. Why is it important to have math skills for the jobs of today?

2. Why should people be prepared to change careers?

3. List five guidelines for job success.

4. List the ten fields in which job prospects appear to be encouraging.

5. You have a low-paying, unskilled job. List five steps that you could take to obtain employment in a higher-paying, skilled area.

2

The Job Search

INTRODUCTION
▼▼▼▼▼▼▼▼▼▼▼▼▼▼▼▼▼▼▼▼

In today's job market you need an edge to get a job. It's not enough to have the skills and qualifications for a job—you need to be able to find and convince employers that you should be hired. Unit 2 will take you through the job search process step by step: locating job prospects, gathering personal information, preparing résumés, writing covering letters, and having interviews.

6

Locating Job Prospects

OBJECTIVES
▼▼▼▼▼▼▼▼▼▼▼▼▼▼

After completing this chapter you should be able to:

• Identify sources of job information.

• Explain some common abbreviations used in job advertisements.

• Analyse job advertisements to see if they match your qualifications and meet your requirements.

INTRODUCTION
▼▼▼▼▼▼▼▼▼▼▼▼▼▼▼▼▼▼▼▼

Thousands of people are unemployed across the country, but there are also thousands of job vacancies. Every day the job situation changes: people are promoted, transferred, offer their resignations, get fired, or die. An average of 4% of all jobs are always available. New jobs are created because of the establishment, expansion, or reorganization of businesses. Even in periods of high unemployment, vacancies exist.

To find a job, you need to discover where these vacancies are. Your first reaction might be to look in the help-wanted section of a newspaper, but it's a well-known fact that many jobs are not advertised because they are filled by personal referrals. Making personal contact with employers, whether by telephone, letter, or in person, will uncover job possibilities not found in the newspaper or through employment services. Figure 6.1 on the next page shows the results of one survey on how most jobs were found.

SOURCES OF JOB INFORMATION
▼▼▼▼▼▼▼▼▼▼▼▼▼▼▼▼▼▼▼▼▼▼▼▼▼▼▼▼▼▼▼▼▼▼▼▼▼▼▼

Employment and Immigration Canada: The federal government operates Canada Employment Centres across the country to assist workers to find jobs and to assist employers to find employees. Job seekers should register at their local Employment Centres. Lists of available local jobs are displayed there, along with lists of job openings across Canada.

When you go to an Employment Centre, a representative will give you a form to complete and then will ask some questions about your job preferences. Have a look at the job openings posted on the bulletin boards. If something suits you, the representative will give you the telephone number and/or address so that you can contact the employer. If nothing suitable is available, the representative will file your application and give you a call when something comes up.

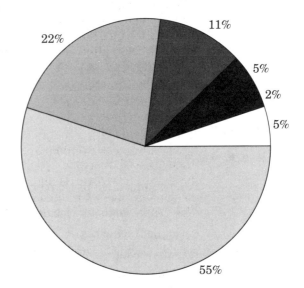

Figure 6.1 Sources of employment identified by young people

11%

5%

2%

5%

22%

55%

☐ Personal contacts (friends, family, acquaintances)
☐ Approaching an employer directly
▨ Through advertisements
■ Through a Canada Employment Centre
■ Through a private employment agency
☐ Other

Source: Canadian Youth Foundation. *Canada's Youth "Ready for Today."* Canadian Gallup Organization, 1985.

Provincial and Municipal Government Employment Services: Government is the largest employer in the country, and there are usually many jobs available.

Friends, Relatives, Neighbours, Acquaintances: Word of mouth is still one of the best ways to locate jobs. Let people know you're looking for employment. They might know of job openings or can give you advice about who might be hiring. Obtain all the information you can and then follow it up. Remember to thank people for their help, particularly when you've been successful.

Former Employers: Depending on the reasons for your leaving, former employers might be glad to welcome you back.

Newspaper Help-Wanted Section: It's important to check the advertisements every day and to answer all appropriate advertisements. Be prompt, because many employers stop accepting applications once they have a reasonable number of suitable applicants.

Newspaper Business Section: If new businesses are opening in your area or if a business is expanding, it's often reported by the local media. These businesses might be hiring new employees.

Group Job Search Programs: You might be interested in participating in a job search program if one is available in your community. Trained personnel assist participants in organizing their job search. Moral support from group leaders and fellow participants has helped many participants to succeed in finding employment.

Private Employment Agencies: Employers pay these agencies to locate and screen prospective employees. You register with the agency, usually complete tests that indicate your skills, and are then contacted if an appropriate job opening is available. For best results, you should be able to specify the type of job you want. Be ready to go for interviews on short notice. Some agencies also charge job applicants a fee, so be sure to check this out.

Some of these agencies also are commissioned by companies to locate and screen both skilled and semi-skilled temporary workers. Working as a temporary or part-time employee could provide a source of income while you look for a full-time job. You would also be gaining experience and using your job skills.

Union Offices of Various Trades: Hiring for jobs in some fields is done through union hiring halls. These jobs are available only to people who belong to the particular union.

Business Directories: It might be possible to obtain a directory of businesses in your area from the library or from a local or regional business development organization. There is sometimes a charge for these directories; however, these lists could give you important information about a business, such as the name of the owner, the number of employees, and the products produced. This can give you an idea of which companies need your particular skills.

Journals, Trade Papers, and Magazines: Consult your local library for these specialized publications. Look in the classified sections for job possibilities.

Help-Wanted Notices Posted in Public Buildings: Study public bulletin boards carefully.

Plants and Factories in Industrial Areas: In one day, you could canvass a dozen or more prospective employers.

Construction Sites: Job-opening notices are sometimes posted at building sites.

New Office Buildings, Shopping Centres, and Factories: Workers are usually needed, including security guards, word processors, clerks, secretaries, computer personnel, and sometimes managers. Three or four suitable jobs might be available in one new office building alone.

Yellow Pages of the Telephone Book: Prospective employers can be found by looking in the Yellow Pages under various services and products related to the field in which you want to work.

Companies that Hire Temporary or Part-Time Personnel: Contact taxi companies, security services, and office cleaning companies if this is the type of employment that you want. Full-time jobs also are often available.

Based on Ontario Ministry of Education. *Work and Employability Skills Program.* Senior Division. 1982, p. 28.

1. UNDERSTANDING JOB ADVERTISEMENT ABBREVIATIONS

Many newspapers use abbreviations to save space in their job-offer ads. Below is a list of abbreviations that are often used. In your notebook, write down each abbreviation and then supply the definition of it.

1.	appt.	9.	eqpt.	17.	mgr.
2.	apt.	10.	exp.	18.	min.
3.	ASAP	11.	ext.	19.	p.t.
4.	asst.	12.	hqtrs.	20.	refs.
5.	bldg.	13.	hrly.	21.	rep.
6.	const.	14.	hvy.	22.	temp.
7.	c.v.	15.	inf.	23.	trnee.
8.	dept.	16.	K	24.	wk.

2. ANALYSING THE JOB ADVERTISEMENTS

Answer the following questions about the job advertisements in Figure 6.2.

1. Which job offers would you respond to with a letter?

2. Which job requires the use of more than one language?

3. Which jobs would definitely require working nights? Which jobs would probably require working nights?

4. Which jobs do you think would require heavy physical work?

5. Which job ad asks for the most education?

6. Which jobs do you think would require computer experience?

7. Which jobs require a résumé?

8. Which job ads don't ask for experience?

9. If all of the jobs were in your region, which jobs would you apply for?

3. EXTRACTING INFORMATION FROM JOB ADVERTISEMENTS

Consult one of your local newspapers to find an advertisement for a job that fits in each of the following categories. Write the name of each category in your notebook and then use the information in the advertisement to answer the questions that follow the list of categories.

- Office and Sales (secretary, administrative assistant, clerk, computer operator, salesclerk, sales representative)
- Mechanical and Industrial Services (mechanic, shop foreman, engineer)
- Medical and Food Services (nurse, nursing assistant, doctor, X-ray or lab personnel, cashier, server)
- Personal Services (counsellor, lawyer, teacher)

1. What is the job title?

2. What qualifications does the job require?

3. Whom are you supposed to contact regarding the job?

4. How are you supposed to contact the prospective employer (in person, by telephone, by letter, etc.).

CHAPTER SUMMARY EXERCISES

▼▼

1. This survey is designed to provide information about the way in which you look for a job. Picture yourself in each of the situations described on page 62 and indicate how likely it is that you would respond in the described manner. If you have never searched for a job before, answer according to how you think you'd respond. Write the letter of each statement in your notebook and then put beside it the letter in the following key that best describes your response to each statement.

A = Very Unlikely   B = Unlikely   C = Likely   D = Very Likely

Figure 6.2   Samples of help-wanted ads

Bilingual Person Friday/18K plus
Distribution centre seeking someone energetic and well organized to work in conjunction with sales department and warehouse. Requirements: Bilingual (excellent English and French grammar), word processing (WordPerfect), knowledge of inventory control. Renumeration based on exp. Fringe benefits. Send résemé to C.G. Industrial Products, 564 boulevard Felix, Montreal, PQ H4L 1J5.

wanted. Northern BC and AB, spring & fall. Call 1-604-582-5660 before Monday, Feb. 26th.

Ambitious individual required by plastics products manufacturer. Experienced in use of power tools (precision work). Responsibilities include estimating, planning production, and dealing with customers by phone. For interview, call 842-2714.

Full-time job opportunity available with prominent retail store chain. Many positions open for present & future stores. Candidates with some exp., please call Michele, 854-7831.

Shop Foreperson
Dynamic automobile dealership requires an enthusiastic leader and motivator of people. Applicants must be able to diagnose electronic components and must have a thorough knowledge of EFI/fuel systems. We offer top salary, bonus, and company car. Refs. required. Send c.v. to: The Star, Dept 274, P.O. Box 2000, Dominion Place, Hamilton, ON L3V 5A8

Data Entry

Experienced individual needed for data entry in order-processing department of modern textile operation. Conscientiousness and intelligence are prime assets. Send résumé (including inputting speed) to: Dorcas Creations, 654 Leonard St., Winnipeg, MB R4H 3H8, Attention: Mr. G. Santori.

Servers
Original fast-food concept requires dynamic, serious personnel; must be available immediately. Hrly. salary and performance bonus. Flexible schedule. Apply in person ASAP at 594 Main St. E., 1 p.m., Mon.-Wed.

Exp. dependable person responsible for cleaning team in office complex, east end, night shift. 243-0770.

Elevator Repair Person

Experienced Skilled Technician
Only experienced skilled technicians need apply. Several openings for electro/mechanical (more mechanical experience than electrical) technicians to trouble-shoot and service various types of industrial weighing equipment. Technical education helpful but not essential, depending on job experience. Person must be willing to relocate to the Maritimes (Saint John). Company is the largest industrial-skill company in NB. Contact, enclosing work history: The Sentinal, Dept 256, P.O. Box 5000, Station C, Toronto, ON M5T 8J8

Warehouse Worker

Person needed for general work in distribution warehouse. Must have exp. Apply 766 Industrial Drive from 8-11 a.m.

• **Industrial carpet sewers** with exp. needed by west-end manufacturer.
•**Shipper**, min. 3 yr. exp.
•**General help** also required. Call for appt.: 685-3396.

Wire display company looking for general workers, full-time, urgently needed. Apply in person: 183A Portland Blvd.

Bilingual Person F 18K plus
Distribution centr someone energetic organized to work i tion with sales depa warehouse. Requ Bilingual (excelle and French gramn processing (Wor knowledge of inve trol. Remuneration exp. Fringe bene résumé to C.G. Products, 564 boule Montreal, PQ H4L

TREE PLAN

wanted in Northe AB, spring & fall. 582-5660 before M 26th.

Ambitious individu by plastics product turer. Experienced power tools (precis Responsibilities in mating, planning p and dealing with cu phone. For interviev 2714.

CASHIER/SALE

Full-time job op available with prom store chain. Many open for present stores. Candidates exp., please call Mi 7831.

a) When asked to indicate my previous experience, I'd mention only my paid work experience.

b) If I hear someone talking about an interesting job opening, I'm reluctant to ask for more information unless I know the person.

c) I'd ask employers who don't have an opening whether they know of other employers who might have job openings.

d) I'd downplay my qualifications so that an employer wouldn't think that I'm more qualified than I really am.

e) I prefer to use an employment agency to find a job rather than apply to employers directly.

f) Before an interview, I'd contact an employee of the organization to learn more about that organization.

g) I hesitate to ask questions while being interviewed for a job.

h) I believe that an experienced employment counsellor would know which types of jobs I should seek better than I would.

i) If a secretary told me that a potential employer was too busy to see me, I'd stop trying to contact that employer.

j) I feel that getting the job I want is largely a matter of luck.

k) I prefer to contact directly the person for whom I'd be working rather than the personnel department of an organization.

l) I'm reluctant to ask my present or previous teachers to write letters of recommendation for me.

m) I wouldn't apply for a job unless I had all of the qualifications listed in the published job description.

n) I'm reluctant to contact an organization about employment unless I know that there is a job opening.

o) If I didn't get a job, I'd call the employer and ask how I could improve my chances for a similar position in the future.

p) I feel uncomfortable asking friends about job openings.

q) Since the job market is so tight, I feel that I should take whatever job I can get.

r) If the personnel office refused to refer me for an interview yet I felt qualified for the position, I'd contact directly the person for whom I wanted to work.

s) If an interviewer said, "I'll contact you if there are any openings," I'd feel that there was nothing else I could do.

t) I'd check out the available job openings before deciding on the type of job that I'd like to have.

u) I'm reluctant to contact someone I don't know for information about career fields in which I'm interested.

v) I'd telephone a company on the chance that there was a job opening.

2. Visit your local Canada Employment Centre and read the job notices posted on the bulletin board. In your notebook, write the details of five jobs that appeal to you or that you're presently qualified to do. Then prepare a report that summarizes, for each job, the type of job, qualifications required, salary and benefits offered, and any other details provided.

Adapted from Ontario Ministry of Education. *Work and Employability Skills Program.* Senior Division. 1982, p. 77.

7

Preparing for the Job Search

O B J E C T I V E S
▼▼▼▼▼▼▼▼▼▼▼▼▼▼▼

After completing this chapter you should be able to:

- Obtain a Social Insurance Number.
- Do the necessary preparation before beginning a job search.
- Prepare a personal information form.

I N T R O D U C T I O N
▼▼▼▼▼▼▼▼▼▼▼▼▼▼▼▼▼▼▼

Effective preparation for your job search involves gathering together the items and information that you'll need. If you're well prepared, you'll save time and be ready to take advantage of opportunities that the unprepared could miss. The following are some important preparations that you must make.

1. *Social Insurance Number:* You must have a Social Insurance Number. This number officially registers you with the federal government and is required by all employers. To obtain a Social Insurance Number, go to your local Employment and Immigration Canada office and ask for a form to complete. After you have sent the form in, you should receive a card within six weeks.

2. *Identify* what type of job you are looking for.

3. *Personal information:* You need to gather all of the appropriate personal information that an employer might need: résumé, copies of certificates and diplomas, etc.

4. *Obtain references:* Contact people whose names you might want to use as references. These are people whom the employer could contact to vouch for your character and ability. Naturally, you want references who will speak favourably of you. Prepare a record of their names, titles, full addresses (including postal codes), and telephone numbers.

5. *Appearance:* You need to be well groomed and have appropriate clothes to wear to meet prospective employers. Remember, you are the product, so package yourself appropriately. Do you need to buy some suitable clothes? Do you need a haircut?

6. *Maintain records:* You need to maintain records of contacts you make with prospective employers, so that you can take appropriate follow-up action.

7. *Job search techniques:* You must know where and how to look for a job.

8. *Positive attitude:* You need to maintain a positive attitude.

COLLECTING PERSONAL INFORMATION

▼▼▼▼▼▼▼▼▼▼▼▼▼▼▼▼▼▼▼▼▼▼▼▼▼▼▼▼▼▼▼

To be well prepared for your job search, you should gather together all of your personal information. You can use this information in preparing your résumé, completing application forms, and answering questions during interviews.

The best way to collect this information is to write everything down on a personal information form, using the following guidelines.

1. *Full name,* including any middle names.

2. *Date and place of birth.*

3. *Address,* including apartment number (if applicable) and the postal code.

4. *Marital status* (Are you married? single?).

5. *Social Insurance Number.*

6. *Telephone number* including the area code.

7. *Driver's licence number.*

8. *Three references:* List the names of three people who know your skills and what type of person you are. They can be previous teachers or employers. Record their full names, job names or titles, addresses, and telephone numbers. *Make sure you have permission to use their names.*

9. *Past employment:*Where have you worked before? How long did you work there (start and end dates)? Who was your supervisor? What type of work did you do?

10. *Education:* List the schools you have attended, but only as far back as high school.

1. OTHER IMPORTANT PERSONAL INFORMATION

1. In your notebook, write the heading *Business Machines* and then, under this heading, write the names of the machines that you can operate.

typewriter	calculator	fax
word processor	computer	others (list)
adding machine	cash register	

2. Under the heading *Shop Tools and Machines*, list the ones that you can use.

3. Under the heading *Household Tools and Appliances*, list the ones that you can operate.

washer/dryer	drill	sander
dishwasher	handsaw	others (list)
vacuum cleaner		

4. Under the heading *Vehicles*, list the ones that you are licensed to operate.

car	bus	truck	motorcycle	others (list)

C H A P T E R   S U M M A R Y   E X E R C I S E S

▼▼

1. List five important items that have to be looked after before you begin your job search and explain why each is important.

2. Prepare a personal information form using the headings listed in the section entitled "Collecting Personal Information." At the end of the form, add the lists of machines, tools, etc., that you prepared in Exercise 1. When you actually begin your job search, make sure that you always have this form on hand.

8

Résumés

O B J E C T I V E S
▼▼▼▼▼▼▼▼▼▼▼▼▼▼▼▼

After completing this chapter you should be able to:

- List and explain the parts of a résumé.
- Prepare two types of résumés.
- List "do's" and "don'ts" in résumé preparation.
- Prepare your own résumé.

I N T R O D U C T I O N
▼▼▼▼▼▼▼▼▼▼▼▼▼▼▼▼▼▼▼▼

When you begin looking for a job, it's important that you make a summary of your qualifications and experience in a résumé. A résumé is a type of self-advertisement that summarizes relevant information about you for prospective employers. Sometimes referred to as a *curriculum vitae*, a résumé consists of details about your educational background, paid and unpaid work experience, and other pertinent personal data.

You might ask, "Why do I need a résumé? The employer will have all the information on an application form." A résumé is different, because the applicant has greater control over the image presented to the employer. A résumé can be tailored to present to an employer a positive image of you that emphasizes the experiences and skills you possess that are most relevant to the position for which you are applying. Also, résumés can be used in situations where you'll not immediately be filling out an application form, such as answering advertisements in newspapers that request submission of a résumé.

A résumé is usually only one or two pages long. You should be concise and to the point in your descriptions.

P A R T S   O F   T H E   R É S U M É
▼▼▼▼▼▼▼▼▼▼▼▼▼▼▼▼▼▼▼▼▼▼▼▼▼▼▼▼

- Personal information
- Career objective (optional)
- Education

- Work history
- Hobbies and interests
- References

PERSONAL INFORMATION

Three pieces of personal information are essential: your name, full address, and telephone number. Optional information includes your date of birth, languages read, written, and spoken, marital status, weight and height, state of health, Social Insurance Number, and citizenship.

Generally, it's a good idea to include only optional information that pertains to the job. If you were applying for a job that involved travelling, perhaps it would be helpful to mention if you're single and have a car. If you wanted to work with children, it might be a good idea to mention that your health is excellent.

CAREER OBJECTIVE

This section could pose some difficulty. Perhaps you haven't yet identified your career objective or perhaps your career objective doesn't fit with the job for which you're applying. Use your judgment about including this section. It might be more appropriate for you to include it in the covering letter that you send with your résumé.

EDUCATION

If you're relatively new to the work force, provide details of your educational background first, otherwise begin with your work history (see the next section) and follow it with the information about your education.

List your most recent educational background, ending with high school. You can use short sentences or write this section in point form. You must mention:

- Name of the institution
- Time period of attendance
- Course or program taken

- Certificate, degree, or diploma attained

In this section you should mention any scholarships, bursaries, or other awards you might have received during this time. Also include any technical skills such as inputting, shorthand, business machine operation, or computer skills that you possess.

WORK HISTORY

As in the education section, you begin with your most recent job experience and list backwards. You should mention:

- Name and location of each employer
- Period of employment
- Title of position

- Duties performed, indicating level of responsibility
- Name and telephone number of supervisor

When writing this section, try to relate some aspect of your work history to the job for which you are applying.

HOBBIES AND INTERESTS

In this section you should include:

- Clubs of which you've been a member
- Volunteer work you've done
- Any elective positions you hold or have held (these could indicate
- characteristics of leadership or responsibility
- Sports you enjoy or take part in
- Hobbies you enjoy

REFERENCES

You're not obliged to give the names of your references; you can simply state, "References available on request." If you do choose to list your references, make sure that you give for each reference:

- Name
- Business position
- Address and telephone number

Don't provide reference letters. The employer will contact your references directly.

TYPES OF RÉSUMÉS
▼▼▼▼▼▼▼▼▼▼▼▼▼▼▼▼▼▼▼▼▼▼▼▼▼▼▼▼▼▼

Two of the most popular types of résumés are the chronological résumé and the modified functional résumé. The chronological résumé presents your education and work experience in historical sequence, starting from the most recent and moving backwards.

The modified functional résumé format is becoming increasingly popular, since it offers the author flexibility without annoying the busy human resource officer who wants to be able to see at a glance just what you've done. It gives you the freedom to describe your skills and interests, while including a section that lists your work experience chronologically.

You should try to fit your résumé onto one page. If necessary, however, you may use two pages.

Examples of chronological and modified functional résumés appear on pages 70-72.

RÉSUMÉ DO'S AND DON'TS

1. *Do* key your résumé. Prepare it on a computer or word processor if possible, so you can update it readily or change it somewhat to fit each job application situation.

2. *Don't* use fancy gimmicks such as coloured paper, exotic lettering, or illustrations. Good-quality white paper of a standard letter size is preferable, and the résumé should be set up in an easy-to-read, attractive manner.

3. *Don't* put a date on your résumé.

4. *Do* keep your résumé short; two pages should be enough.

5. *Do* put your career objective near the beginning of your résumé, but remember that it must fit with the job for which you're applying.

6. *Do* keep descriptions short and space them properly. List information in point form.

7. *Do* use lots of action verbs, such as "supervised," "organized," "developed."

8. *Do* emphasize your skills and accomplishments but don't exaggerate them or give misleading information. If prospective employers uncover even the smallest of "errors," they might doubt the truth of your entire résumé.

9. *Don't* include salary requirements. Prospective employers might be unfavourably influenced by figures that are either too high or too low. If an ad asks for expected salary, research what the job usually pays (and make sure that this is enough for you to live on) and state an appropriate amount in your covering letter.

10. *Do* ensure that your résumé is neat and error-free. Have someone check it for grammar and spelling and ask that person to give you his or her general impression.

11. *Do* make photocopies of your résumé so you'll always have some on hand.

12. *Don't* include your list of references. If you're asked to provide references with your résumé, list them in your covering letter.

13. *Don't* include your photograph. If you're applying for a position for which a prospective employer has a *legal* reason for asking for a photograph, attach it to your covering letter. Human rights legislation protects job applicants from discrimination based on gender, race, or age, facts that could be revealed by a photograph.

14. *Don't* mail your résumé to a prospective employer without a covering letter.

15. *Do* carry your résumé in an envelope or briefcase to avoid getting it dirty or wrinkled.

EXAMPLE OF A CHRONOLOGICAL RÉSUMÉ

Paul Pearson
492 Galt Avenue
London, ON
N5Y 2B2

(519) 654-5677 (residence)   (519) 657-9525 (business)

Date of Birth:	November 23, 1968
Social Insurance No.	211 346 523
Languages	
Read and written: Spoken:	English, French English, French, Spanish
Marital Status:	Single
Citizenship:	Canadian
Career Objective:	To market Canadian travel destinations to foreign visitors.

Education

1986-1988	Fanshawe Community College, 300 Price Street, London, ON N6A 4N9 • Obtained a first-class diploma in travel marketing; took additional courses in accounting, micro-computers, and French
Summer 1986	Six-week, intensive French course at St. Ignace Summer School, 106 rue Desjardins, Quebec, PQ G1G 4E8
1982-1986	Forest City Comprehensive High School, London, ON N6H 4E1 • Graduated with a Grade 12 certificate

Work History

1989-Present	Travel Agent: Sam Smith Travel Inc., 106 Wellington St., St. Thomas, ON N5S 3P7 Supervisor: Beverley Anselmi (519) 637-1890 • Market travel packages; arrange itineraries and make necessary bookings by computer for clients. Handle office books and arrange advertising in local newspapers.
1988-89	Salesman: Share Bay Condominiums, 16 Lake Street, Grand Bend, ON N0M 1T0 Supervisor: George Nemeth (519) 367-4513 • Sold holiday packages for families and private and corporate groups (including for conferences) for four-season resort.
Summer 1987	Chief Information Officer: Summer Information Booth, Forestland Park, 1086 Springbank Drive, London, ON N6A 5J1 Supervisor: Marc Lalonde (519) 679-1167 • Answered visitors' questions and supervised two other information officers.

Community Service

French immersion teacher's aide; camp counsellor; leader in high school recycling program; Big Brother

Hobbies

Reading, travelling, cycling, softball, hiking

References available on request

Victoria Mannelli
4076 Roncey Place
Edmonton, AB
T5S 1B6

(403) 821-4318 (residence)
(403) 821-2313 (business)

Career Objective

- To gain experience in counselling and/or instructing people
- Ultimate goal: Teacher

Education

Graham Collegiate and Vocational Institute
8001 Girard Road
Edmonton, AB
T5X 2T4

1988-1990:   General vocational, English, mathematics, inputting

Spenser Junior Secondary School
1000 Logan Avenue
Langley, BC
V3A 4J3

1985-1988:   General vocational, child care, and computer courses; class assistant

Work Experience

Counselling: Volunteer, children's after-school program, Langley Community Centre (5 months)

- Planned and supervised children's activities
- Organized outings and fun days
- Assisted children with their homework

Tutoring: Class assistant at Spenser Junior Secondary School (3 years)

- Acted as tutor
- Assisted slow learners and the mentally handicapped in studies

Human Relations:	Companion to the elderly at The White House

- Dealt with patients aged 50 to 97
- Provided conversation and entertained lonely patients
- Assisted customers at The Treasure Chest and BonBons

Child Care:	Baby-sitter

- Baby-sat 3 children, including one handicapped child, on a daily basis for 8 months
- Assumed responsibility for the children's needs and various household chores

Other Experience

- Operated emergency switchboard and contacted the right people in cases of emergency
- Operated cash register; totalled sales; made cash deposits; assisted in ordering for large parties, birthdays, and weddings

Work Chronology

- The Treasure Chest, 154 Queen Street, Edmonton, AB T6E 4H2
  Working Student project: July 1989
  Supervisor: Pamela Konno (403) 232-1641

- The White House, 2630 Portland Blvd., Edmonton, AB T5K 1A2
  Working Student project: Aug. 1988
  Supervisor: Carl Lind (403) 369-1181

- Bonbons, 54 Goldstream Drive, Langley, BC V0X 1A0
  Cashier: October 1987-January 1988 (part-time)
  Supervisor: Sonya Harris (604) 211-8732

- Wanda Leon, Langley, BC V3A 6H4. (604) 211-6490
  Baby-sitter: 1985

Activities and Interests

- Reading
- TV documentary programs
- Baseball, swimming, weight lifting
- Sewing: Design and make my own clothes, sell clothes to friends

Personal information

- Languages spoken, written, and read: English
- Additional language spoken: Italian

References

- Available on request

1. **ALL ABOUT RÉSUMÉS**

    Write the following sentences in your notebook, inserting the missing words or phrases.

    1. A résumé is ___.

    2. A résumé usually consists of ___ sections. They are ___.

    3. Personal information that is optional includes ___.

    4. Your career objective is not included in your résumé if ___.

    5. Six "don'ts" to remember when preparing a résumé are ___.

    6. Nine "do's" to remember when preparing a résumé are ___.

CHAPTER SUMMARY EXERCISE
▼ ▼

Prepare your résumé and give it to your teacher. Choose one of the two types of résumés presented in this chapter. Be sure to follow all of the suggestions given to prepare an effective résumé.

Covering Letters

O B J E C T I V E S
▼ ▼ ▼ ▼ ▼ ▼ ▼ ▼ ▼ ▼ ▼ ▼ ▼ ▼ ▼ ▼

After completing this chapter you should be able to:

- Explain the purpose of a covering letter.
- List what should be included in the letter.
- Choose an attractive format for it.
- Define the major parts of a covering letter.
- Write an effective covering letter.

I N T R O D U C T I O N
▼ ▼ ▼ ▼ ▼ ▼ ▼ ▼ ▼ ▼ ▼ ▼ ▼ ▼ ▼ ▼ ▼ ▼

When you send a résumé to a prospective employer, you should always enclose a covering letter. This letter should be designed to:

- Introduce your résumé and stimulate the reader's interest in it.
- Make a favourable impression on the employer.
- Obtain an interview.

This section presents details on what you should include in your covering letter and ways of ensuring that it makes a good impression on the employer.

W H A T   T O   I N C L U D E   I N
Y O U R   C O V E R I N G   L E T T E R
▼ ▼

Before you actually begin writing your covering letter, write an outline of the information you should include. As a guideline, ask yourself the following questions each time you write such a letter.

1. Why am I writing this letter?
2. What position am I seeking?

3. What type of work does it involve?

4. What do I have to offer that the employer might be looking for?

5. How is my training relevant to the job I'm seeking?

The answers to these questions provide the framework for your letter.

Now that you know what you want to say, how do you put it all together? First of all, write a paragraph about each major point, then arrange these paragraphs in order of importance. The body of the letter usually has three main paragraphs:

- First paragraph: State your reason for writing. Offer your services to the employer, stating the name of the position in which you're interested. If you're responding to an advertisement, mention the name of the newspaper and the date the advertisement appeared.

- Second paragraph: Tell the employer why you're interested in the job and give reasons why you think you're qualified (mention any special skills). Refer the reader to your résumé for more details.

- Third paragraph: Request an interview with the employer. Identify general times when you'll be available for an interview and specify where and when you can be contacted to set up the interview.

Your letter is essentially a sales letter. Salespeople know that an advertisement should be patterned after two formulas: AIDA (A-ttention, I-nterest, D-esire, A-ction) and KISS (K-eep I-t S-hort and S-imple).

COVERING LETTER FORMATS

Your letter should be keyed, single-spaced, on one side of the page only, in one of the two most common formats:

- *Full block:* Everything begins at the left margin, including the date and complimentary closing.

- *Semi-block:* Each paragraph is indented (usually five spaces) from the left margin. The date and complimentary closing are aligned with each other, starting at the centre or to the right of the centre of the page.

Examples of these two formats appear later in this chapter.

The letter should be positioned on the page so that it is surrounded by a balanced amount of white space on all sides. Some white space should be left between each part of the letter (date, inside address, etc.), as detailed later. The amount of space left will depend on the length of the letter and the way it fits on the page.

Plain white paper of good quality is preferable, and most business letters are prepared on 21.5- by 28-cm (8½- by 11-inch) stationery.

FINE-TUNING
THE COVERING LETTER
▼▼▼▼▼▼▼▼▼▼▼▼▼▼▼▼▼▼▼▼▼▼▼▼▼▼▼▼▼

No prospective employer will be favourably impressed if your letter contains incorrect grammar, spelling, or punctuation. Remember, you never get a second chance to make a good first impression.

- **Grammar**: Make sure that you use proper English. Do not use any contractions such as "don't" or any abbreviations.

- **Spelling**: If you're not sure how a word is spelled, look it up in a dictionary.

- **Punctuation**: Study carefully the sample letters provided later in this chapter, paying close attention to the use of commas and periods.

- **Other**: Make sure that you send a clean, neat letter; cross-outs are not acceptable.

PARTS OF A LETTER
▼▼▼▼▼▼▼▼▼▼▼▼▼▼▼▼▼▼▼▼▼▼▼▼▼▼▼▼

The parts of a letter are described here and are illustrated by the sample letters that appear on pages 79 and 80.

Date: The date appears on one line at the top of your letter. Either the numeric (19– 06 21) or standard (June 21, 19–) is acceptable.

Your address: Leave a few spaces after the date line and insert your full address. Do not include your name. You could put your telephone number here or incorporate it into your letter.

Inside address: The inside address consists of the name of person to whom the letter is being sent, that person's business title, the name of the company, and the full address, including postal code. Each item should be on a separate line (see the example of the full block letter) unless the length of the person's name and title makes it possible for these to be on one line without that line extending too far into the white space (e.g., Mr. Kim Ito, President).

Salutation: When you know the name of the person to whom you are writing, the usual salutation is, for example, "Dear Mr. Ito." If you don't know the name of the letter recipient, simply use "Dear Sir or Madam." The best idea, however, is to telephone the company and ask for the name of the person who should receive your letter, confirming the correct spelling of the person's name. Even Smith has alternative spellings, such as Smithe or Smyth. Also ask for the person's title and, if the person is a woman, ask whether she should be addressed as Miss, Mrs., Ms., Mlle, or Mme.

Body: The body is the main part of the letter, in which you present the necessary information and ask for a job. All paragraphs in this section begin either at the left margin or are indented five spaces, depending on the format you've chosen.

Complimentary closing: The complimentary closing is situated either at the left margin or in line with the date and your address. The most commonly used closing is "Yours truly."

Identification line and signature: The identification line is your keyed name, and should be located four to seven line spaces under, and aligned on the left with, the complimentary closing. Always sign your letters in ink.

Envelope: The final step is to prepare the envelope. Choose the size of envelope that suits the size of your stationery and the thickness of your enclosures. Double-check to make sure that all of the information and spellings are correct. Figure 9.1 shows an example of a properly addressed envelope.

Figure 9.1 Sample of properly prepared envelope

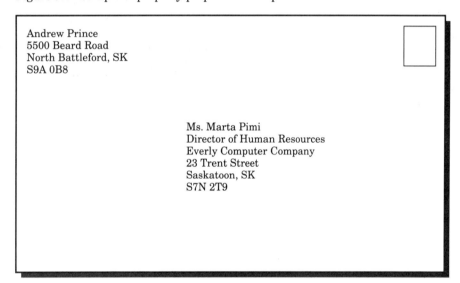

1. COVERING LETTER FACTS

Answer the following questions in your notebook, explaining each answer in detail.

1. What is the purpose of a covering letter?

2. What questions should you ask yourself before writing a covering letter?

3. The body of a covering letter usually has three main paragraphs. Describe the role of each of these main paragraphs and the order in which they should be arranged.

4. What do AIDA and KISS mean?

5. What are the two most common letter formats? Describe each format.

6. What type and size of stationery should be used for a covering letter?

7. What is involved in "fine-tuning" a letter?

8. List the parts of a letter and explain the function of each part.

9. If you don't know the name of the person who should receive your letter, what should you do?

10. What size of envelope should you use for your covering letter?

Samples of full block and semi-block covering letters appear on the following two pages.

SAMPLE OF FULL BLOCK
COVERING LETTER

19— 06 21

↓ 4-6

5500 Beard Road
North Battleford, SK
S9A 0B8

↓ 3

Ms. Marta Pimi
Director of Human Resources
Everly Computer Company
23 Trent Street
Saskatoon, SK
S7N 2T9

↓ 2

Dear Ms. Pimi

↓ 2

In reply to your advertisement in the Saskatoon Daily News of June 20,
19—, I would like to be considered for your Management Training Program.

↓ 2

reliable + well organized

The enclosed résumé highlights my education and work experience. I recently
graduated from the University of Saskatchewan with a degree in Computer Sciences,
specializing in Data Management. I have had supervisory and management experience
in the food industry, get along well with people, and am self-motivated.

↓ 2

I would very much appreciate the opportunity to discuss the advertised *co-op*
position with you in person. My telephone number is 362-1088, and I am usually
there between 9:00 a.m. and 12 noon. Thank you in advance for your consideration.

↓ 2

400 and 9

Yours truly

↓ 4-6

Andrew Prince

↓ 2

Encl.

SAMPLE OF SEMI-BLOCK COVERING LETTER

my name

551 Brook Lane,
Portage La Prairie, MB.
R1N 0H4
↓2
(204) 673-1982.

↓4-6

September 28, 19—.

↓4-6

Mrs. Rinata Sadler,
Personnel Manager,
Mayfair Classic Creations,
894 Queen Boulevard,
Winnipeg, MB.
R2P 0X3
↓2
Dear Mrs. Sadler:
↓2
    I would be interested in discussing with you the possibility of employment as general secretary. I have been fascinated by the progress your company has made in the gift industry.
↓2 (or close up for longer letters)
    I have just successfully completed a two-year course in Office Technology at Goodfellow College. The school received glowing reports of my work from my field placement supervisors. I am sure you would find me to be a conscientious and capable worker. Enclosed is a résumé of my educational background and work experience.
↓2 (or close up)
    Since I would like to be able to discuss with you personally the possibility of employment with your company, I will call you in a few days to see whether an interview could be arranged. Thank you for your consideration.
↓2
Yours truly,

↓4-6

Christa Berndt.
↓2

Encl.

Note that in the sample full block covering letter no punctuation has been used at the end of the date line, at the ends of lines in the address blocks, or after the salutation, complimentary closing, or identification lines. This is called *open punctuation*. When abbreviations appear at the end of lines, however, periods *are* used, as in the case of "Encl." or "Ltd."

In the sample semi-block covering letter, punctuation has been used at the ends of all lines in the address blocks (except after the postal code, which is never puncuated), at the ends of the telephone number and date lines, and after the salutation, complimentary closing, and identification lines. This is called *closed punctuation*.

CHAPTER SUMMARY EXERCISE
▼▼▼

Pretend that you're applying for a job at Jetco Enterprises Inc., 2450 Delisle Road, (name of your community and your own postal code), and prepare a covering letter to go with the résumé you prepared in the last chapter. You're addressing the letter to Mr. Alfred Gallo, Human Resource Director. Choose the type of format and punctuation style you prefer from one of the two samples shown in this chapter.

Application Forms

OBJECTIVES
▼▼▼▼▼▼▼▼▼▼▼▼▼▼▼▼

After completing this chapter you should be able to:

- Explain the purpose of application forms.
- Understand the instructions on an application form.
- Identify the types of employment discrimination that are illegal in your province or territory.

INTRODUCTION
▼▼▼▼▼▼▼▼▼▼▼▼▼▼▼▼▼

When you inquire about employment, many places will give you an application form to complete. This is one situation in which the personal information form you prepared in Chapter 7 will come in handy.

The application form is usually from one to four pages long and consists of questions that include everything from personal facts to the last job you had. This is a compact way for the employer to keep your name and qualifications on file.

WHAT IS THE EMPLOYER LOOKING FOR?
▼▼▼▼▼▼▼▼▼▼▼▼▼▼▼▼▼▼▼▼▼▼▼▼▼▼▼▼▼

The main information that the employer is looking for on the application form is:

1. How well you follow instructions.
2. What type of employee you would be.
3. What you have achieved.
4. How well you hold a job.
5. How thorough you are.

When employers have positions to fill, they check through the perhaps dozens of completed application forms that they have on file. Their first step usually is to discard any sloppy or incomplete ones, because these indicate that the applicant is sloppy, cannot follow instructions well, or is not thorough. Application forms can indicate a lot about applicants.

APPLICATION FORM COMPLETION TIPS

1. Read the entire form carefully before you start to complete it; otherwise you might discover later that you've put some information in the wrong place.
2. Always be neat. Use a pen to fill out the form or, if you are allowed to take the form home, key it.
3. Double-check your spelling and grammar.
4. If possible, ask for two forms so you can use one as a rough copy.
5. Always answer all of the questions. Blank spaces give the impression that you're sloppy and missed questions or that you didn't understand questions.
6. If you find a question that doesn't apply to you, print "N/A" (not applicable) to indicate that you didn't miss the question. If you feel that a question does not apply to you or you feel that you don't have to answer it, state your reason.
7. Always ask for clarification if you don't understand a question.

Study carefully the two sample application forms on pages 86-90 so you'll know what to expect when you apply for a job. Make sure that your personal information form contains all of the details you'll need to complete such forms.

D I S C R I M I N A T I O N
I N   E M P L O Y M E N T
▼▼▼▼▼▼▼▼▼▼▼▼▼▼▼▼▼▼▼▼▼▼▼▼

Notice that neither of the application forms at the end of this chapter asks for information about date of birth, gender, race, national or ethnic origin, religion, or marital status. This is in line with human rights legislation that is in effect in every Canadian province and territory. Such legislation prohibits discrimination in employment, and employers usually are careful to abide by it.

There are some situations in which an employer might be justified in asking certain questions or refusing to hire a person on certain grounds, such as situations in which a person's age or a physical handicap might affect the legal or physical performance of a job.

The following table summarizes the types of employment discrimination that are illegal federally and in various provinces and territories. The items under the *Federal* heading apply to all companies and departments controlled by the federal government across Canada. As you can see, employment discrimination is illegal federally and in all of the provinces and territories on the basis of:

*   Race
*   National or ethnic origin
*   Colour
*   Religion
*   Gender

*   Age (with limitations in some provinces)
*   Marital status
*   Physical handicap or disability

PROHIBITED GROUNDS OF DISCRIMINATION IN EMPLOYMENT*

Jurisdiction	Federal	British Columbia	Alberta	Saskatchewan	Manitoba	Ontario	Quebec	New Brunswick	Prince Edward Island	Nova Scotia	Newfoundland	Northwest Territories	Yukon
Race	•	•	•	•	•	•	•	•	•	•	•	•	•
National or ethnic origin[1]	•	•	•	•	•	•	•	•	•	•	•	•	•
Colour	•	•	•	•	•	•	•	•	•	•	•	•	•
Religion or creed	•	•	•	•	•	•	•	•	•	•	•	•	•
Age	•	•	•	•	•	•	•	•	•	•	•	•	•
Gender	•	•	•	•	•	•	•	•	•	•	•	•	•
Pregnancy or childbirth	•		•	•	•		•						•
Marital status[2]	•	•	•	•	•	•	•	•	•	•	•	•	•
Family status[2]	•				•	•	•					•	•
Pardoned offence	•						•				•		
Record of criminal conviction		•				•	•						•
Physical handicap or disability	•	•	•	•	•	•	•	•	•	•	•	•	•
Mental handicap or disability	•	•			•	•	•	•	•	•	•	•	•
Dependence on alcohol or drug	•												
Place of residence												•	
Political belief		•			•		•			•	•		•
Assignment, attachment, or seizure of pay[3]											•		
Source of income					•								
Social condition[3]							•						
Language							•						
Social origin[3]											•		
Sexual orientation[4]					•	•	•						•
Harassment[4]	•				•	•	•				•		•

[1]New Brunswick includes only "national origin."

[2]Quebec uses the term "civil status."

[3]In Quebec's charter, "social condition" includes assignment, attachment, or seizure of pay, and social origin.

[4]The federal, Ontario, and Quebec statutes ban harassment on all proscribed grounds. Ontario, Nova Scotia, and Newfoundland also ban sexual solicitation.

*Any limitation, exclusion, denial, or preference may be permitted if a bona fide occupational requirement can be demonstrated.

Based on information supplied by the Canadian Human Rights Commission. © Minister of Supply and Services Canada, 1989. Cat. No. HR 21-26/1989.

In some cases, the type of protection varies in the different jurisdictions. For example, some jurisdictions that protect individuals on the basis of age set the upper limit at age 65, meaning that if you're younger than 65 you can't be refused employment on the basis of age. In some jurisdictions, age 18 is the lower limit of this protection, while in others the age is 19.

If you're not sure whether you're protected under federal or provincial legislation, contact your local human rights commission. Representatives can provide you with the information you need, advise you about your rights, and help you make a formal complaint if it appears that you have been treated unjustly.

1. EMPLOYMENT DISCRIMINATION

Study the "Prohibited Grounds of Discrimination in Employment" table and list the grounds for discrimination that apply in your province or territory. Then look in the telephone book under the provincial government listings and write down the telephone number you would call to contact your local human rights commission. If you don't understand any of the categories listed in the table, call your local commission and ask for an explanation. Check first with your classmates to ensure that several of you don't call about the same category.

CHAPTER SUMMARY EXERCISES
▼▼

1. Answer the following questions in your notebook.
   a) What does a prospective employer hope to learn from a completed application form?
   b) What might cause an employer to discard an application form?
   c) What does a messy or incomplete form indicate about the applicant?

2. List the guidelines for completing an application form properly.

3. Do research at a library about court cases in your province that have involved charges of discrimination in employment practices. The cases could involve discrimination in hiring, treatment on the job, or wrongful dismissal, which means to fire someone without a reason that is recognized by law. For example, a person can be fired for stealing from his or her employer, for being consistently late for work, or for frequently taking time off without permission. If necessary, ask the librarian for help in locating this type of material.

   Then, choose one of the cases and prepare an essay that contains as many details of the case as possible, including:
   a) The name of the plaintiff (the person who laid the charge) and his or her age and occupation.
   b) The details of the charge that was laid by the plaintiff.
   c) The name of the defendant (the person or company sued).
   d) The date(s) that the case was heard in court.
   e) The judge's decision of the case (whether the plaintiff won or lost, and the judge's explanation of why).
   f) If the plaintiff won, provide details of what the judge directed the defendant to do and/or how much the person or company was ordered to pay the plaintiff.

PEPSICO FOOD SERVICE INTERNATIONAL

A DIVISION OF PEPSI COLA CANADA LTD

Pizza Hut

APPLICATION FOR EMPLOYMENT

PepsiCo Food Service International is a large and successful company. We are proud to be an important part of the largest restaurant group in the world today: PepsiCo. With Taco Bell and Pizza Hut, PepsiCo owns or franchises over 15,000 restaurants all over the world. We know how to run restaurants that give our valued guests the quality of food, speed of service, cleanliness of surroundings, and hospitality of treatment they expect and deserve. We are proud of our company and the people that work for us.

AND WE'VE GOT HIGH STANDARDS, ARE YOU WILLING TO:

- Pitch in with the teamwork to get a job done?

- Work shifts when some of your friends are out socializing?

- Abide by our hair cut and personal grooming rules?

- Wear shoes that comply to our safety standards and uniform guidelines?

- Do physical work, including plenty of cleaning?

- Show up consistently on time so we can count on you?

WE REALLY VALUE SOME THINGS THAT YOU SHOULD BE AWARE OF:

- Hospitality: We want only the friendliest people to serve our guests.

- Quality: We serve only the freshest, hottest product made from the freshest ingredients and made to our guest's order.

- Service: We insist on fast and friendly service procedures.

- Cleanliness: We require clean kitchens, dining rooms, parking lots and bathrooms.

AND WE THINK OUR PEOPLE LEARN A LOT IN THE JOB, FOR EXAMPLE:

- Technical Skills: Through our crew training programs.

- Customer Service Skills: Something needed in any job.

- Social Skills: As you become a valued part of our team.

- Business Knowledge: As you learn the various components of a successful enterprise.

- Organizing and Planning: Through the logic of our work design.

- Responsibility: By adherence to our high standards.

HOW WOULD YOU RATE YOURSELF ON OUR SUCCESS PROFILE?

(1 = Unsure 2 = Improvement needed 3 = Solid 4 = Strength 5 = Superstar)

_____ Hospitality: Your natural friendliness and customer service skills.

_____ Energy Level: Your enthusiasm, self-motivation and sense of urgency.

_____ Reliability: Your dependability, attendance, self-discipline and dedication.

_____ Communication skills: Your ability to listen well, express yourself clearly and accept feedback.

_____ Personal Pride: Your appearance, hygiene and achievement.

_____ Teamwork: Your cooperation with others and team spirit.

"PepsiCo: Where friendly people make the difference."
Still interested? Turn the page and complete the application.

The information requested is essential to a proper evaluation of your application. Kindly provide complete and legible answers to all questions.

PERSONAL

DATE AVAILABLE:

POSITION APPLIED FOR:

NAME:

SALARY DESIRED:

(LAST)　　　　　(FIRST)　　　　　(MIDDLE)

ADDRESS:

STREET　　　　　CITY　　　　CODE

TELEPHONE

If you are under 18, how old are you? _____

Do you have the legal right to be employed in Canada?　☐ Yes　☐ No

Do you want to work　☐ Full-Time　☐ Part-Time.

Specify days and hours you want to work _____

Do you have a reliable means of transportation to get to work? _____

What prompted you to apply
for work here?　☐ Company Image　☐ Agency　☐ Friend　☐ Relative　☐ Newspaper　☐ Other _____

List any relatives employed by Pizza Hut / Taco Bell _____

Have you ever been employed by Pizza Hut / Taco Bell before?　☐ Yes　☐ No　If yes, list dates & location _____

Have you ever been bonded?　When? _____　For Whom? _____

Personal Interests _____

EDUCATION

	DATES		SCHOOL	GRADE	DIPLOMA
	From	To			
SECONDARY					
TECHNICAL or VOCATIONAL					
UNIVERSITY					
SPECIAL TRAINING					

EXPERIENCE

START WITH NAME AND ADDRESS OF MOST RECENT EMPLOYER

1. Company Name		
Position Held	Dates Employed	
	From:	To:
Reason for Leaving	Name of Supervisor	Salary
		Start:	End:
2. Company Name	Address	
	Phone No.	
Position Held	Dates Employed	
	From:	To:
Reason for Leaving	Name of Supervisor	Salary
		Start:	End:
3. Company Name	Address	
	Phone No.	
Position Held	Dates Employed	
	From:	To:
Reason for Leaving	Name of Supervisor	Salary
		Start:	End:

Are there any other experiences, skills, or training which you feel would qualify you for work with the company? _____

Provide information that you would like us to consider in the selection process. Do not give any information prohibited by law. Pizza Hut / Taco Bell does not make employment decisions based on race, sex, colour, religion, national origin, age, handicaps, marital status or record of offences.

"RATE YOURSELF" SECTION

YES	UNSURE	NO	
☐	☐	☐	Have you ever worked a cash register?
☐	☐	☐	Have you ever worked an electronic "Point-of-Sale" (POS) cash register?
☐	☐	☐	Have you ever held or been elected to a leadership position?
☐	☐	☐	Do you know anyone that works at this restaurant?
☐	☐	☐	Do you think hard work can also be fun?
☐	☐	☐	Do you consider yourself a hard worker?
☐	☐	☐	Would you describe yourself as a happy, enthusiastic person?
☐	☐	☐	Could you be smiling and happy through your full shift?

If you had a choice, would you rather:

☐ Work in front with customers? or

☐ Work in back cooking and preparing the food?

REFERENCES

LIST THREE (3) SCHOOL, BUSINESS OR PERSONAL REFERENCES AND INDICATE IF WE MAY CONTACT THEM (Exclude Names of Ministers of Religion)				May We Contact?
Name	Address	Occupation	Tel:	
Name	Address	Occupation	Tel:	
Name	Address	Occupation	Tel:	

I declare my answers to the questions on this application are true and give PIZZA HUT/TACO BELL and its affiliates the right to investigate all information given and to secure additional information, if necessary.

I understand that the completion of this application does not assure me of a position with this Company and does not obligate the Company to me in any way.

I further understand that any misleading or incorrect statements or the incomplete filling out of this application may render this application void and, if employed, may be cause for immediate discharge.

SIGNATURE OF APPLICANT   DATE

If you are hired, you must provide a valid Social Insurance Number. Before you start to work you will present to the selecting manager your Social Insurance Card.

SOCIAL INSURANCE NUMBER ☐☐☐ ☐☐☐ ☐☐☐

Source: Pepsico Food Service International (a Division of Pepsi-Cola Canada Ltd.).

Copp Clark Pitman Ltd.

EMPLOYMENT APPLICATION FORM

Name	Phone

Address

Type of Work Desired

EDUCATION:	Name & Address	Course Taken/Degree	From	To
High School				
College/University				
Other				

List any previous duties, skills or achievements which may be relevant to position applied for:

_____

_____

_____

EMPLOYMENT HISTORY: Show Current or Last Employer First

Employer's Name	From	Positions Held:
Address	To	
Name of Last Supervisor/Manager		End Rate
Employer's Name	From	Positions Held:
Address	To	
Name of Last Supervisor/Manager		End Rate
Employer's Name	From	Positions Held:
Address	To	
Name of Last Supervisor/Manager		End Rate

89

REFERENCES:

Name & Occupation	Address	Tel. No.	Business Or Personal Ref.

Signature _____

Date _____

Job Interviews

OBJECTIVES
▼▼▼▼▼▼▼▼▼▼▼▼▼▼▼

After completing this chapter you should be able to:

- Prepare properly for an interview.
- Identify the types of questions an interviewer might ask.
- List some "do's" and "don'ts" of interviews.
- Answer an interviewer's questions effectively.

INTRODUCTION
▼▼▼▼▼▼▼▼▼▼▼▼▼▼▼▼▼▼▼▼

The interview is probably the most important part of the job search and therefore requires much consideration and preparation.

When at the interview, you are the interviewee and the person asking the questions is the interviewer. Your main purpose in speaking to him or her is to ask for a job. You want to convince the interviewer that you are the best candidate.

In this section you will learn how to prepare for an interview, what to expect when you get there, and how to make a good impression. This section will also show you how to evaluate your performance after an interview, so that you can improve this skill for future interviews.

PREPARING FOR AN INTERVIEW
▼▼

When you are granted an interview, you have only one chance to make the best possible impression. Five basic rules will help you to do this:

1. **Be clean and neat**: The interviewer's first impression will be based on your appearance. You and your clothing should be clean and neat, and your clothing should be appropriate for the position for which you are applying. Use perfume or aftershave sparingly or not at all, and be moderate in applying make-up. Hair should be clean, combed properly, and styled appropriately, and beards, mustaches, and fingernails should be clean and trimmed.

2. **Know where you're going**: Unless you're already familiar with where the company is located, check beforehand to find out how to get there.

Then determine the appropriate type of transportation and how long the trip will take. Being late for an interview is guaranteed to make a bad impression. If you have time, it would be smart to actually make a trial run to ensure that your understanding of the location and your estimate of the time necessary to reach it are correct. In any case, allow yourself at least five minutes more than your estimate. If circumstances beyond your control occur (bus breakdown, etc.), find a telephone if at all possible and let the interviewer know what has happened. Be sure, too, that you ask where you are to report when you actually arrive at the building. Then, when you arrive, tell the receptionist your name and that of the person with whom you have the appointment. If you have to wait, do so with a minimum of fidgeting.

3. **Have a positive attitude**: You're not going to get every job you apply for, but this doesn't mean that you're a failure. Usually it means that the job just wasn't right for you and that perhaps the next job interview will result in the job you want. So, approach each interview positively and enthusiastically. Even if it doesn't result in a job offer, the interview experience will mean that you are even better prepared next time.

4. **Know something about the company**: Find out basic information about the employer and the position you are applying for before the interview. What does the company do? Is it well established in the area? Sources of this information could include company literature (brochures, advertisements), friends in the area, the local Chamber of Commerce or Board of Trade, municipal records, other employees with whom you are acquainted, etc.

5. **Bring necessary paperwork**: Have with you additional copies of your résumé, originals and copies of reference letters and school records, and samples of your work if you are applying for the type of job that might require these, such as drafting, art, design, etc. Also, bring a copy of your list of references, complete with addresses and telephone numbers. These are often asked for at interviews.

INTERVIEW QUESTIONS MOST COMMONLY ASKED
▼▼▼▼▼▼▼▼▼▼▼▼▼▼▼▼▼▼▼▼▼▼▼▼▼▼▼▼▼▼▼▼

The interviewer will ask you many questions in an effort to determine what type of employee you would be. Your answers will also indicate how well you know yourself and your goals. The interviewer will be impressed if you know about the company, because this will demonstrate your sincere interest in working for the organization.

The following questions are ones most commonly asked by interviewers. Study them carefully and make sure that you can answer them before an interview.

QUESTIONS RELATED TO THE COMPANY

1. Why do you think you would like a job with our company?

2. What do you know about our company?

3. What interests you about the products and/or services we offer?

4. If you had the choice, what job would you choose with our company?

5. When are you available for work?

6. What kind of salary do you need?

QUESTIONS ABOUT YOUR SKILLS

1. What type of job interests you?

2. Why did you choose this type of job?

3. What are the qualities needed to succeed in the work you have chosen?

4. What are your most outstanding qualities?

5. Give examples of times when you have shown initiative.

6. Are you a leader? Give me an example.

7. What languages do you speak? write? read?

QUESTIONS ABOUT PAST JOBS

1. What was your last job?

2. Why did you leave this job?

3. How often were you absent from your last job?

4. What have you learned from your past work experiences?

QUESTIONS ABOUT YOUR JOB PREFERENCES

1. How important are wages to you?

2. Are you willing to move to another geographical location?

3. Do you like to work alone? in a group?

4. How do you feel about jobs that involve a lot of routine?

5. How do you feel about teamwork?

6. How do you feel about overtime?

7. Do you work well under pressure or tight deadlines?

PERSONAL QUESTIONS

1. What do you do to keep fit?

2. What are your hobbies?

Adapted from Employment and Immigration Canada. *How to Find a Job in Today's Market.* Publication No. LM-016/11/89.

THINK BEFORE YOU ANSWER

▼▼▼▼▼▼▼▼▼▼▼▼▼▼▼▼▼▼▼▼▼▼▼▼▼▼▼▼▼▼▼▼▼▼▼▼▼

All

Sometimes interviewers will ask questions that should be thought about very carefully by the responder. The following are some of these questions, along with suggestions for answering them.

1. **Tell me about yourself.**

   The interviewer doesn't want to hear your life story. She or he is interested in your achievements and what you're looking for in a job.

2. **What is your greatest strength?**

   You shouldn't tell the employer about something that has nothing to do with your working life. Maybe you're able to keep a cool head in tense situations. Maybe you're always determined to see a job through to completion. But don't tell the person that you're a strong swimmer unless it applies to the job.

3. **What are your weaknesses?**

   Too many people respond to a question like this by willingly listing all of their weaknesses—and talk themselves out of jobs. The basic rule here is to never give a negative answer, to try to come up with a positive response while still being honest. And mention only items that relate to the job for which you're applying—it doesn't matter if you don't know which fork to use at a formal dinner if you're applying for a job as a fork-lift operator!

4. **What do you think your previous boss would name as the main area in which you need improvement?**

   Again, try to avoid a totally negative response. If there was some area in which your former employer found you somewhat lacking, name it but explain the steps you took to improve it, stressing some of your positive qualities.

5. **How long are you planning to stay in this job?**

   Unless for some reason you *have* put a time limit on how long you plan to remain in the job, your answer to this question might relate to your career goal and therefore to promotion to a better job.

6. **Why do you want to work here?**

   The interviewer wants to know how your skills and career goals might contribute to the company.

7. **Why should I hire you?**

   You should assure him or her that you'd be an asset to the company because of some skill or ability that you possess.

8. **Where do you see yourself five years from now?**

   The interviewer wants to know where you're heading and if you have a definite career goal.

9. **Have you ever had a problem on the job?**

   Assure the interviewer that if you ever have had a problem, you have learned from it and taken steps to ensure that it won't happen again.

10. **Are you applying for other jobs?**

   If you are, say so. The interviewer would expect you to be looking elsewhere if you're seriously job hunting.

11. **What do you do in your spare time?**

   Many employers prefer employees who have outside interests. These people are usually better workers on the job.

12. **What did you like the most or least about your last job?**

   The interviewer wants to know the type of atmosphere in which you work best.

13. **Do you have any questions?**

   You should be ready with some questions. Avoid asking questions about benefits that come with the job, but rather concentrate on questions that show your interest in the job itself.

Employers are taking risks whenever they hire new employees. An interviewer's job is to reduce this risk as much as possible. Some of the risk employers take are that:

- You don't have the necessary skills and experience.
- You won't work hard enough.
- You'll be absent often.
- You'll take the job, receive training, and then leave shortly thereafter.
- You won't get along with the other workers.
- You won't show initiative.
- You won't take orders.
- You have a character flaw that will affect your work.
- You're dishonest.

You might have had some past experiences that could cause an employer to have some of these fears. Prepare yourself to present these experiences in a positive light.

1. ANSWERING INTERVIEW QUESTIONS

The following questions are typical of ones frequently asked in an interview. Assume that you're being interviewed for a position. In your notebook, write out a brief answer to each question as you would answer it in an actual interview.

1. What is your career goal?

2. In what type of position are you most interested?

3. Why did you choose your particular field of work?

4. What qualifications do you have that make you feel you'll be successful in this job?

5. What are your ideas about salary?

6. How much money do you expect to be earning in ten years?

7. Do you prefer working with others or by yourself?

8. Are you primarily interested in making money or do you feel that service to humanity is more important?

9. How does your course of studies relate to this job?

10. Do you like routine work?

11. Do you like regular hours?

12. What jobs have you enjoyed most?

13. How do you spend your spare time?

14. Are you willing to go where the company sends you?

2. ROLE-PLAYING

Your teacher will assign partners to role-play an interviewer/interviewee situation. The interviewer will take a few minutes to choose four questions from the ones that appear in this chapter and will then ask the interviewee these questions, making notes of the answers received. The partners will then switch roles and repeat the process. In each case, the person playing the interviewer will give her or his notes to the other person. Review these notes and decide whether you would have made a good impression in an actual interview situation.

INTERVIEW DO'S

▼▼▼▼▼▼▼▼▼▼▼▼▼▼▼▼▼▼▼▼▼

1. Dress appropriately and be well groomed.

2. Make sure that your credentials are up to date.

3. Have extra copies of necessary papers.

4. Let the interviewer take the lead in the conversation.

5. Show respect for the interviewer.

6. Exhibit poise and self-control.

7. Try to overcome nervousness.

8. Act naturally. Maintain eye contact.

9. Be pleasant and friendly. If a hand is offered, give a firm handshake.

10. Listen very carefully.

11. Answer questions clearly and fully. Avoid one-word answers.

12. Answer all questions honestly.

13. Make yourself understood.

14. Stress your qualifications for the job and your interest in it.

15. Speak in terms of specific jobs, rather than saying "I'll take anything."

16. Be realistic when discussing wages.

17. Ask sensible questions.

18. Thank the interviewer for his or her time as you leave, holding out your hand for a handshake.

19. Make notes after the interview so you will remember details of the discussion.

20. Send a thank-you note after the interview.

INTERVIEW DON'TS

1. Bring other people to the interview.

2. Be late.

3. Smoke (decline if invited to smoke).

4. Chew gum.

5. Interrupt the interviewer while she or he is talking.

6. Criticize former employers.

7. Make salary the main theme.

8. Mention personal, domestic, or financial problems.

9. Freeze or become tense.

10. Become emotional.

11. Become impatient.

12. Limit your time for the interview.

13. Use negative body language.

14. Prolong the interview.

15. Suggest how the employer should run his or her business.

16. Be overconfident.

17. Talk too much.

18. Feel that the world owes you a living.

19. Display a feeling of inferiority. For example, don't sound unsure of yourself by making statements in a questioning tone of voice.

FOLLOWING UP JOB INTERVIEWS

After the interview, you should sit down and write a thank-you letter. Not only is this polite but also it reminds the prospective employer of who you are and what position you're applying for. In addition to thanking the person for the privilege of the interview, you could express your increased interest in the job because of the interview and perhaps mention again the skills and personal characteristics that you feel qualify you for the position. This is a prime example of professionalism and, if by any chance the interviewer has someone else equally qualified in mind for the job, such a gesture could tip the scales in your favour. Even if you don't get the job, another opening could occur in the near future and the interviewer is more likely to remember you if you've sent a follow-up letter.

Other letters that should be written to interviewers include ones that accept an offer of employment, acknowledge a rejection, decline a job offer, or explain that you are no longer available.

A letter accepting a job offer should confirm your acceptance of the job, whether the offer was made verbally or in writing, and confirm the terms of your employment (starting date, working hours, salary, etc.). This is particularly important if the job offer and terms of employment were stated verbally, not in writing. Employers *should* put such details in writing and, at some point in your career, it might be advisable to insist on this.

If you don't get the job, simply thank the interviewer for considering your application, express your disappointment, and mention that you hope you'll be kept in mind for future job opportunities.

If you don't know *why* you've been rejected, ask for the reason, explaining that perhaps there is some area in which you need improvement and that you'd appreciate knowing the interviewer's assessment of you and your skills.

If you're declining a job offer or are no longer available, again thank the interviewer for considering your application and explain the circumstances. Such courtesy makes an excellent impression on prospective employers—and you never know when you might want to apply to that company again.

If you haven't heard from the interviewer within the time period that was probably indicated at the end of your interview, a follow-up telephone call is in order. Remind the interviewer of who you are and what position you applied for, and ask whether a decision has been made yet. Or you could call a day or so before the expected time of notification and ask politely if you are being considered for the job. Sometimes a little reminder helps. Be careful, however, not to call more than once; otherwise you could end up irritating the interviewer.

CHAPTER SUMMARY EXERCISES

1. What is the main purpose of an interview?

2. List the five basic rules for preparing for an interview.

3. You're being interviewed for a job in your chosen field. The interviewer asks you what your weakness are. How would you reply?

4. List eight interview "do's."

5. List eight interview "don'ts."

6. Write a brief example of the letter you would send if:
   a) You were hired.
   b) You were not hired.
   c) You didn't want the job or were no longer available.

7. Are follow-up telephone calls advisable? Explain your answer.

3

Success on the Job

INTRODUCTION
▼▼▼▼▼▼▼▼▼▼▼▼▼▼▼▼▼▼▼▼▼▼▼▼▼

The change from student to employee is a dramatic one; the rules are very different. For example, many of your new employer's expectations will not be stated and you'll be expected to find out what these are. This unit will discuss how to handle your first day at work and employer expectations relating to attendance at work and to efficiency on the job.

First Day on a New Job

O B J E C T I V E S
▼▼▼▼▼▼▼▼▼▼▼▼▼▼▼

After completing this chapter you should be able to:

• Accept that being nervous at the start of a new job is normal.
• Define the term *probation period*.
• Plan ahead, so that your first day on a job will be less stressful.
• List ten important "do's" and "don'ts" for a successful first day on a new job.

I N T R O D U C T I O N
▼▼▼▼▼▼▼▼▼▼▼▼▼▼▼▼▼▼▼▼▼

The first day on a new job can be one of the most tension-filled days of a person's life. Many things in an employment situation are different from those you've experienced at school. The environment will be less casual, the grading will be different, and the work will be done for real, instead of for practice.

The adjustment period can be difficult if you go about it the wrong way. Two important keys to success are: *getting along with your fellow workers* and *relating to your supervisor*. If you exercise tact, co-operation, and patience you'll enhance your chances of starting off on the right foot.

Starting a new job requires you to become used to new situations, both physical and psychological. You'll be meeting new people and might find yourself in situations where problems already exist. Be assured, though, that most people have at one time or another been just as nervous in a new-job situation.

T H E   P R O B A T I O N   P E R I O D
▼▼▼▼▼▼▼▼▼▼▼▼▼▼▼▼▼▼▼▼▼▼▼▼▼▼▼▼

Usually new employees are hired on a trial basis for a certain length of time, which is called a *probation period*. This period could be from a week to six months long, as determined by the employer. It's a critical time for the new employee: your work habits are analysed, your conduct is graded, your ability to perform the job functions is rated, and your reaction under pressure is observed.

The probation period gives you the chance to show your employer the type of employee that you can be. During this time, you must prove to your supervisor that you are capable of doing your job well and that you possess the other necessary characteristics of a good employee.

APPEARANCE COUNTS
▼▼▼▼▼▼▼▼▼▼▼▼▼▼▼▼▼▼▼▼▼▼▼▼▼▼ ▼▼

You were hired and are scheduled to start Monday morning. What should you wear? Remember, you only get one chance to make a good first impression on your new supervisor and co-workers.

On some jobs you'll wear a uniform, so clothing won't be a problem. Other jobs require protective clothing over street clothes, which lessens the problem. For many jobs, however, you will have to make decisions every day on what to wear.

Wearing appropriate clothing is most important. It can affect not only how confident you feel but also how others judge you. Imagine your co-workers' opinion of you if you arrived for an office job dressed in a sweatsuit and dirty sneakers, or if you wore a three-piece suit and tie to your job as an auto mechanic!

Basically, the type of clothing you wear will be determined by the type of job that you do. Dressing inappropriately not only could make you look ridiculous and feel uncomfortable, but also could be a safety hazard. It also might be an indication of a lack of understanding of your role or a lack of commitment to success in your job.

It might help to look at your co-workers' clothing. Sometimes a company has an image, either formal or informal, that it wants to project, which might be quite different from that of other similar companies. Usually your co-workers' clothing will reflect that desired image.

Good grooming is equally as important as appropriate clothing in making a good impression. Greasy hair, dirty fingernails, or bad breath can cancel out the good impression made by a smart suit, dress, or uniform.

1. CLOTHING AND GROOMING

1. In the occupation you would like to have, what clothing would be suitable? Name the occupation first, then describe the type of clothing required.

2. List ten examples of good grooming (e.g., clean, trimmed fingernails).

PLANNING AHEAD
▼▼▼▼▼▼▼▼▼▼▼▼▼▼▼▼▼▼▼▼▼▼▼

You know what date you're starting work and what clothes you will wear. What else should a new employee consider?

WORK SCHEDULE

What time are you supposed to report for work? When do you finish? When are the coffee and meal breaks? What is the company policy concerning overtime (hours worked in addition to the usual schedule)? Will you be doing shift work? The majority of these questions can be answered within the first few days by someone in the personnel or human resource department or by your supervisor.

TRANSPORTATION

You'll have to determine ahead of time how you'll get to work. If you plan to take public transportation, you should call the transportation company to confirm the schedule and the pick-up and drop-off locations. If you'll be riding in someone else's car, you should consider the cost and inconvenience to that person. Perhaps you could contribute some money toward the cost of gas. If you'll be driving your own car, make sure it's in good operating order and reliable. If you can walk to work, you should figure out ahead of time exactly how long the walk will take. Whatever mode of transportation you use, plan to arrive a little early on your first day, to allow for any possible problems.

FOOD SERVICES

If your work hours include a meal break, you'll need to find out what food service facilities are available. Some typical situations include:

- A cafeteria. Is it open during your shift?
- A food truck, which goes from company to company selling hot and cold snacks.
- Vending machines. Sometimes the company provides a microwave oven for heating the food.
- A kitchen where you can store food in a refrigerator and perhaps heat it up on a stove or in a microwave.
- Just a kettle (useful for hot soup and coffee, etc.).
- A nearby restaurant.

PERSONNEL FORMS

When you first begin work you'll probably be required to complete a number of official forms. These are necessary to register you as an employee, to determine your tax situation, and to enrol you in company insurance and pension plans. To help you complete these forms, bring to work the personal information form you prepared in Chapter 7. Don't hesitate to ask the personnel officer for help in completing forms—they can be complicated.

FIRST-DAY DO'S AND DON'TS

The boxed information on the next page offers a few do's and don'ts to help you have a successful first day on a new job. Actually, these are good suggestions for *every* day on the job.

DO:

1. Get a good rest the night before.

2. Set your alarm. Allow yourself plenty of time to get ready without rushing.

3. Eat breakfast; it'll give you much-needed energy.

4. Get to work on time. In fact, plan to arrive a little early.

5. Be cheerful and friendly with co-workers.

6. Be co-operative.

7. Show your willingness to learn.

8. Carry out your tasks with care.

9. Ask questions if you don't understand something, but try to use your initiative.

10. Listen and observe carefully, and write down necessary information.

DON'T:

1. Ask too many questions.

2. Bother people unnecessarily.

3. Be too aggressive.

4. Be a show-off.

5. Speak critically about anyone or anything.

6. Try to become too familiar with co-workers or your supervisor.

7. Bring personal problems to work.

8. Use the telephone for personal calls.

9. Smoke, unless special areas are provided for this. If this is the case, smoke only during your official breaks.

10. Show any strong emotions. Always remain calm and polite, no matter what the problem is.

CHAPTER SUMMARY EXERCISES

1. What is meant by the phrase *probation period*?

2. In the job that you intend or want to do, what type of clothing will be appropriate? If you have a job now, describe your usual on-the-job clothing. Give details, explaining why the clothing you wear (or will wear) is appropriate, takes safety precautions into account, etc.

3. List five things you should do during your first day on a job.

4. List five things you should *not* do.

Job Attendance

O B J E C T I V E S
▼▼▼▼▼▼▼▼▼▼▼▼▼▼▼

After completing this chapter you should be able to:

- Explain the importance of punctuality on the job.
- Define the word *flextime*.
- Discuss what are and what are not good reasons to be absent from work.
- List the guidelines for calling in to report that you will be absent from work.

I N T R O D U C T I O N
▼▼▼▼▼▼▼▼▼▼▼▼▼▼▼▼▼▼▼▼

In the work world, *you* will have the main responsibility for being *where* you should be, and *when*. In school you had help: the bell rang to start classes, end classes, start lunch, end lunch, and so on. At work you're expected to keep track of time yourself. There are no bells to remind you.

You must be on the job for your complete work schedule. To an hourly paid worker, coming in three minutes late means the loss of a quarter-of-an-hour's wages! Being late could not only earn you your supervisor's disapproval, but also could be possible grounds for dismissal.

To be successful at work, you'll need to develop a mature and self-reliant attitude concerning punctuality. Regardless of the reason, you are responsible for the consequences of being late. Punctuality applies not only to starting and finishing times, but also to coffee and meal breaks.

If you don't wear a watch or you don't own one, buy or borrow one. You might not always be near a clock when it's important for you to know what time it is. Don't always be dependent on someone else to tell you the time, because you'll be bothering that person and interfering with her or his work.

If your work schedule is irregular, you'll have to be particularly careful. Write your schedule down and put it somewhere that you'll see it often.

And remember, you have a commitment to your job. If your schedule interferes with your social life, that's unfortunate but can't be helped. Your employer depends on you to be at work as scheduled. And if you don't honour that schedule, you'll be out of work and will have difficulty obtaining future jobs. Unpunctuality and excessive absenteeism are major offences in the work world.

F L E X T I M E
▼ ▼ ▼ ▼ ▼ ▼ ▼ ▼ ▼ ▼ ▼ ▼ ▼ ▼

Employees of many organizations today are able to take advantage of flextime. Flextime is a work schedule that allows employees to choose their job-starting and job-ending times, although they are usually required to be at work during certain specified hours, which are called *core time*. For example, core time might be 10 a.m. to 3 p.m. Other than these hours, employees would be able to choose their own schedules, providing that the number of hours worked added up to the required total. So, if an eight-hour shift was required, some employees might choose to work from 7 a.m. to 3 p.m., while others might work from 9 a.m. to 5 p.m., or 10 a.m. to 6 p.m., or any other combination that suited their needs.

Just remember: whether the company you work for uses flextime or regular-time schedules, you must be responsible for your timetable and ensure that you work the required minimum number of hours.

♭ 1. PUNCTUALITY QUIZ

Decide what your reaction would be to each of the following situations and write your answer in sentence form in your notebook. In certain cases more than one answer might be suitable. Include them all in your answer.

1. You have to be at your job, ready to work, by 8 a.m. You must change clothes at work before you start. How much earlier should you get to your place of work?

    a) 5 min   b) 15 min   c) 60 min

2. Being late for school and being late for work are:
    a) Different because being late for school can result in suspension.
    b) Different because being late to work can result in your being fired.
    c) The same.

3. Getting back to work on time after lunch is as important as:
    a) Leaving at the right quitting time.
    b) Taking your coffee break at the right time.
    c) Getting to work on time in the morning.

4. When a person you work with is always on time, you can:
    a) Depend on that person.
    b) Count on him or her to fill in for you.
    c) Hope that he or she doesn't make you look bad.

5. When employees are often late for work, their employers and co-workers will think that those employees:
    a) Don't care about their jobs.
    b) Can't be depended on.
    c) Are an asset to the company.

6. A good way to form the habit of being on time is to:
    a) Be on time for school every day.

b) Always be on time when you're supposed to be in a certain place at a certain time.

c) Arrive late when you feel like it.

7. You're supposed to start work at 8 a.m. but the bus stops at your place of work only at 7:30 and 8:30 a.m. You should:

a) Arrive at work at 7:30 a.m.

b) Arrive at work at 8:30 a.m.

c) Alternate from day to day.

8. You live 32 km from work and drive in every day. If you wake up to a bad snowstorm, you should leave:

a) At the usual time.

b) Earlier than usual.

c) Late, because everyone will probably come in late.

2. THOUGHTS ABOUT PUNCTUALITY

1. List three thoughts that an employer might have about a worker who is always on time.

2. List three thoughts that an employer might have about a worker who is always late.

3. What are some tricks that you could use to help you to be punctual?

IF YOU CAN'T GO TO WORK
▼▼▼▼▼▼▼▼▼▼▼▼▼▼▼▼▼▼▼▼▼▼▼▼▼▼▼▼▼▼▼▼▼▼▼▼▼▼

One expectation an employer has is that an employee will be on the job as scheduled. If you're not there, no one else might be available, or able, to do your work, and the company's business activities might suffer. Then, too, when you do return to work, you'll have to work twice as hard to catch up. Also, if other employees have to do your work as well as their own too often, they'll probably become resentful. So you should always be at work unless you have a good reason not be be. If you *must* miss work, be sure that you always follow the guidelines illustrated in the following scenarios.

1. You have terrible flu symptoms. You feel that you should stay home to avoid spreading germs and also because, in your present condition, you'd be inefficient. Yes, you probably have a good reason to stay home.

2. You have a good reason to stay home from work, so are you just going to turn over in bed, thinking, ''I'll call the boss later''? No, it is your responsibility to let your employer know as soon as possible that you are unable to work. This gives your employer time to make arrangements to ensure that your absence won't interfere with business or put too much of a load on your co-workers.

3. It's 8:30 a.m. and your place of business is open. You call in and speak to the receptionist, asking that a message regarding your absence be

passed on to your supervisor. *Now* you can go back to bed, right? Wrong! Never leave such a message with someone who might be too busy to pass the message on right away, or who might not appreciate what your absence will mean to your supervisor and co-workers. If you can't reach your supervisor when you call in, leave a message with the most responsible person you can, asking that your supervisor call you for a fuller explanation when convenient.

4. If you think that "I'm not coming in today. 'Bye." is all you need to say when you call in, you're wrong. You must explain clearly and fully why you're unable to go to work. If you can, identify when you will be able to return to work and offer to make up the time you're missing. This should make a very good impression on your supervisor—but be prepared to work that extra time.

5. If your job for that day involves an urgent task, inform your supervisor of this and offer to provide over the telephone any help you can to the person who will have to do the task. Your supervisor will undoubtedly appreciate such a responsible attitude.

Being off work for special occasions (weddings, family reunions, etc.) is something that should be arranged well in advance, as soon as you know about the event. Then your employer will be able to set up a work schedule that takes your absence into account. And, of course, you shouldn't expect to be allowed to take time off very often for such events.

3. CALLING IN

The following are telephone conversations between employers' receptionists and employees who are going to be absent from work. In each case, write a possible continuation of the conversation in your notebook. Include what you think the person's supervisor's reaction will be and explain how the caller did or didn't follow the guidelines for calling in to report an absence. If you can think of a compromise that might help both the employer and the employee in any of the situations, include that too.

1. **Receptionist:** Good morning. Mackis and Company.
   Employee: Hi, Andrew. It's Ryan. I won't be in for my four o'clock shift today. I've got some type of stomach flu and I've been awake almost all night. I feel awful.
   Receptionist: Oh, that's too bad. I'm sorry to hear it.
   Employee: Well, I need to let my supervisor know. May I speak to Ms. Singh, please?
   Receptionist: Ms. Singh isn't here at the moment, but she should be back soon. Would you like me to pass on your message that you're sick and won't be in?

2. **Receptionist:** Season's greetings. Rinaldo Enterprises
   Employee: Hi, Evelyn. It's Nikki.
   Receptionist: Oh, hi, Nikki. How are you?
   Employee: Not great! Just between you and me, I was out partying last night and I just can't handle coming in to work.
   Receptionist: Again!
   Employee: Oh, come on! I don't take that much time off! That's why I figured I was entitled to take today.
   Receptionist: You mean you're not coming in *at all?* I think your

department is really counting on you today—Mr. Eastman's not going to be too happy. I'll transfer your call to his office.

3. **Receptionist:** Good morning. Bibeau Industries.
Employee: Oh, Gord, it's Alina. I totally forgot until this morning that I have a dental appointment at eleven, so there's no point coming in to work until after.
Receptionist: Uh-oh! Mrs. Gamit has already said that she needs you as soon as you come in. This'll be really inconvenient for her.
Employee: Oh, that's too bad. Well, tell her I called.

4. **Receptionist:** Gillis and Company, your communications specialists.
Employee: Hi, Ramesh. Guess what! I've just had a call from my favourite cousin. She's going to be in town for four hours and wants to spend the time with me. I'm heading out to meet her now, so I won't be in until later.
Receptionist: That's great for you, but I think you'd better check with Mr. Demers first. He might really need you for something this morning.

5. **Receptionist:** Good morning. Fujimoto Enterprises.
Employee: Danica, it's Leo. I'm not coming in today. We've had this great three-day family reunion at the cottage planned for months, so I'm leaving for there now.
Receptionist: Oh, then I guess your department's known for some time that you'll be away today.
Employee: Well, no. I figured it would be less of a hassle to just call in and let them know on the day of the reunion. That way, I'm sure of getting the time off.
Receptionist: If you do things like that, you might end up getting more time off than you'd like! I'd better transfer you to Miss Walters.

6. **Receptionist:** Good morning. Smith Storage.
Employee: Hi, Rose. It's Malcolm. I can't come in today. Our babysitter is sick and I have to look after my little sister.
Receptionist: Where's your mom?
Employee: Oh, she has a job.
Receptionist: So do you.
Employee: Oh, well, her job's a lot more important than mine.
Receptionist: Not to our company! You'd better talk to Mr. Bradette.

CHAPTER SUMMARY EXERCISES

▼▼▼▼▼▼▼▼▼▼▼▼▼▼▼▼▼▼▼ ▼▼▼▼▼▼▼▼▼▼▼▼▼▼▼▼▼▼

1. Why is being punctual for work important?

2. Explain what the word *flextime* means.

3. When you are planning to be absent from work, what five guidelines should you follow?

4. In paragraph form, describe three situations that you think would be acceptable to an employer as reasons not to report for work.

Efficiency on the Job

O B J E C T I V E S
▼▼▼▼▼▼▼▼▼▼▼▼▼▼▼▼▼

After completing this chapter you should be able to:

- Explain why employers value efficient employees.
- Remember new people's names better.
- Realize the importance of using company equipment and supplies carefully and efficiently.
- Discuss why both quality and quantity of work are important.
- Assess the quality and quantity of your work.

I N T R O D U C T I O N
▼▼▼▼▼▼▼▼▼▼▼▼▼▼▼▼▼▼ ▼▼

One of the most desirable characteristics of an employee is efficiency. Efficiency on the job is the ability to do your work without wasting time, energy, supplies, etc. Efficient work habits are developed. Becoming efficient starts with learning the best way to do your job, discovering who is who at work, where to find what you need to do your job, how to take care of equipment and materials, and being able to distinguish the difference between quality of work and quantity of work.

W H O ' S   W H O   A T   W O R K
▼▼▼▼▼▼▼▼▼▼▼▼▼▼▼▼▼▼▼▼▼▼▼▼▼▼▼

When you begin a new job, you're introduced to many new people. This can be very confusing! However, these are the people you will need to communicate with to get your job done, so the sooner you can remember their names, the sooner you will be productive in your new employment. The following are a few tips that might help.

REMEMBERING NAMES

1. Ask for a list of employees' names, such as an internal telephone list. Refer to this to jog your memory and to make sure you spell names correctly.

2. When you are introduced, repeat the person's name and try to identify one outstanding feature of the person (e.g., unusual glasses, jutting chin, etc.). Mentally link the person's name with the unusual characteristic you

observed. For example, Mr. Carpenter enjoys working with his hands, so you might picture him working with carpenter's tools and remember that his name is "Carpenter." Or you might make the mental connection of "snow" to remember Mr. White's name.

3. Listen to how the other employees refer to each other. Do they use first names or family names? Is it Marie or Mrs. Brown? Roy or Mr. Smith? In some companies, everyone is informal and only first names are used. In others, some people are addressed by their first names but others are addressed as "Mr.," "Ms.," or "Miss." Follow the lead of the majority of your co-workers. Addressing someone appropriately will make you both feel comfortable.

GETTING ORGANIZED

No matter what your job, you'll need some materials to produce results. An office worker needs paper, scissors, a stapler, pen, and so on. An instrument technician needs a lab coat, tools, a magnifying glass, etc. An auto mechanic needs items such as protective clothing, tools, and spare parts.

The time you spend assembling your materials before you start to work is not productive. If you have to make several trips, production time is lost. If you have to ask someone the location of every item, even more time is wasted.

To avoid this situation, find out during the first day or two the location of all the basic supplies you'll need and the procedures required to obtain them. Is someone's permission necessary or can you just help yourself? Sometimes you'll need to fill in a requisition form and perhaps indicate a budget code. A budget code identifies the department to which the cost of the materials is to be charged. If a budget code is required, write it down and keep it in your work area for future reference.

Whenever you run out of a particular material and need to pick up more, take a moment to consider what other supplies also are low. Thinking ahead will reduce the number of interruptions and, therefore, the amount of time spent away from your job. Equipment and supplies are a major expense item for most companies, so it's important for all employees to use and conserve these carefully. The following are some basic guidelines for doing this.

CARE AND HANDLING OF EQUIPMENT AND SUPPLIES *

1. Before using a new piece of equipment, read the operating instructions and follow them carefully. If you are still unsure about the correct way to use the equipment, ask your supervisor or an experienced worker to show you how to do it.

2. Even if it takes longer, follow safety procedures when using equipment. Accidents happen to people who take chances. Remember, safety rules

---

*The rest of this chapter is adapted from: Guidance Centre, University of Toronto, in co-operation with Employment and Immigration Canada. PLACE. *Guided Steps to Employment Readiness*. "Part D: Doing Well on the Job." © Minister of Supply and Services Canada, 1984, pp. 27-30, 37-47. Reproduced with the permission of the Minister of Supply and Services Canada, 1990.

are based on previous accidents—if it happened to someone else, it could happen to you. Your basic rule should be: The safe way is the right way.

3. When you have finished with tools or equipment, put them away or turn them off. This will help to prevent them from getting lost, broken, or wearing out, and turning off the power conserves energy.

4. If the equipment you're using doesn't seem to be working properly, immediately report the problem to the person in charge. Often a minor flaw that is found early can save a major breakdown later. Also, it is difficult to produce high-quality work if the equipment you are using is defective.

5. Don't waste company supplies. In the following case study, for example, Renée wasted fifty sheets of paper by running the photocopy machine carelessly. Then she added to her wastefulness by throwing the paper away. Paper, pens, erasers—all types of supplies—cost money.

6. Don't steal from the company. This costs everyone money—workers and consumers alike. Stealing includes stealing time from your work to run personal errands, stealing supplies or equipment, and "borrowing" things for your own use. Also, remember that theft is against the law. Not only can you be fired for it but also you can be prosecuted.

CASE STUDY

Read the following case study and then answer the questions that appear at the end of it.

Renée was furious. "The equipment they give us around here is useless," she fumed to herself, giving her computer terminal an angry shove. "Especially this machine. Something's always going wrong with it. Yesterday the data set wasn't working. This morning the paper jammed. Half the time it doesn't accept the sign-on sequence. And now it won't even start! The thing is a pain in the neck."

She flicked the power switch a couple of times, then stood and glared at the machine.

Just then Nadia walked by. "What's the matter?" she asked with concern when she saw the expression on Renée's face.

"I don't know. The darn thing won't start."

"Here, let me look," Nadia said helpfully. She tried the power switch, made sure the data set was hooked up, then walked to the back of the machine. "Here's our problem," she said after a moment. "Someone's unplugged it. Must have been the cleaning staff. There, it should work now." Sure enough, the terminal hummed happily.

"Thanks, Nadia. I wouldn't even have thought of anything so simple," Renée said, sitting down to start work.

Things didn't seem to get any better during the day. When she went to photocopy her printout, the photocopy machine was out of paper. She tried loading it, but it wouldn't work. She had to go and ask Mrs. Hansen to help. Renée knew it was part of her job to load the machine, but she just couldn't seem to get it right. The paper always got jammed or she forgot to press the right switch. It was easier to get someone else to do it.

When the paper was loaded properly she started to make her copies, still feeling flustered. She needed fifty copies of each page. "At least this time I remembered to set it for the right number of copies," she thought.

While waiting for her copies, she rushed to her desk to make a personal telephone call. When she got back to the machine, she noted with a sinking sensation that the copies were blank. She'd put the original in wrong side up! Looking guiltily over her shoulder, she threw the fifty blank pages into the waste basket.

"I just won't record those copies in the record book," she decided. "After all, I didn't really make the copies and they don't ask us to list every page we have to throw away."

At 3:30 her supervisor went out, saying "I'll be back in an hour, Renée." Great! Now she could get the paper and stuff that her roommate had asked her to bring home. "After all," she argued, justifying her actions to herself, "the company is making lots of money. They won't even notice that the stuff is missing. Besides, my roommate really needs it. She's just a student and she can't afford it like the company can." Gathering up several lined pads and some typing paper, pens, paper clips, and pencils, she made a neat pile on her desk. "I'll just wrap them up in some of this brown paper," she thought, and did so.

Halfway through her task, she got a creepy feeling and looked up. There stood her supervisor, looking very stern. "Oh, you're back already. Was the meeting shorter than you expected?" Renée asked breathlessly, trying to hide what she was doing.

"What are you doing, Renée?" he asked, ignoring her question.

"Oh, this . . . well . . . you see . . . my roommate is a student and she asked me to bring some . . . uh . . . paper and stuff home . . . uh and . . . well . . . ," her voice trailed off.

"Yes, I do see," Mr. Kelly answered, rather grimly. "I think you and I had better have a talk. Come into my office, please."

Renée sat nervously in the chair while Mr. Kelly looked out the window for a moment. Finally he turned and said, "I've been thinking for some time now that I should speak to you about your attitude toward company equipment and materials. You don't seem to understand that you have a responsibility to use them carefully and efficiently.

"For example, look at the way you use the photocopy machine. I've noticed that you waste a lot of paper. And even though it's part of your job, you haven't learned to load it properly. So you're costing the company money in two ways. First, you're increasing the cost of supplies, and second, you're keeping another employee from her work. If everyone was like you, the company would go bankrupt.

"Now I've caught you stealing. Stealing company supplies as well as company time. Everyone who works here, as well as everyone who buys our products, ends up having to pay for that kind of behaviour.

"When you decided to help yourself to company supplies, you probably figured that the company was rich and could afford the loss. Imagine what would happen if everyone behaved like you.

"Now, I'm going to give you one last chance. But I expect you to learn to operate the business machines properly and to stop wasting and stealing company supplies. Treat company materials as if they belonged to your best friend. You wouldn't steal from her or mistreat her property, would you?

"O.K. You can go now. But be warned, next time you'll lose your job."

1. In what ways did Renée misuse her company's supplies and equipment?

2. What would happen if every employee behaved like Renée?

3. Do you think it's a good idea to treat company materials as if they belonged to your best friend? Explain your answer.

In the case study, Renée showed her lack of concern about company equipment and materials by treating the equipment roughly, not learning to operate it properly, wasting supplies, and stealing company materials Like many people, she took the attitude that ''the company can afford it.'' But employers *can't* afford to keep employees like Renée. It costs them money to fix or replace equipment that's damaged or broken by careless workers. And supplies cost money too. Careless, wasteful, and dishonest employees could, in the long run, cause the company to close its doors. Then Renée and her co-workers would lose their jobs. Also, the amount of money that a company has to spend on its office and plant is built into the prices that it charges for its products or services, so Renée, her co-workers, and the general public have to pay more for these.

Careless use of equipment and materials can have other serious effects also. For example, if you use large or dangerous machinery without proper care, you could injure yourself or others, and if your equipment is damaged, other employees might not be able to do their jobs either.

1. ASSESSING YOUR USE OF EQUIPMENT AND SUPPLIES

1. Do you wait until something goes wrong before you bother to read the operating instructions?

2. When a machine isn't working, do you kick or shake it to try to get it going again?

3. When you've finished with a piece of equipment, do you leave it lying around?

4. Do you ''borrow'' company supplies or equipment for your personal use?

If you've answered ''Yes'' to more than one of these questions, you should examine your behaviour regarding your use of company equipment and supplies.

QUALITY OF WORK
▼▼▼▼▼▼▼▼▼▼▼▼▼▼▼▼▼▼▼▼▼▼▼▼▼▼▼▼

At school and at work your teachers and your employer expect that the quality of work you produce will meet acceptable standards. Usually people produce poor-quality work not because they can't do better, but because they can't be bothered to do their best. Perhaps they don't like school or their jobs, maybe they think that a few mistakes don't matter, or maybe they're more concerned about getting their work done quickly then about doing it well.

The quantity of work produced is important, but the quality of that work is also extremely important. First of all, the mistakes you make can cause problems for other workers and increase company costs. This is particularly obvious on a production line. For example, Ali works in a bakery, taking buns out of the oven and placing them on a conveyor belt. If Ali jiggles the trays when he lays them on the belt, the buns end up out of position and don't get iced properly. The next workers in the sequence, who inspect and package the buns, have to remove all of the buns that aren't iced properly. This makes extra work for them and results in a lot of waste. By taking a little more time and being more careful, Ali can help to improve the overall productivity of his unit.

In some sense, in almost every job the individual worker is part of a production line. We are all dependent on the work of others in the organization. Take a few minutes to think about where your work fits in with the work of others and you'll realize that the quality of your work affects the overall production of the entire organization. This is why employers value employees who produce good-quality work.

GUIDELINES FOR IMPROVING THE QUALITY OF WORK PRODUCED

1. Before starting a task, make sure you understand the instructions. Obviously, if you don't know what you're supposed to be doing, it'll be sheer luck if you do it correctly. Write down the instructions or repeat them to your teacher or supervisor to make sure you understand. Ask questions if you don't. If you are really unsure, do one example, then take it to your teacher or supervisor to check that you are on the right track before going further.

2. The first times you do a task, follow the instructions exactly. Only when you're completely familiar with the work should you start looking for shortcuts.

3. From time to time, check back over your instructions to make sure you haven't forgotten anything. It's easy to slip into bad habits or sloppy work procedures.

4. Concentrate on doing work properly. If your mind is on other things, you are more likely to make mistakes. You won't notice your mistakes unless you are concentrating on what you are doing.

5. Before you pass your work to the next person, double-check it. Everyone makes mistakes from time to time, so it's worth spending the few minutes it takes to check your completed tasks. It's particularly important to check your work the first few times you perform a new activity.

6. Be aware of and deal with problems you encounter in your work. Sometimes, for example, you might find yourself in situations for which you've received no instructions. If the problem is a minor one, try to solve it yourself. If it is something you don't feel comfortable handling, however, report it to someone in authority right away. Don't ignore it in the hope that it will solve itself.

7. Accept the fact that you are responsible for the quality of your work. Don't look for excuses or blame others for your mistakes.

2. ASSESSING THE QUALITY OF YOUR WORK

1. If you make a mistake do you let it go, thinking that someone else will find it?

2. Do you fail to double-check your work because you assume that you did it correctly the first time?

3. Do you tend to rush through your work as quickly as possible?

4. Does your teacher or supervisor criticize you for sloppy or inaccurate work?

5. When doing routine tasks, do you find that you let your thoughts wander?

If you have answered "Yes" to more than one of these questions, you should make an effort to improve the quality of your work.

QUANTITY OF WORK

In any organization, a slow worker can cause just as many problems as a careless worker, so the quantity of work produced is also important. For example, if the bakery worker, Ali, is slow getting the buns out of the oven and onto the conveyor belt, two holdups result: the baking of the next batch of buns will be delayed, and the people after Ali on the production line, the people who inspect and package the buns, will be left with nothing to do. So Ali's slowness affects everybody involved in the production of the buns.

In many jobs, employers set production quotas, which means that employees are expected to produce a certain number of products or perform a certain number of tasks in a set period of time. In other occupations, employees are paid for piecework, which means that their income depends on the number of items they produce. Even when formal production quotas aren't set, employers expect employees who are doing similar types of work to produce approximately the same quantity of work.

As an employee, therefore, you should aim to produce about the same quantity of work as the people you work with. If you're very slow, you'll interfere with the work of others, and they'll probably feel that you're not doing your share. At work, you're part of a team and you have a responsibility to the other team members. Your aim should be to do your fair share of work quickly and well.

GUIDELINES FOR IMPROVING THE QUANTITY OF WORK PRODUCED

1. *Find out how much you are expected to produce.* When you start an assignment, your teacher or supervisor will usually tell you what tasks you are responsible for. Make a list of these tasks and use it to prepare a daily schedule. If you're not given specific instructions about the amount of work you should produce, find out what is expected by watching or asking other students or people with whom you work.

2. *Plan a daily routine.* Decide on the order in which you're going to do each of your assigned tasks and give yourself a time limit for each one. Having a routine helps you to save time because you don't have to stop after each activity and take time to decide what to do next.

3. *Before you begin a task, make sure you have all the necessary materials and equipment.* If you have to keep jumping up to get things you've forgotten or run out of, your productivity will decrease. By organizing yourself before you begin, you'll find that you get more done in the same amount of time.

4. *Work at a steady pace.* It's easy to waste a lot of time jumping up to get things, making personal phone calls, making unnecessary trips to the washroom, daydreaming, or chatting with other workers. You should try to avoid interruptions and keep your mind on the task at hand.

5. *When you've finished one task, don't sit and wait for someone to tell you what to do next.* Move on to the next activity you've planned as part of your daily routine. If you've finished your work for the day, you might either start on work that's due later or ask your teacher or supervisor for something else to do.

6. *Try to finish one task before beginning another.* Each time you switch to a new activity, it takes a few moments to get your thoughts organized. Obtain an in-basket and ask people to leave their work there. Then finish what you're doing before starting on the next thing in the basket.

7. *Try to avoid worrying about the work you still have to do.* This is easier said than done, but if you've planned a realistic daily routine, you should be able to get everything finished. Worrying about what's still to be done just slows you down.

3. ASSESSING THE QUANTITY OF YOUR WORK

1. Do you always seem to fall behind in your assignments?

2. Do you often have to stay late at school or work to finish your tasks?

3. Does your teacher or supervisor usually ask for your work before you've finished it?

4. Do you usually meet your work deadlines?

5. Has your teacher or supervisor criticized you for slowness or poor productivity?

7. Do the people you work with regularly produce more work than you?

8. Do you spend a lot of time gazing around or talking to others?

If you've answered ''Yes'' to more than one of these questions, you're probably producing an inadequate quantity of work during your regular work hours. It's possible that your assigned workload is too heavy. To judge this, you should discuss the problem with your teacher or supervisor. However, if others doing similar tasks have the same amount of work and seem able to handle it, the problem must be poor productivity on your part and you should review the guidelines for improving the quantity of work produced.

CASE STUDY

Read the following case study about two young employees who work for the same employer but have quite different working habits. Then answer the questions that appear at the end.

Sam and Marita are the two newest employees in a cafeteria located in a large, busy mall. They've been there only two weeks but already the difference in their work habits is clear to everyone.

As far as Sam was concerned, today had been the worst day yet. Here it was, only two o'clock, and it felt like he'd been there forever. He was rushed off his feet and everything was going wrong.

"How can I be expected to serve properly if I can't even find the trays?" he asked himself crossly as he stuffed everything into one small bag. "Here you go," he smiled, handing the bag to his waiting customer, only to watch, horrified, as the bottom of the bag tore, spilling food and a soft drink all over the counter. Sighing, he cleaned up the mess and started over.

Out of the corner of his eye, he saw one of his regulars looking impatient. She must have been waiting ten minutes already, he groaned to himself, "Well, what'll it be today?" he asked, hurrying to her.

"I think I'll have a small cola, a cheeseburger, and do you have any chocolate ice cream?" she asked.

"Just a minute, I'll go check," he said, rushing off.

On his way, another customer interrupted. "Could you tell me where to find the straws?" he asked. "Right over there," Sam pointed.

"There aren't any there," the customer persisted. Sam turned back. Sure enough, they had run out of straws. "I'll get some more from the back," he promised, and started off.

When he came back with the straws, he noticed his first customer. What was it she'd wanted to know about? Oh yes, chocolate ice cream. He hurried back with the answer.

"Fine, I'll take two cones." she said.

As he reached for the cones, he realized with a sinking sensation that there wasn't enough ice cream. "I'll be right back with more," he called over his shoulder, diving into the back room.

"You'll have to wait a minute, there's none open," said Ferdie, the manager, when Sam explained what he wanted. So Sam waited.

Five minutes later, when Sam got back, he noticed that his customer had disappeared. Oh, there she was, at Marita's counter, He grabbed an ice cream cone and rushed over to her. "Here you go," he panted. "Is this what you wanted?"

The customer looked at him coldly. "Never mind," she said. "I got tired of waiting and decided to get something else instead."

Sam felt angry. Grumbling, he walked back to his counter and looked around. Well, at least there weren't any customers at the moment. He knew he should tidy up his area a bit, but first he'd have a drink and relax.

Sipping his drink, he looked over at Marita, who was working busily behind her counter. She seemed to have a really easy time of it. "Look at her now, cleaning up her counter when it doesn't even need it," he thought to himself. "I guess it's easier on her side of the restaurant. Besides, all my customers are in such a hurry." Still, he wondered.

At three o'clock, when he and Marita went for their coffee break together, the question was still on his mind. "You always look so cool." he said. "When I was going crazy trying to do three things at once and that customer was on my back, I looked over at your counter and there wasn't even anyone waiting. How do you do it?"

"Well, I don't know. It got pretty busy at my counter for a while there!" Marita answered, surprised. "I just don't let myself get upset. Instead, I concentrate on serving one customer at a time. I find that when I try to do more than that, I get mixed up and forget what everyone wants. It just slows me down.

"I try to be prepared, too. When it slows down a bit, I check to make sure there are enough trays and I tidy up under my counter, making sure that I have enough condiments, cups, plates—you know, the stuff that runs out. Then I don't have to keep running to the back when I need them.

"When I arrive in the morning, I like to follow a regular routine. For example, I always start by cleaning and tidying up my counter. That way I don't have to think about it later on. Then I read the price lists and try to memorize any changes. I find it saves time when customers come in, because I don't have to keep checking. And I'm trying to learn where everything is kept. That way I don't have to waste time searching for things. And once I've finished with something, I try to put it back in the same place each time. It makes it faster to find things."

Sam looked impressed. "So that's why you always manage to look cool. Maybe I should try it."

QUESTIONS

1. Who do you think did more work during an average day, Sam or Marita? Give reasons for your answer.

2. Why do you think it's important for your work to meet acceptable standards of quality? What happens when these standards are not met?

3. List ways of improving the quality of your work.

4. What can you do to improve the quantity of work you produce?

5. In what ways can being organized and tidy in your work habits lead to greater efficiency?

CHAPTER SUMMARY EXERCISES

▼▼▼▼▼▼▼▼▼▼▼▼▼▼▼▼▼▼▼ ▼▼▼▼▼▼▼▼▼▼▼▼▼▼▼▼▼▼▼▼▼

1. What does the word *efficiency* mean?

2. What does being efficient on the job involve?

3. Describe some methods you can use to remember co-workers' names.

4. What is the first step you should take before beginning a task?

5. Briefly describe six things that are important in relation to the care and handling of company equipment and supplies.

6. Is it O.K. to take company supplies such pens, paper, etc., for personal use? Explain why or why not.

7. Why is the quality of work produced important?

8. Why is the quantity of work produced important?

9. List four ways in which the quality of work can be improved.

10. List four ways in which the quantity of work can be improved.

11. Read again the case study at the end of this chapter and make notes of each thing Sam did that you think was the result of inefficiency. Then, in paragraph form, describe each example of inefficiency and explain how he could have avoided the problem.

4

Attitude, Interpersonal Skills, and Stress on the Job

INTRODUCTION
▼▼▼▼▼▼▼▼▼▼▼▼▼▼▼▼▼▼▼▼

Success in the workplace depends on more than a person's knowledge, practical skills, attendance, and efficiency. Having a positive attitude, demonstrating professionalism, getting along well with supervisors and co-workers, and effectively handling stress are also very important.

This unit discusses these aspects of work life, including chapters on how to be assertive, not aggressive; how to handle anger; and how to really *listen*, not just hear, including a section on telephone skills.

Importance of a Positive Attitude

OBJECTIVES
▼▼▼▼▼▼▼▼▼▼▼▼▼▼▼

After completing this chapter you should be able to:

- Explain the importance of a positive attitude in all situations.
- Assess your own attitude.
- Accept orders and follow instructions effectively.
- Define your own level of trustworthiness.
- Explain what the word *professionalism* means.
- List some of the ways in which professionalism can be demonstrated.

INTRODUCTION
▼▼▼▼▼▼▼▼▼▼▼▼▼▼▼▼▼

The word *attitude* means a way of thinking, acting, or feeling. Attitudes can be either positive or negative. Negative attitudes lead to negative results, so a positive attitude is necessary for you to make the most of your life, both personally and on the job. A positive attitude is a greatly valued characteristic of an employee.

A positive attitude makes every situation more enjoyable for everyone. At work, the employer feels that any reasonable request will be willingly handled by an employee with a positive attitude. If you enjoy what you're doing, you'll probably have a positive attitude toward your work. Even if you *don't* enjoy what you're doing, however, a positive attitude helps.

Attitudes colour every aspect of our lives. A positive attitude brightens our lives with every colour of the rainbow, while a negative attitude darkens the world to grey and black. Which attitudes colour your world?

1. IS YOUR ATTITUDE SHOWING?

The following survey will help you to assess your attitude toward others and toward situations in which you might find yourself. The results will indicate if your attitude needs improvement. In your notebook, write down the number of each question and then put beside it the number in the key below that best describes your first reaction to the question.

5 = Yes   4 = Usually Yes   3 = Sometimes Yes/Sometimes No
2 = Usually No   1 = No

1. Are you friendly and outgoing?

2. Do you avoid being a complainer?

3. Can you be optimistic when others are depressed?

4. Do you refrain from boasting or bragging?

5. Do you have a sense of duty and responsibility?

6. Do you control your temper?

7. Do you speak well of your employer?

8. Do you feel well most of the time?

9. Do you follow directions willingly, asking questions when necessary?

10. Do you keep promises?

11. Do you organize your work and stay on schedule?

12. Do you readily admit your mistakes?

13. Can you be a leader without being bossy?

14. Is it easy for you to like most people?

15. Can you stick to a tiresome task without being prodded?

16. Do you know your weaknesses and attempt to correct them?

17. Can you stand being teased?

18. Do you avoid feeling sorry for yourself?

19. Are you courteous to others?

20. Are you neat in your personal appearance and work habits?

21. Do you respect the opinions of others?

22. Are you a good loser?

23. Can you adapt to new and unexpected situations readily?

24. Are you tolerant of other people's beliefs?

25. Do you refrain from sulking when things go differently than you'd like?

26. Are you a good listener?

27. Are you the type of friend that you expect others to be?

28. Can you disagree without being disagreeable?

29. Are you punctual?

30. Do you drive carefully?

31. Do you generally speak well of others?

32. Can you take criticism without being resentful or feeling hurt?

33. Are you careful to pay back all loans, however small?

34. Do you generally look at the bright side of things?

35. Does your voice usually sound cheerful?

36. Can you work with people you dislike?

37. Are you pleasant to others even when you feel displeased about something?

38. Do you show enthusiasm for the interests of others?

39. Do you tend to be enthusiastic about whatever you do?

40. Are you honest and sincere with others?

Attitude Scoring

There are 40 questions; a perfect score would be 200. Total your score and rate yourself according to the following scale.

175-200:   You're terrific.
150-174:   Your attitude toward others is admirable.
110-149:   Your attitude needs polishing in certain areas.
Below 110: Take a close look at your attitude. You might need to pay particular attention to those questions you answered with a 1 or 2. Can you see any room for improvement there?

QUESTION

How can negative attitudes be changed to positive attitudes? Give some examples.

CHARACTERISTICS OF A PERSON WITH A GOOD ATTITUDE

If you have a good attitude, you are:

Helpful	Polite
Willing	Persistent
Orderly	Even-tempered
Co-operative	Responsible
Considerate	Interested in work
Cheerful	Enthusiastic
Prompt	Eager to improve
Trustworthy	Accepting of criticism

2. TAKE A LOOK AT YOURSELF

In your notebook, write down the numbers of the following questions. Then, beside each number, answer each question by writing "Yes," "No," or "Not sure."

1. Do you always wish it were the weekend?

2. Do you look forward to your future?

3. Do you enjoy tackling new challenges?

4. Can you keep a secret?

5. Do you feel that you don't get what you deserve?

6. Are you always late?

7. Do you often do things at the last minute?

8. Do you trust your own judgment?

9. Do you find it difficult to concentrate on finishing one task at a time?

10. Are you understanding about other people's problems?

11. Are you a good listener?

12. Are you able to work alone without supervision?

13. Do you always look for the easy way out?

14. Do you feel confident about your skills and abilities?

15. Do you find it difficult to meet new people?

16. Are you able to admire other people's accomplishments without feeling jealous?

17. Do you refrain from gossiping?

18. Are you tolerant of other people's opinions?

19. Do you know the difference between what you can change and what you can't?

20. Do you give and accept praise graciously?

21. Are you neat in your personal appearance?

22. Are you sympathetic? Do you try to put yourself in the other person's situation?

23. Do you frequently interrupt other people while they are speaking?

24. Do you enjoy meeting new people?

25. Are you patient with other people?

QUESTIONS

1. Which questions did you answer "Not sure"? Why?

2. Identify the questions that you answered "No" and explain why you answered this way. Could the attitude indicated by your answer to these questions determine the type of employee you are or might be?

3. Describe the characteristics of a person with a positive attitude toward her or his work.

3. AN INTERVIEW

What does it mean to have a positive attitude in the workplace? What's it like to work with people who have a positive attitude—and with people who don't ? How does having a positive attitude affect the way the negative aspects of a job are handled? Ask someone who likes his or her job some questions like the following ones. Add some questions of your own.

1. Why do you like your job?

2. Are there people you work with who make your job easier? How?

3. Are there people you work with who make your job more difficult? How?

4. Do you think that one person's attitude can affect the company as a whole? How?

5. What do you dislike about your job?

6. How do you handle it when you really don't feel like going to work?

7. How do your co-workers handle it when they don't want to go to work? What's your opinion of their methods?

ACCEPTING ORDERS
▼▼▼▼▼▼▼▼▼▼▼▼▼▼▼▼▼▼▼▼▼▼▼▼▼▼▼▼▼▼

Like it or not, most people have to take orders from others for at least part of their working lives. Remember that the person who is giving orders is in that position because he or she has demonstrated an ability to do that job well or to make sure that it is done properly.

By indicating your willingness to take and carry out orders, you show your willingness to co-operate in doing what your employer feels is best for the company. So, when you are given an order:

1. Look willing.

2. Make sure you understand what is required.

3. Respond positively and cheerfully.

4. Carry out the task to the best of your ability.

CASE STUDIES

Read the following case studies to see how some employees accept and carry out orders. In your notebook, rewrite these case studies so that they follow the four guidelines for accepting orders. Finally, use your own part-time job experience to write your own case study about a person who accepts orders well.

1. Shawna's supervisor asked Shawna to interrupt her work in the stockroom to help at the cash desk during a busy period. Shawna shrugged and said, "O.K., but don't blame me if the new stock doesn't get sorted today."

2. When Dimitri arrived at the restaurant for his shift, his supervisor was very glad to see him. "We're so short-handed today! Would you please help to clear the tables, instead of your usual job of helping to make desserts?" Dimitri's face fell. "I guess so, he said. He worked as slowly as he could, to show his supervisor how annoyed he was.

3. Maral worked part-time at the local library. She enjoyed working at the check-out desk and meeting the library patrons. One day, her supervisor said, "I'd like to look after reshelving the books and making sure that the shelves are tidy." Maral thought that this would be a boring job, but she nodded, smiled, and began to carefully put books away in their proper places on the shelves.

4. GETTING THINGS STRAIGHT

You're following directions properly when you do things in the right order. If you're not sure what the right order is, you should ask your teacher or supervisor. Read the following scenarios and, in your notebook, write down the letters that indicate the order in which you think the tasks should be done.

1. You work in a small coffee shop. Your supervisor has told you that attending to patrons and making sure that they're comfortable must always be your first priority. The various jobs you do in the coffee shop involve:

   a) Clearing and wiping tables.

   b) Sweeping the floor and mopping up spills.

   c) Serving glasses of water to customers when they first sit down.

   d) Emptying ashtrays.

   e) Refilling napkin and condiment containers.

   f) Regrouping chairs and tables as necessary.

   You've just had an extremely busy lunch hour. All of your tables are now dirty, and you're busy cleaning up a sticky spill on the floor. Suddenly, a group of ten people comes in, wanting to sit together.
   In what order would you carry out your tasks? Explain why.

2. You work in a clothing store. The owner has told you that the customer always comes first. Your job involves:

   a) Helping customers to find the items they want.

   b) Working on the cash desk.

   c) Directing customers to the fitting rooms.

   d) Keeping shelves stocked with merchandise.

   e) Recording new stock as it arrives.

   f) Keeping the store neat and tidy.

   One day, while you're busy with a customer, new stock is delivered and left in the main store area instead of in the stockroom. Just as you're about to move it, start updating your records, and refilling some of the almost-empty shelves, a customer asks you where to find a certain size of a garment and if it's possible to try it on. At the same time, another customer rushes up, saying, "I'm in a terrible hurry. Will you please take the money for this purchase right away?"
   In what order would you carry out your tasks? Explain why.

3. You are the customer. You're ordering a meal in a fast-food restaurant. Your server has to:

   a) Take your order.

b) Obtain your food and drink.

c) Take your money for the meal.

d) Provide ketchup and vinegar.

e) Inform the customer of reasons for any delay.

f) Check on the progress of food preparation.

You order a hamburger, French fries, and a glass of milk. Your server notices that all of the pre-prepared hamburgers have been used during the lunchtime rush, but figures more are probably being prepared. Some fries are ready, so he puts them in a container and puts the container on your tray. He then pours milk from the milk dispenser and places it on your tray. He leans against the counter, waiting for the hamburger.

After a while, you hear one of the cooks call, "Any more burgers needed? We can start on them now." Your server announces that you have ordered one. Several minutes later, the hamburger is ready. Your server now adds up your order and asks for the money. You pay, take several steps away from the counter, and are stopped by the server calling, "Oh, 'scuse me, but do you need ketchup and vinegar?"

As the customer, in what order would you have preferred that your server carry out his tasks?

4. You have a part-time job in an office. You assist your supervisor by:

a) Keying letters and memos.

b) Keeping files up to date.

c) Delivering interoffice mail.

d) Sending out external mail.

e) Operating the photocopier.

f) Operating the fax machine.

Your supervisor will be in a meeting all day and has left you some notes regarding the work that must be done today. The instructions include:

- Key the handwritten letters in the attached folder. Sign them for me and make sure they get out in the last mail pick-up at 16:00.

- Key the memo to Ms. Lum. She'll need the information in this memo in order to write a letter that must go out today.

- Send the attached fax to our Vancouver branch. It must arrive there first thing this morning (don't forget the time difference—it's three-hours earlier there).

- Do the big photocopying job that you'll find on my desk. It'll probably take a couple of hours. Good thing we have the automatic multi-page photocopier, right?

- There are two documents regarding the Baron Corporation somewhere in the pile of filing that I've left on your desk. They and the rest of the file will be needed for a meeting tomorrow morning. The rest of the pile can be filed any time.

In your notebook, write down the order in which you'd do these tasks. Explain why.

Figure 15.1 Calendar for Exercise 5

OCTOBER

SUNDAY	MONDAY	TUESDAY	WEDNESDAY	THURSDAY	FRIDAY	SATURDAY
	1 Coffee machine this week: Vida. Thanksgiving Charity Drive all week: 12-1 p.m. daily-cafeteria. Come and donate your time.	**2** New employees' orientation meeting 9-10 a.m.	**3**	**4** Accounting Dept. meeting 3-4 p.m.	**5**	**6**
7	**8** THANKSGIVING DAY Holiday	**9** Coffee machine this week: Les	**10** Community Blood Donor Clinic: Please plan to attend. 12-2 p.m.	**11**	**12** All-employees meeting to demonstrate new telephone system: 10-11 a.m.	**13**
14	**15** Coffee machine: Baldeo	**16** Farewell party for Ann Sava at 4:30 in the cafeteria. Wine + cheese	**17**	**18** Employee Job Appraisal meetings to be held all day in the boardroom.	**19**	**20**
21	**22** Managers' meeting: 9-12 Coffee machine: Carla	**23**	**24** New security system goes into effect. Before 7 a.m. and after 6 p.m. every day, use front doors only.	**25**	**26** Warehouse closes at 2 p.m. for inventory.	**27**
28	**29** Coffee machine: Hawk	**30**	**31** HALLOWEEN Halloween Lunch presented by the Social club, 12 p.m. All invited. $3.50 each.			

129

5. CALENDAR EXERCISE

Figure 15.1 on the previous page shows a calendar in an office. It tells employees when various events are happening. Read the notes on the calendar and answer the questions below.

1. What is the date and time of the Accounting Department meeting?

2. Patty arrived to work at the Thanksgiving Charity Drive at 2 p.m. on Monday. Did she come in at the right time?

3. What time should Joe go to the farewell party for Ann?

4. Who is in charge of the coffee machine during the second week?

5. At 6:10 p.m. on October 29, Andrea left the building. How should she have left?

6. What must Social Club members do before lunchtime on October 31?

7. By when should the employees be ready for their job appraisals?

8. If Ann's dad comes on October 26 at 3 p.m. to pick up an order from the warehouse, will he be able to get it?

9. What type of meeting should all new employees attend? When?

10. If Len wants to attend the Blood Donor Clinic, when should he go?

11. When do employees have a long weekend?

12. Should employees be at the information meeting regarding the new telephone system first thing in the morning?

GETTING ALONG WITH SUPERVISORS
▼▼▼▼▼▼▼▼▼▼▼▼▼▼▼▼▼▼▼▼▼▼▼▼▼▼▼▼▼▼▼▼

It's important to have a good working relationship with your supervisor. Your work environment will be pleasanter and you'll have a greater sense of satisfaction in your job if you get along well with the people in authority.

6. PROBLEMS WITH SUPERVISORS

Read the following scenarios and note the words in boldface that describe a supervisor's actions or attitude. Note also how the employee responded to the supervisor in each case. In your notebook, write your opinion of whether the supervisor's actions were acceptable or unacceptable, and whether the employee made an acceptable or an unacceptable response to the supervisor. In each case, explain your opinion. If you feel that the actions or attitudes of either person were unacceptable, state what you think the other person should have done.

1. Vida worked at a food concession at a busy convention centre. She enjoyed working with the public and took pride in being efficient and cheerful. **Her supervisor never complimented her, however, but always seemed to be pointing out what Vida should do next.** Vida

would promptly start on the next task, but began to wonder if she was doing her job as well as she should or could.

Once the convention season was in full swing, another person was hired to work in the booth. Vida noticed that **the supervisor gave the other person the job of serving most of the time, while Vida was told to keep the area clean and make sure that there were always plenty of supplies.** Vida felt that the supervisor was playing favourites and that her skills weren't being used properly. She wondered if she should discuss the situation with the supervisor, but never got around to doing so.

Eventually, Vida became resentful and put less and less effort into her job. **The supervisor told her that her work was unsatisfactory, but didn't explain in what way.** Vida became angry, and quit.

Months later, after being unable to find another job, Vida wondered if there might have been some other way to resolve her difficulties with her supervisor.

2. Lee had always had a good working relationship with the supervisor of the warehouse where she worked. **Her supervisor gave her a variety of tasks to do, to find out what Lee did best**, and Lee did well at each task.

One day, the supervisor told Lee that a new shipping procedure was going to be used in the warehouse. **She didn't have time to explain it very well, but said that she was sure that Lee would "pick it up quickly."**

Lee felt a little nervous about the new procedure. There were other people who knew how it worked, but Lee didn't bother to ask them, figuring it would all work out all right.

A short time later, **Lee's supervisor angrily called Lee into her office.** An important order for which Lee was responsible had gone astray. The mistake would probably cost the company a lot of money.

"You're the one who's stupid," Lee told her supervisor. "How can you expect me to do the job when you don't explain it to me? The mistake is your fault!"

BEING TRUSTWORTHY
▼▼▼▼▼▼▼▼▼▼▼▼▼▼▼▼▼▼▼▼▼▼▼▼▼▼▼▼▼▼

Trustworthiness—being dependable, reliable, and honest—is another very important trait, whether on the job, in school, at home, or with friends and acquaintances.

7. RATING OTHERS' TRUSTWORTHINESS

If you're trustworthy, your employer can depend on you to do your job, even when the supervisor isn't watching you. In your notebook, describe what you think would be the most trustworthy thing to do in each of the following situations.

1. Mario's employer always found it easier to pay Mario cash, since Mario didn't work many hours and his shifts varied. One day, Mario realized that he had been overpaid. He told a friend about this, and the friend's opinion was, "You might as well keep the extra money.

It's cash, so your boss won't have a record of it. Besides, he can afford it.'' What should Mario do?

2. Reba's supervisor often sends her out of the office on errands. Reba enjoys the chance to get out. Lately, she's started to go into stores and look around while out on errands. She hurries to do the errands to give herself extra time to shop. She feels that she isn't doing anything wrong, particularly since her supervisor has never said anything about how long the errands have taken.

3. Ron works in a small variety store. One day, a customer comes in and buys a number of items. When Jack has finished adding up the various prices, the customer asks, ''Did you charge me the sale price for the facial tissues?'' Jack hadn't realized that the tissues were on sale. If he changes the price now, he'll have to write out a ''Void'' slip for the store owner. This will take time, and several customers waiting in line. It's possible that the customer won't check her sales slip—he could even ''forget'' to put it into her bag. What should Jack do?

8. RATING YOUR OWN TRUSTWORTHINESS

When someone trusts you, that person expects to be able to count on your behaving in a certain way. This puts a certain responsibility on you. If you behave in a trustworthy manner, employers will respect you and will probably give you greater responsibility.

In your notebook, make two columns, one headed ''Yes'' and the other ''No.'' In whichever column best represents your reaction to each of the following statements, write the number of the statement.

1. In my job, I try to give good value for my wages.

2. I always do what's expected of me at work.

3. I work hard and only take longer breaks than I should when I know if won't affect anyone.

4. I speak well of my employer when I'm away from work.

5. I believe in being truthful, so I let everyone know that my employer is a jerk.

6. I take good care of my employer's equipment and supplies.

7. If I break something, I admit that I did it.

8. If I break something that I know I couldn't afford to replace, I keep quiet about it.

9. When my supervisor gives me more money that is necessary to buy coffee and doughnuts for a meeting, I always return the extra money.

10. If my supervisor asks me to do something that isn't part of my job, I cheerfully do it.

11. When quitting time comes, I quit, regardless of the work I've left unfinished.

12. I always tell new employees about everything I think is wrong with the company.

1. Take a look at your results. In which areas could you improve?

2. Have you ever been in a situation that you found hard to deal with honestly? Try to come up with suggestions on different ways in which this situation could have been dealt with honestly and comfortably.

PROFESSIONALISM

Being professional on the job means more than doing your job competently. Professionalism, which means demonstrating the habits and attitudes of a professional, involves having a personal code of ethics in relation to job attendance and punctuality, dependability, loyalty, self-control, gossip, personal appearance, and maintenance of work equipment and work area.

BEING ON THE JOB — AND ON TIME

As discussed in Chapter 13, punctuality and being on the job when you're supposed to be are very important. Even if you don't have to sign in or punch a clock, being even a few minutes late is not professional and is actually cheating your employer. And staying away from work because you partied too well the night before is also a betrayal of your employer's trust.

DEPENDABILITY

A true professional takes responsibility for properly completing all projects and tasks that have been assigned. Making up excuses for failure or blaming someone else for it are not acceptable behaviours. If you have a problem with some aspect of your work, speak to your supervisor and ask for help or guidance.

LOYALTY

Don't tell outsiders any information that your company might consider to be confidential. Don't bad-mouth your company or your supervisor to outsiders or co-workers. If you have a lot of complaints, perhaps it's time you looked for another job.

SELF-CONTROL

Having self-control means more than just avoiding tears or outbursts of anger on the job. It also means keeping your mind on your work and not letting your personal life infringe on your work life. Try to arrange to make and receive as few personal telephone calls as possible. Don't discuss your personal problems with anyone at work or spend valuable time broadcasting details about what a great or miserable weekend you had.

GOSSIP

Always remember that there's a big difference between facts and gossip. If someone is gossiping to you, ask yourself: "Why is this person telling me this?" "Should I trust a person who gossips?" "Would I like to be the subject of such gossip?" Gossiping takes time and thought away from work. Also, if you're the gossiper and the rumour proves to be untrue, your trustworthiness will always be in question. Look for ways to compliment other people and to speak well of them. Always heed the old saying: "If you can't say anything nice, don't say anything at all."

PERSONAL APPEARANCE

As discussed in Chapter 12, you should dress appropriately for your job but always be as clean and tidy as possible. Your appearance affects the way in which your supervisor, co-workers, and clients or customers react to you. Many studies have shown that people tend to judge other people's personal qualities and characteristics based on their clothing and grooming. People are more likely to respect and trust a well-groomed, neatly dressed person.

Be aware that personal image is negatively affected by the use of bad grammar and too much slang or street language, as well as by mannerisms such as chewing gum, cracking knuckles, fussing too much with hair, and coughing or sneezing without covering the mouth.

EQUIPMENT AND WORK AREA MAINTENANCE

The importance of properly caring for company equipment and maintaining a tidy work area were discussed in Chapter 14. Besides the major items of concern, you should also think of the little things. For example, if you occasionally have to eat your lunch at your desk or workbench, dispose of the remains carefully. Your co-workers wouldn't appreciate smelling your tuna sandwich all afternoon! Also, avoid overpersonalizing your work area with photos, clippings, knick-knacks, etc.

CHAPTER SUMMARY EXERCISES

▼▼

1. What does the word *attitude* mean?

2. What are the benefits of having a positive attitude?

3. Should you work well even when you're not being supervised? Explain your answer.

4. How can you demonstrate a positive attitude when you're receiving an order?

5. Why is it important to receive criticism with a positive attitude?

6. What positive attitudes are required to co-operate with others?

7. Describe in detail a work situation in which trustworthiness is required.

8. Why is it important to demonstrate to your employer that you're a reliable worker?

9. List seven areas in which professionalism on the job is important.

Assertiveness *Is Not a Bad Word*

OBJECTIVES
▼▼▼▼▼▼▼▼▼▼▼▼▼▼▼▼

After completing this chapter you should be able to:

- Describe the characteristics of assertive, aggressive, and passive people.
- Act assertively in situations.
- Accept and give criticism constructively.

INTRODUCTION
▼▼▼▼▼▼▼▼▼▼▼▼▼▼▼▼▼▼▼

People want to feel as if they have some control over their lives, and to make their own choices. Some people, however, spend most of their time trying to be "nice," no matter how they *really* feel inside. These are passive people. Others react aggressively to almost every situation, demanding that things go their way. Happily, there's a middle road that doesn't involve being "good" or being "bad." People have the choice to be assertive.

ASSERTIVE, AGGRESSIVE, OR PASSIVE?
▼▼▼▼▼▼▼▼▼▼▼▼▼▼▼▼▼▼▼▼▼▼▼▼▼▼▼▼▼▼▼▼▼

To be assertive, you don't have to be pushy and nasty. Assertive people:

- Are confident and certain of their likes and dislikes.
- Honestly express their feelings without being rude or unpleasant.
- Choose for themselves what they want to do or not do, based on their values.
- Allow and encourage others to achieve their goals.
- Respect themselves and others.
- Understand and like themselves.
- Avoid behaviour that makes them feel helpless, depressed, or dissatisfied, but don't do things that infringe on the rights of others.

So, assertive people are well-balanced and know how to achieve happiness and success without hurting anyone else in the process. Aggressive people, however:

- Achieve their own ends at the expense of others.

- Express their feelings without thought for the sensitivities of others.

- Impose their opinions and choices on others.

- Think only of themselves and their desires.

- Have no respect for other people.

- Always think that they're right and everyone else is wrong.

Just as unbalanced, but in the opposite direction, are passive people, who:

- Have a poor sense of their own self-worth; are always putting themselves down.

- Don't express their real feelings even though they often feel hurt and anxious; are afraid people won't like them if they do.

- Allow others to make choices for them, so they seldom get what they want; look to others to solve their problems or tell them what to do.

- Feel that they're always wrong and others are always right.

- Are often disappointed because other people don't live up to their expectations.

- Are often taken advantage of by aggressive people, who identify the weakness of passive people.

CASE STUDIES

Read the following case studies and then explain how each person could behave assertively in the situations described.

1. Diane spent a lot of time with her three friends, Petra, Saiko, and Louise. Lately, she was getting tired of spending time with them. It seemed that, every weekend, one of them was planning something they would do together. Sometimes she didn't want to go out with them but since she didn't have anything planned, she would say yes. Sometimes she regretted later that she had spent her money on a movie she didn't really want to see or a meal at a restaurant that she really couldn't afford.

2. Paul's sixteenth birthday is in two weeks, in late May. He has lots of things to look forward to, but he's not looking forward to his birthday. Every year his parents invite his aunts, uncles, and cousins over for a barbecue on the night of his birthday. He doesn't feel comfortable with the tradition anymore. It was fun when he was a kid but now he's embarrassed by all the fuss his mother makes and he doesn't like people feeling that they have to give him presents. He usually doesn't like the presents but he has to act grateful for them. He'd like to be able to invite some of his friends over for his birthday instead.

3. After the high school prom there's going to be a party where Corey expects there will be drinking. He's anxious to go to the party because all of his friends will be there. After talking to his date, Dana, about the party, he doesn't know what to do. Dana would like to please Corey but she doesn't want to go because she's afraid they might have to get a ride home with someone who has been drinking.

CASE STUDIES

Study the following list of common characteristics of aggressive people and then identify which person in each case study should be more assertive. Aggressive people:

- Manipulate others to achieve their own ends.
- Want things done their way.
- Often speak without thinking.
- Know it all.
- Are very critical of other people.
- Demand a lot of attention from others.

1. Susan and her mother often go shopping together for clothes. Susan receives a small clothing allowance from her parents and she baby-sits occasionally. Four weeks ago Susan put a winter coat on a lay-away plan with a store. On a Friday night she and her mother go shopping and Susan makes sure that they go to the store where the coat is on lay-away. Susan arranges for her mother to see the coat and then explains that she has put a $50 deposit on it and will lose the deposit unless her mother buys the coat for her tonight or tomorrow.

2. Yasif and Steven have worked part-time as clerks in a sporting goods store for more than a year. Part of their wages are based on commissions. When a customer comes in who looks fairly well off, Yasif makes sure that he serves that person.

3. Lee has had a crush on Danny for several months. He doesn't appreciate her attention so he came up with a plan that he hoped would divert Lee's attention from him: on Valentine's Day, he sent flowers to her house, but signed the card with another young man's name.

4. Janet and Marna share an apartment. Janet is the best cook so she usually cooks supper on week nights. Marna does the cleaning up but resents it. Hoping that Janet will realize she hates cleaning up, Marna has started leaving a few dishes unwashed in the sink.

5. Erica would like to see her boyfriend Ian more frequently. Often when she wants to go out, he tells her that he has to play pool first. When Ian does get to her house, it's usually too late to go out. Erica also thinks he's not being honest with her. Sometimes she wonders if he's seeing someone else.

6. Midori has had a job at a popcorn store at the mall for three months. She usually enjoys her job, but lately she's started to feel uncomfortable around the assistant manager, Mark. He often calls her into the back for no good reason and then asks her personal questions, which she tries to avoid answering. Mark has offered to drive her home a few times, but she always refuses. Midori doesn't want to have anything to do with him. She just wants to get through her shifts without incident when he is on duty.

MAKING CRITICISM
WORK FOR YOU
▼▼▼▼▼▼▼▼▼▼▼▼▼▼▼▼▼▼▼▼▼▼▼▼▼▼▼

The word *criticize* can mean to judge, appraise, assess, evaluate, estimate, examine, analyse, survey, and comment on. It also can mean to attack, disapprove, find fault with, shoot down, condemn, denounce, blame, censure, reprove, reproach, take exception to, take offence.

As you can see from these possible synonyms, not all of the actions described would lead to good communication. Some of the inappropriate, negative actions are used by aggressive people in criticizing other people's ways of doing things. To be able to accept and give criticism in an assertive and constructive way, however, are important skills that can help to smooth the process of working and living with other people.

To have good relationships on the job it's essential to have good communication. When you have a job, you're part of an organization that has goals. A supervisor might criticize your actions when he or she thinks that a change in these would assist the organization to achieve its goals. The giving and taking of constructive criticism require care and much thought if the result is to be of benefit to the people involved and to the organization.

Who criticizes you now? Perhaps it feels as though many people do but that there are only certain people from whom you will accept criticism without feeling hurt. On the job you'll have to learn to accept criticism from your supervisor and co-workers, and you must be aware that criticism doesn't need to bring anger or hurt. A suggestion for improvement should be welcomed.

Criticism and putdowns are not the same thing. If you're feeling unsure of yourself, however, you might interpret any critical comment as an attempt to belittle you. Constructive criticism, however, can help you to be better at your job, and is offered with caring, respect, and a genuine desire to help the other person. Everyone has different strengths, weaknesses, and perceptions. You can profit from the experience and skills of others if you're willing to listen to different ideas and suggestions.

Nobody enjoys being criticized, but we can't expect to be able to please everyone all of the time. If you interpret every comment as an unfair criticism or if you believe that any criticism you receive is proof of your worthlessness, you're setting yourself up to feel upset.

At work you'll be with people of different ages, backgrounds, and levels of experience. Sometimes people disagree and sometimes people make mistakes. No one is perfect all the time. Taking and giving constructive criticism well is a skill that can avoid unnecessary conflict in the workplace, at school, and at home. The following are some guidelines for accepting and giving criticism constructively.

ACCEPTING CRITICISM CONSTRUCTIVELY

1. It helps to remember that neither you nor anyone else is perfect, so everyone deserves criticism at least some of the time.
2. It's often very difficult for the person who is criticizing you. He or she might feel uncomfortable and worried about hurting your feelings. If you keep in mind that constructive criticism will help you to grow and improve in your job, you could make it easier for the other person to help you. For example, you could demonstrate by means of your body language and facial expression that you are prepared to listen positively.
3. Looking as though you're listening is important, but you must also *hear* what is being said to you. Ask questions if you need to clarify certain aspects. Repeat the criticism in your own words so that both you and the other person know that you understand.
4. Try to put yourself in the other person's shoes. How would you feel about your performance on the job if you were in her or his position? What does this person (or the organization) require from you that you are not providing?

GIVING CRITICISM CONSTRUCTIVELY

Listening to criticism requires certain attitudes, but giving criticism requires skills as well. The following guidelines should help.

1. Give some forethought to the person and the task. Your goal is to contribute to the organization by helping the individual develop in his or her job. Ask yourself whether you're being too critical or not critical enough. When a person is new on the job, you might need to help him or her understand the "big picture"—how that job fits into the company program and how the details fit into the job. If the person understands the scope of the job, the details will have more meaning and are more likely to be attended to.
2. Try to understand from the other person's point of view why she or he is doing the job in a way you consider to be faulty. Has the person understood completely what is expected? Does she or he believe that the job is actually being done correctly and efficiently? Give the individual an opportunity to explain. For example, rather than saying, "This isn't the way you're supposed to do this," you might say, "I wondered why you chose to do it this way."
3. Explain why the job must be done in the manner you require, letting the person know that other ways might well be acceptable, but this is the most efficient way anyone has identified so far.
4. End the discussion on a positive note, taking into account the positive aspects of the person's job skills and accomplishments. Be sincere. Most people can tell when you're saying something positive just to be "nice." Make sure that, when you see improvement in the person's performance, you remark on it to the individual concerned.

CASE STUDIES

Read each of the following case studies and imagine that you are the person's supervisor. In your notebook, write a brief description of how you, as the supervisor, would handle each situation.

1. Bill works at an insurance office. He was in a car accident a few months ago. Twice a week, during working hours, he goes for physiotherapy on his knee. Sometimes he forgets to tell his supervisor that he's leaving work for an appointment.

2. Shannon is a waitress in a restaurant. Sometimes the cook can't read her handwriting.

3. Nick enjoys teasing the women with whom he works. His teasing is so annoying that none of the women want to work with him. Nick's supervisor is aware of the tension among the staff.

4. Ina sometimes forgets to punch out from work. Sometimes her supervisor is not sure how many hours she has worked.

CHAPTER SUMMARY EXERCISE
▼▼

Put yourself in the following situations and, in paragraph form, suggest assertive ways of dealing with them.

1. You'd like to buy two bananas, but all of them are priced and packaged in large quantities.

2. Two weeks ago someone borrowed some money from you. The person has not returned the money, and this week you are low on cash.

3. It's ten o'clock on a Saturday night. Your neighbour telephones you and says, "You're coming over. We're having a party." You're tired and you want to go to bed.

4. Someone pushes ahead of you in a movie line.

5. A car cuts in front of you on the highway.

6. You're invited to a party at which everyone will probably be dressed up. You really want to go, but you don't want to dress up.

7. You're filling out an application form and you notice that some of the questions are illegal.

8. Your best friend cancels a planned outing for a reason you don't think is very good.

9. Your mother telephones. You've just started eating dinner.

10. You buy some fruit in a store. The cashier weighs the fruit and asks you for an amount that seems to be very high.

11. Your neighbours are playing music so loud that you're getting a headache.

12. You're telling a story to a group of friends and one of your friends keeps finishing your sentences for you.

13. Someone is telling you gossip that you think was given to that person in confidence.

14. You receive an electricity bill that you think is unreasonably high.

15. You're driving around a new town, looking for a good, moderately priced restaurant where you can eat lunch.

16. You're invited to a reception. You go to the reception and you don't know anyone.

17. You receive your bill at a restaurant. You're disappointed with the quality of the food and displeased with the service.

18. A friend has planned a surprise party for a mutual friend. You know the friend will feel uncomfortable at being surprised.

19. At a social gathering you're cornered by someone who's boring you.

20. You've had positive feedfack about your performance from your supervisor. You feel that you deserve a raise or promotion.

21. You've just had your hair cut and you're very pleased with it. Your mother asks why you didn't have it cut shorter.

22. You take your four-year-old nephew to the grocery store with you. He insists that you buy him a box of cereal that contains a prize instead of the cereal his mother requested.

23. You're having lunch with a friend whom you see infrequently. Another friend comes to the table and asks to join you. You'd prefer to be alone with the first friend.

24. Your brother and sister-in-law always bring their dog to family gatherings. The dog slobbers, sheds hair, and jumps up on everyone.

25. Provide an example of your own.

Handling Anger

OBJECTIVES
▼ ▼ ▼ ▼ ▼ ▼ ▼ ▼ ▼ ▼ ▼ ▼ ▼ ▼ ▼ ▼

After completing this chapter you should be able to:

- Accept that everyone becomes angry sometimes.
- Understand the negative consequences of insulting or belittling people.
- Handle anger in a positive manner.
- Recognize situations in which an apology is advisable.
- Take steps to diffuse anger.

INTRODUCTION
▼ ▼ ▼ ▼ ▼ ▼ ▼ ▼ ▼ ▼ ▼ ▼ ▼ ▼ ▼ ▼ ▼ ▼ ▼

Everyone becomes angry sometimes. It can happen anytime, anywhere. Your roommate left the apartment in a mess again and anger wells up inside you. Someone says something you think is unfair and you feel angry. A passing bus splashes you, or a co-worker is rude and unco-operative. Some days everything seems to go wrong and you feel anger and frustration building inside you.

Even if you're usually good-natured, you'll sometimes become angry when things don't go well at work or at home. It's normal to have both negative and positive feelings. Anger isn't something to fear or ignore: it's a signal that something is wrong. Analysis of the situation that's making you angry usually clarifies how a particular problem can be solved. It's necessary to handle anger constructively and to deal with others' anger toward us. In this way, we can control our feelings instead of having them control us.

While anger is a natural reaction to some situations, if it gets out of control or is kept inside, anger can be dangerous and destructive. Displays of uncontrolled anger toward other people can lead to hurt feelings and damaged relationships, or even to violence.

On the other hand, if we don't express anger when something upsets us, the repressed anger simmers deep inside us. It doesn't just go away. This is called *repressed anger* and can actually lead to physical and mental illness, including high blood pressure, tension, and depression.

Prevention is always better than a cure for this very powerful emotion. The best prevention is open and direct communication with other people. This helps in avoiding the misunderstandings and hurt feelings that can cause anger.

Do you feel that you're being treated unfairly? Do you think you're getting less than you deserve? Are you being misunderstood? What's your style for resolving life's conflicts? Do you shout it out or do you grin and bear it?

POSITIVE WAYS TO DEAL WITH ANGER

▼▼▼▼▼▼▼▼▼▼▼▼▼▼▼▼▼▼▼▼▼▼▼▼▼▼▼▼▼

1. **Identify the real source of your anger**. Ask yourself the following questions.

   - What is the real issue here?
   - What is it about the situation that makes me angry?
   - What do I want to change?
   - What do I want to accomplish?
   - What are the things I will or won't do?
   - Am I trying to control or change a person who doesn't want to change?

2. **Control yourself**. Erupting in anger might clear the air in some relationships, but you wouldn't want to do this at work. Use some control techniques, such as silently counting to ten. Postpone getting angry. Take time to sort your thoughts out. If you do have an angry outburst, apologize and admit that you should have controlled yourself.

3. **Appreciate the fact that everyone is different**. No two people see a situation the same way and rarely is one person totally right or totally wrong. Different perspectives and ways of reacting are not necessarily wrong. Arguing about what's "right" won't resolve the conflict. It's pointless to tell someone what they should feel or think; they have a right to their own feelings and thoughts.

4. **Recognize that each person is responsible for his or her own behaviour and feelings**. No matter what the situation, it's not the other person's fault that you're angry. You *choose* to react with anger, so don't blame other people for how you feel.

5. **Show respect for yourself and for the other person**. Blaming, preaching, lecturing, and ridiculing won't resolve anything. Make it clear that you value the other person and simply want to clear up a specific problem.

6. **Listen to what the other person is saying**. Are you really trying to understand that person's point of view? Or are you just hearing what you want to hear?

7. **State your feelings calmly and clearly**. Use the word "I" often as you explain your feelings: "I think...," "I'm afraid...," "I want..." Saying "You did..." or "You are..." makes your statements accusatory, and could make the situation worse. Remember, we are responsible for our feelings; the other person is not *making* us be angry. Also, saying something like "Everyone thinks you're..." doesn't help either. Speak for yourself.

8. **Avoid gossip**. If you're angry with someone, tell that person, not everyone else. Avoid getting other people involved with your problems. Talking over a problem with a responsible person might help you to feel better, but you still must resolve your problem with the person involved in it. If you're angry with someone, that's the person you should tell.

9. **Offer suggestions to resolve the conflict**. Let the person know specifically what you want. You can't expect other people to know what you want if you make vague requests.

AVOIDING NEGATIVE REACTIONS
▼▼▼

Insulting or belittling the other person when we're angry might offer some satisfaction at the moment but always creates new problems. We might feel guilty or embarrassed later, the other person is probably feeling resentful, onlookers might be negatively impressed, and nothing has been accomplished in solving the problem. The consequences of such a reaction can be short-term or long-term and can be direct or indirect.

If a person reacts to an insult with another insult, the typical result is an argument that no one can win. Nothing is resolved and things are said that might be regretted later.

In a work situation, the after-effects of an unresolved argument can be very disruptive. The "wronged" individual might be unwilling to work and co-operate with the other party, affecting the quality and quantity of work produced. Gossip and attempted sabotage of the other person's work are also possibilities.

1. HANDLING ANGER NEGATIVELY

The following are negative ways of handling anger. In your notebook list two ways in which each response could make life more difficult for you or for other people.

1. Insult the other person.

2. Control your anger with the person involved but take it out on your family.

3. Control your anger, walk away, and try to forget the problem.

4. Say nothing; keep all your anger inside.

2. HOW DO YOU HANDLE YOUR ANGER?

Write the following statements in your notebook, completing each with the word or phrase that best describes how you usually react. If none of the items describes your reaction, add your own description.

1. When I'm angry I usually:
   a) Yell.
   b) Sulk.
   c) Explain what's wrong.

Immediately I feel: (emotion)	a) Guilty.
	b) Relieved.
	c) Powerful.

Later I feel:	a) Foolish.
	b) Content.
	c) Guilty.

2. Last time I was angry I: (behaviour)
   a) Yelled.
   b) Sulked.
   c) Explained what was wrong.

   Immediately I felt: (emotion)
   a) Guilty.
   b) Relieved.
   c) Powerful.

   Later I felt: (emotion)
   a) Foolish.
   b) Content.
   c) Guilty.

3. How does your teacher or supervisor react when he or she becomes angry?

4. How does your parent or guardian handle her or his anger?

5. How does your best friend handle his or her anger?

A P O L O G I Z I N G

An apology is defined as "an acknowledgment of some fault, injury, or insult, with an expression of regret and a plea for pardon." So an apology has two elements:

1. Admitting that we are at fault.

2. Asking for forgiveness.

An apology can be an excellent way to reduce stress and to deal with a situation that makes us angry. Everyone makes mistakes from time to time and a simple apology can heal hurt feelings.

Whatever the situation, we have to face the consequences of our actions. We add to the stress if we try to defend inappropriate behaviour. Such defence can result in even more stressful emotional levels, exaggeration, and even lying, perhaps making the situation worse and definitely making it more difficult to apologize. It is far easier to admit our weaknesses or errors, apologize, and correct the situation immediately.

On the other hand, if you find yourself always apologizing, that too can signal a problem. Take a look at the situations and why you're apologizing so often. Perhaps you have trouble areas that you could work to improve. On the other hand, you might be apologizing too often for situations that aren't your fault. Talking to a parent, teacher, co-worker, or supervisor might help you to figure out what is wrong and to find a solution.

3. ANALYSING APOLOGIES

1. Think of some apologies that you have heard in the last few days. Write down an example. Did the person sound sincere? Did the apology seem to clear the air?

2. Do you have different ways of apologizing to different people?

3. How do you feel when someone says "I'm sorry" to you?

4. How do you react to an apology?

5. What do you say to the person who is apologizing?

6. In each of the following situations, an apology is in order. With a classmate, role-play each situation twice, so that each of you has the opportunity to play the apologizer. Write down ahead of time what you will say.

   a) You promised to telephone a friend and you didn't.

   b) You're talking to your friend and your little sister interrupts rudely.

   c) You borrowed something and didn't return the item when promised.

R E S P O N S E S   T O   A N G E R
▼▼▼▼▼▼▼▼▼▼▼▼▼▼▼▼▼▼▼▼▼▼▼▼▼▼▼▼▼▼▼

Sometimes when we're angry we respond in an apologetic manner and don't express our real feelings. We hide our hurt and disappointment and do nothing to solve the basic problem. Then again, sometimes we erupt in anger at another person and don't give that person a chance to respond. We condemn or insult the person, perhaps unfairly, or blow the whole incident out of proportion.

The sensible, positive way to handle anger is to express calmly and clearly how we feel and what is making us feel that way. Then we should specify what we would like changed and motivate the person to make that change. The motivation could be either positive (an explanation of how the change would improve the situation) or negative (a warning of the possible consequences if the change is not effected).

C A S E   S T U D I E S

Read the following case studies and choose what you think would be the best response in each case. Give reasons for your choice.

1. Shane and Megan decided to go to the fair one August evening. When they left for the fair at 6:30 p.m., their sister Erin wasn't home yet. Usually she was home from her summer job by 5 p.m. They had discussed going to the fair the night before and Erin had said that she'd like to go too. So they had made tentative plans to leave at 5:30 p.m. When they came home at 10:30 p.m., Erin was waiting for them and she was angry because they had left without her. Which of the following

reactions would indicate that Erin handled her anger in a positive manner? Explain your answer.

a) You could have waited for me. You always leave me out of things. I don't feel as though I'm a part of this family. We didn't set a definite time to leave and you *know* I wanted to go, too. I can never depend on you to keep your word.

b) I'm sorry you waited for me for an hour. I was disappointed that I didn't get to go with you but I can understand that you really wanted to see the Musical Ride at seven.

c) I'm really disappointed. I wanted to go to the fair with you and I thought we'd agreed that we'd go when I got home. Next time I'd like you to phone me at work if you decide something at the last minute, or maybe we should make more definite plans in future. I know you don't want me to feel left out. We won't be able to spend much time together next year, so we should take advantage of the time we can have together this summer.

2. Grant and Paula have gone out together a few times and usually have a good time. Grant is upset because, at a party last night, Paula left him and went to talk to some old friends on the other side of the room. What would be the probable results if Grant handled his anger in each of the following ways?

a) I was disappointed that you didn't introduce me to that couple last night. I would have felt more comfortable if you'd introduced me to them. Instead, you left me in the corner with boring Gerald. I'll hesitate to go to parties with you again if you keep forgetting to introduce me to your friends.

b) Grant says nothing to her about the incident, although he's really hurt. He's now regretting that he agreed to go to a surprise birthday party for one of her friends.

c) I didn't know you were such a snob. Did you think I couldn't handle meeting those people last night? You were really thoughtless to leave me with that bore Gerald. Now I don't want to go to that stupid birthday party.

3. Without consulting her, Ruta's mother bought her a winter jacket last night that Ruta doesn't really like. It looks exactly like something her mother would buy for herself. It even fits her mother. Ruta had agreed to shop for a jacket with her mother next week. Ruta and her mother rarely agree about clothes, although they get along well otherwise. Ruta doesn't want this to happen again, but she also doesn't want to upset her mother. How should she handle the situation? Explain your answer.

a) You're always trying to get me to wear clothes *you* like. Some mother you are. You bought that jacket for me so you could borrow it!

b) I'll wear it but I'm not going to like it.

c) I'm upset you went ahead and bought me a jacket when we had agreed to go out next week together. I would feel much more comfortable if you would let me make my own decisions.

GUIDELINES FOR DIFFUSING ANGER

▼▼▼▼▼▼▼▼▼▼▼▼▼▼▼▼▼▼▼▼▼▼▼

1. Postpone showing your anger. Remember to count to ten before saying anything. Once you're able to put it off, you'll have learned control.

2. Keep an "anger journal," recording the time, place, and frequency of the occasions when you get angry. This will help you determine the *real* cause of your anger. The next step is to discuss ways of eliminating the cause.

3. Don't *expect* other people to behave in certain ways. Remind yourself that other people have a right to behave in whatever way they choose.

4. Remember that it's natural for young children to be active and loud.

5. Be aware of how you sound to others.

6. After an angry outburst, apologize for your lack of control and try to discuss the matter calmly and constructively.

7. Learn to tolerate things you might dislike.

8. Be kind to yourself. Don't burden yourself with self-destructive anger.

9. Keep in mind that expressing anger in a positive way is better than storing it up.

CHAPTER SUMMARY EXERCISES

▼▼

1. List five ways of diffusing anger.

2. Why is it a good idea to make apologies?

3. What are the dangers of insulting or belittling people?

4. When you are angry with someone and you want to correct the situation, what are four good rules to follow?

5. In a 250-word essay, describe a situation that made you angry. Then describe how you reacted to the situation. How did you handle your anger? Do you think you handled it positively or negatively? Do you think you would react the same way again? Why or why not?

Are You Really *Listening?*

OBJECTIVES
▼▼▼▼▼▼▼▼▼▼▼▼▼▼▼▼

After completing this chapter you should be able to:

- Explain why listening involves more than hearing.
- Describe the listening process.
- List ways in which you can be a better listener.
- Define the term *non-verbal cues*.
- Recognize non-verbal cues given by yourself and by other people.
- Be a better listener.
- Use your listening skills on the telephone.
- Handle business telephone calls properly.

INTRODUCTION
▼▼▼▼▼▼▼▼▼▼▼▼▼▼▼▼▼▼▼▼

Listening is a skill that involves more than just *hearing* what others are saying. The three basic components of the listening process are:

- Understanding the message that is sent to the brain.
- Evaluating the information the brain has received.
- Reacting or responding to what has been heard.

Interestingly enough:

- We absorb only 25% of what we hear.
- About 45% of our waking time is spent listening.
- People speak at the rate of approximately 100 words per minute, while the brain is capable of absorbing some 600 words per minute.

In a classroom, a teacher once asked a daydreaming student if he had trouble hearing. He replied, "No ma'am, I have trouble listening." Hearing is simply the receiving of sounds, a physical perception, while listening is a mental activity. Listening requires concentration, co-operation, and an open mind.

You might be listening in order to learn how to do a task, to help you make a decision, or to achieve friendly relations with other people. But in every case, it's important to get beneath the surface of what the speaker is saying.

To do that you must listen with more than your ears. You need to be alert to tone of voice, facial expressions, gestures, and body posture. These verbal and non-verbal messages supply added information that will help you to grasp the speaker's full meaning.

Good listening habits are an important ingredient for success. If you practise careful listening, you'll become more efficient in your job, more knowledgeable, and more able to get along with people. You'll understand and remember the information and points of view that you hear. Responsible, patient listening is a rare skill, but it can be developed.

WHAT IS LISTENING?

▼▼▼▼▼▼▼▼▼▼▼▼▼▼▼▼▼▼▼▼▼▼▼▼▼▼▼

1. The ear is focussed by the mind on sounds.

2. According to some psychologists, minds are always listening, detecting, and selecting sounds on which to focus.

3. The purpose of listening is to re-create in the mind of the listener the information that is presented by the speaker.

For our purpose, the listening process can be described in four steps:

- Attention.
- Reception.
- Perception.
- Examination.

Paying full *attention* to a person speaking is probably the most important part of the listening process. If you don't do this, the other parts of the process are ineffective. Attention is an all-or-nothing proposition—there is no such thing as "divided attention." You're either paying attention or you're not.

Attention is conditioned by many factors, some of which are motivation, mood, and situation. The importance to you of what is being said is the motivation. If you really care, you'll listen carefully. If not, your attention will probably wander.

Mood, of course, means how you feel at the time. If you're upset about something, you won't be able to concentrate as much as you should on what's being said.

The situation also affects your ability to concentrate. If you're in a distracting situation, your attention is bound to wander from the speaker.

Reception, or hearing, is the receiving stage of listening. Visual cues (facial expressions, gestures, nodding) are very important to the listening process.

Perception means seeing in the mind. Perception also involves word recognition and association with past experience.

Examination involves the interpretation of the sounds being received. Who is speaking? How is that person feeling? What is the person saying?

Many people don't realize that they have listening problems. When they do stop to think about what happens when they don't listen, they manage to identify quite a few habits (mostly variations on "I was thinking of something else") that interfere with their listening. The following are some that have been mentioned.

- I have a tendency to be too concerned with how people see me.
- I don't listen things out; I jump in before the other person has finished speaking.
- My mind wanders to things I think are more relevant.
- When I'm bored as I listen, I fantasize, do my own thing, or am critical of what's going on.
- Sometimes I stop listening when I become more interested in the speaker's physical features than in what the person is saying.
- When the subject is of personal interest, I anticipate and wait for the other person to stop so I can defend my idea. If I become impatient, I interrupt.
- I'm thinking ahead to what I'll say next.

1. HOW WELL DO *YOU* LISTEN?

Review the explanations given above about why people don't listen. To increase your awareness of the ways in which *you* listen, answer the following questions.

1. When you're bored with what's going on in a discussion or meeting, how do you usually listen?

2. When you're annoyed with another person with whom you want to build a better working relationship, how do you listen?

3. Your supervisor asks you to do something that you're uncertain about being able to do well. You also want to hide the fact that you feel inadequate. How effectively do you think you would listen in this situation? Explain your answer.

EFFECTIVE LISTENING
▼▼▼▼▼▼▼▼▼▼▼▼▼▼▼▼▼▼▼▼▼▼▼▼▼▼▼▼▼▼▼▼▼▼

Employees have to do a lot of listening on the job. Being able to listen to directions from your customers, employer, and other employees is very important, so companies want employees who are good listeners. Good listeners get the job done correctly the first time. The efficiency of many businesses could be doubled if only their employees knew how to listen well.

By listening in a courteous and attentive manner, you create a positive image of yourself and of your company. This calls for active listening: you must not only concentrate on what is being said but also watch for the visual cues that tell you how the speaker feels about what he or she is saying. Active listening will show your supervisor, co-workers, and customers that you care.

Listening is one of the most necessary but least understood communication skills. Since you've been listening all your life, you might be unaware that some improvement is necessary. The following are some techniques that will help you to become a better listener.

1. Look at the person who is talking. This will help you to concentrate on what is being said, and you'll be able to watch for visual cues.

2. Demonstrate that you're listening. The speaker can't be sure of this unless you respond in some way, such as appropriate facial expressions (a smile) or gestures (such as nodding your head).

3. Remain aware of your and the speaker's body language, the visual cues that often say more than words. If you're nodding your head in agreement but thinking, "What an idiot!" this *could* show on your face or in some involuntary movement. Watch the speaker for the same type of signal. A customer might swear that she or he had paid the bill, but not be able to look you in the eye while speaking. This should alert you to a possible problem, although you would investigate carefully before following through on your hunch!

4. Avoid interrupting the speaker. Hear him or her out to make sure that you understand exactly what is being said. This will lessen the chance of negative feelings due to misunderstanding. Save your questions until the speaker is finished.

5. When the speaker has finished, ask clear, concise questions about anything you didn't understand. Listen carefully, and take notes if necessary. Then repeat the instructions or information to ensure that you understood it.

2. GOOD AND BAD LISTENING HABITS

The following is a list of good and bad listening habits. Write the items in your notebook, then beside each write *G* if you think it's a good habit or *B* if you think it's a bad one.

1. Interrupts.
2. Changes the subject.
3. Repeats some of the things said.
4. Asks questions when the speaker is finished.
5. Rushes the other person.
6. Looks at the speaker.
7. Finishes the speaker's sentences.
8. Does not give responses.
9. Pays close attention.
10. Has a wandering gaze.
11. Does not interrupt.
12. Is impatient.
13. Jumps to conclusions.
14. Shows sympathy.
15. Reacts with a nod or smile.

Now think about *your* listening habits and list areas in which you feel you could improve.

3. LISTENING INTERVIEW

To learn what others think about listening habits, ask a person you know well to give you three or more characteristics of a good listener. Ask the same person for three characteristics of a poor listener. Prepare a brief report on the interview results.

4. ANALYSING OTHERS' LISTENING HABITS

Observe the listening habits of two of your classmates or co-workers, then write down your observations of whether they:

1. Look directly at people who are speaking to them.
2. Respond in some way to the speaker.
3. Use only positive body language.
4. Allow the speaker to finish, uninterrupted.
5. Ask questions or repeat the information to make sure they've understood.

5. LISTENING REPORTS

During the next full day of school or work, use some time during your breaks to keep a log of two conversations or listening experiences that you have. Complete a report for each listening experience, summarizing the conversation. You don't need to repeat the conversation word for word or detail who said what. Just briefly describe the conversation as it flowed from one topic to another. You might want to record it in the form of a list. Record the date of each conversation, the location where the conversation took place, who was speaking, and then your summary of what was said.

6. THE WORDLESS GAME

Write the topics listed below on twelve slips of paper, fold the slips so that the statements are not visible, and mix them together. The "speaker" should draw a slip and attempt to communicate the message on it without using words or sounds. The listener's job is to guess which statement the speaker is trying to convey. The listener does not have to give the statement word for word.

1. Come on. Let's get going, we're late.
2. Sh! We don't want anybody to hear us.
3. I don't know. I'm undecided.
4. I'm really hungry. Let's eat.
5. I'm fed up with this whole deal.
6. I'm so sleepy I can hardly keep my eyes open.
7. Look over there!
8. Stop what you're doing and follow me.
9. Did you say something? I can't hear you.
10. This whole thing bores me. I wish I could leave.
11. I'm broke. Can you lend me some money?
12. You and I should talk.

7. IT'S NOT WHAT YOU SAY, IT'S HOW YOU SAY IT

The tone of voice that a person uses to express a thought can alter or even completely change the meaning of words. Read each of the following statements several times out loud, changing the tone of your voice each time. Discuss with your classmates the different meanings that are conveyed each time.

1. Yeah, sure, you can borrow my car. Do you know how to start it? It's kind of tricky. Put it on choke, but don't forget to take the choke off once the engine's warm. No, really, I trust you. Go ahead. Here are the keys.

2. I'm sorry I'm late, but I just can't seem to get everything done. I work all day, and then I have to rush home and do practically another whole day's work. I really envy those people who can go home and relax. I'm not complaining, but there's just nobody but me to keep things going.

3. Oh, you're sick, huh? Gee, that's too bad. Well, I guess we'll just have to go on without you. Maybe you can go another time. We'll miss you.

4. Yes, I feel sure we'll be able to meet the deadline. It doesn't give us much time, but I'm sure we can do it. I don't see any major problems that could cause delays. Yes, I think we're okay.

8. NON-VERBAL CUES

Non-verbal cues are a very important part of the listening process. You must be aware of the type of cues that you use when listening to another person; otherwise, you'll be sending negative messages, no matter what you actually say. In this exercise, put yourself in the place of a person who is speaking and observing the non-verbal cues of a listener. Write each item in your notebook and then, beside each item, write the letter *P* if you think you would interpret this as a positive cue, and the letter *N* if the cue would strike you as being negative.

1. Raises an eyebrow.
2. Smiles.
3. Nods head.
4. Sits forward in chair.
5. Remains silent.
6. Frowns.
7. Looks away from the speaker.
8. Rolls eyes.
9. Relaxes body posture.
10. Touches you.
11. Stiffens body posture.
12. Moves away slightly.
13. Stays absolutely still.
14. Fidgets.
15. Looks at the floor.
16. Lets head almost touch shoulder.
17. Looks delighted.
18. Scowls.
19. Shakes head.
20. Slumps in chair.
21. Folds arms across chest.
22. Looks at the ceiling.
23. Narrows eyes.
24. Stretches.
25. Moves closer.
26. Looks disapproving.
27. Looks straight at you.
28. Drums fingers.
29. Shrugs shoulders.

HANDLING TELEPHONE CALLS
▼▼▼▼▼▼▼▼▼▼▼▼▼▼▼▼▼▼▼▼▼▼▼▼▼▼▼▼▼▼▼▼▼▼▼▼

Good listening skills play an important role in telephone communication. Efficient and personal, the telephone is used to accomplish business that otherwise would have to be carried out in person or by a less immediate means such as by letter.

When you use the telephone at work, you are projecting an image of your employer. The impression the caller receives is the result of many little things. Many times the first contact a person has with a business is by telephone. Most people can recall telephone calls during which they were unfavourably impressed by the manner of the person at the other end of the telephone. Always take time to be courteous. Nothing is gained by a brisk, abrupt manner. Remember the following points when using the telephone.

ANSWERING THE TELEPHONE

Answer promptly: Don't keep callers waiting. Answering promptly shows that you're ready to be of service. Give telephone calls the prompt attention you'd give an actual visitor.

Identify yourself: Your caller likes to know who you are and whom you represent. If you identify yourself, the caller knows at once how to proceed from there. Never simply say "Hello" or "Yes" when answering the telephone; this leaves callers wondering if they've reached the right number. Answer the telephone by saying " ___ Company, ___Department, (your name) speaking" if the call has come directly to you from the outside. Or you could say "___ Department, (your name) speaking. May I help you?" if the call has been forwarded by a switchboard. In some instances it might be appropriate to ask the caller to identify herself or himself. You could say "May I ask who's calling?" Once you know the caller's name, use it. Most people like to hear their names used.

Speak distinctly: It's impossible to speak clearly with gum, candy, or a pencil in your mouth, and don't speak too loudly or too softly. The caller should be able to understand you without difficulty.

Be businesslike and friendly: Being businesslike on the phone doesn't mean being abrupt or hurried. Give your caller your undivided attention and try to be helpful. Make callers feel welcome and glad that they phoned your company. Use the words "May" and "Please" when you need information from a caller.

Take notes: You might need exact details later, so take notes during the call. Try to avoid asking the caller to repeat things. Also, it's inefficient and embarrassing to have to call someone back later for details you didn't write down the first time.

Use a telephone message form: Most companies have a standard telephone message form. If you take a call for someone else, write down enough information to inform the recipient clearly of the purpose of the call and the follow-up action that's necessary. Make sure that you spell the caller's name correctly: ask the caller for the correct spelling. Deliver the message promptly to the person for whom the call was intended.

Try not to delay the caller: If the caller needs information that is not immediately available to you, give the person the option of waiting or hanging up. Ask, "Will you wait, or shall I call you back?" If you have to call the person back, make sure you have the correct telephone number. If you tell the person that you'll call back, keep your promise.

End a call pleasantly: End telephone conversations by saying, "Thank you for calling" or "We're looking forward to your order" or "We'll look forward to hearing from you again." Let the caller say goodbye first and hang up first. If you're overly hasty in hanging up the telephone, you risk offending the caller or missing last-minute orders or instructions. When you're sure that the conversation is finished, replace the receiver quietly.

Be careful about giving out information over the telephone: If the person being called isn't immediately available, say so. It shouldn't be necessary to say why the person isn't available or to give specific details. You never know who's at the other end of the line. The following are some examples of correct and incorrect responses.

Do say:

I'm not expecting her to be in the office this afternoon.

Don't say:

It's such a nice day, she took the afternoon off to go to her cottage.

Do say:

Mr. Dalin isn't at his desk right now. May I help you?

Don't say:

Mr. Dalin is in the washroom right now.

Do say:

Ms. Kirk is out of town until Friday.

Don't say:

Ms. Kirk is away on vacation.

TRANSFERRING CALLS

If you receive a call that isn't for you, transfer the call to the proper person. If that isn't possible, give the caller the correct number to call. Don't show annoyance or impatience at someone else's mistake.

9. COURTEOUS ALTERNATIVES

You work in the advertising division of a large department store. Write an alternative, businesslike version of each of the following statements.

1. Can't you read a phone book? You've reached the advertising division not the credit department.

2. I'm sorry, she's not here. Ms. Jonas must have slept in this morning.

3. What's your name? I'll pass your number on to him to call you.

4. Yeah, yeah. I'll pass the message on.

5. Speak up. I can't hear a word you're saying.

6. Hello.

7. You've got the wrong department. Try personnel.

10. TELEPHONE QUIZ

1. Why is it important to answer your telephone promptly?

2. Why should you identify yourself and/or your company immediately?

3. How can you finish a call pleasantly?

4. Why should you be careful of what type of information you give on the telephone?

5. What is a friendly telephone manner?

6. Why is it important to speak clearly?

11. TAKING TELEPHONE MESSAGES

The majority of organizations provide telephone message forms to ensure that messages are properly recorded. Study the telephone message form shown in Figure 18.1 on the next page and then, in your notebook, record the information that you would record on the message form in each of the situations described below.

1. Janice Porter of Tanaka Inc. (622-1436, Extension 2003) calls to speak to Amy Patrese, who is in a meeting. The date of the call is March 18, and the time is 10:15 a.m. Ms. Porter wants Miss Patrese to call her back.

2. At 11:20 a.m. on March 18, you receive a call from André Campeau of Ace Packing Services (961-3025). He wants to arrange a meeting with your supervisor, Jeff Solinski, at either 3:30 p.m. on March 20 or 11 a.m. on March 21. Your supervisor is to choose the meeting location and let Mr. Campeau know.

3. Peter Hendricks of Myer Communications (342-1699) telephones on March 19 at 1:30 p.m. He wants to speak to Myrna Surtees, who is out of the office. Mr. Hendricks won't be near a telephone all afternoon, so he wants you to tell Mrs. Surtees that the meeting is scheduled for tomorrow morning as they had previously discussed. The meeting will be at 10 a.m. at the Chamber of Commerce office.

4. Aziz Verani returns Katherine Klein's call at 3 p.m. on March 19, but Mrs. Klein is out of the office. Mr. Verani asks you to let Mrs. Klein know that he returned her call and would appreciate her calling him again. He's with Verani & Sung Inc. and his telephone number is 553-0984.

5. At 4:30 p.m. on March 19, Leslie Hoover of Tomco Ltd. (916-0327) calls and asks to speak to Monique Perron. Mme Perron is in

Figure 18.1 Telephone message form

MESSAGE FOR

M ____________________

WHILE YOU WERE OUT

M ____________________

OF ____________________

PHONE NO. ____________________

TELEPHONED		RETURNED YOUR CALL	
CALLED TO SEE YOU		PLEASE CALL	
WANTS TO SEE YOU		WILL CALL AGAIN	

MESSAGE: ____________________

____

____

____

____

DATE ____________ TIME ____________

RECEIVED BY ____________________

a meeting. Mr. Hoover asks you to tell Mme Perron that he'll call back tomorrow morning at 10 a.m. because he is leaving the office.

CHAPTER SUMMARY EXERCISE

In your notebook, copy the following sentences, supplying the missing word or phrase.

1. When others really listen to me I feel ___.
2. When I want to show that I'm really listening to others I ___.
3. One of my family members provides the non-verbal cue of ___to show that he or she is really listening.
4. I think good listeners make friends easily because ___.
5. The most difficult time I have in listening to others is when ___.

6. The communication in my family could be improved if I would ___.

7. What I definitely will do this week to improve my communication skills is ___.

8. When I answer the telephone at work, I am ___ my employer.

9. I will always take time to be ___when handling telephone calls.

10. Five important things to remember when taking telephone calls are ___.

Stress on the Job

O B J E C T I V E S

After completing this chapter you should be able to:

- Define the word *stress*.
- Explain how stress can be good as well as bad.
- Analyse your own level of stress.
- Use stress management techniques.
- Recognize situations in which stress can work *for* you.

I N T R O D U C T I O N

Some stress in our lives is essential and desirable. It helps to keep us alert, stimulated, and interested in what we are doing. Without some stress, life would be boring. Coping with life's stressful demands positively is a challenge and can result in personal growth and increased competence.

Too much stress, however—too many demands, for too long a time—can cause problems. The businessperson who worries continually about work problems while at home or about home problems while at work, the employee who dislikes his or her job but makes no effort to find a better one, and the student who studies all day and works after school and on weekends, are all subjecting themselves to continuous stress. Unless such stress is handled properly, physical or even mental illness could result.

One of the main challenges today is learning how to deal with stress. Stress has been defined as the response of the body to any demand put or made on it. Anything and everything is a possible source of stress: waking up, deciding what you're going to wear, catching a bus, playing hockey, writing an exam, starting a new job, getting married, moving to a new home, meeting a deadline, driving a car.

It's our response to events and not the events themselves that determines whether the stress will have a positive or negative effect on us. Our goal shouldn't be to eliminate stress from our lives, but to make it work for us. Stress is a natural result of almost all activity. We must accept this fact and learn to recognize the danger signals when we are under more stress than we can tolerate. That's when we need to eliminate the factor that is causing the unhealthy level of stress or find some way to make the situation less stressful. In some cases, assertiveness and handling anger positively can reduce stress, as discussed in earlier chapters. Other effective stress management techniques include relaxation, physical exercise, and good sleeping and eating habits.

REACTION TO STRESS
▼▼▼▼▼▼▼▼▼▼▼▼▼▼▼▼▼▼▼▼▼▼▼▼▼▼▼▼▼▼

In the 1930s, Dr. Hans Selye of Montreal, president of the International Institute of Stress, defined stress as the "non-specific response of the body to any demand made upon it." In other words, it is the body's initial reaction to any change it has to deal with.

Dr. Walter B. Canon, a noted Harvard professor of physiology, called the body's response to a stressful stimulus the "flight or fight response." This response prepares us for action in the same way it did our predecessors in the Stone Age. When confronted with danger, people in early civilizations would either stand and fight or flee a life-threatening enemy. Either way, the stressful situation was soon resolved and the people could go back to their everyday ways of functioning.

Today, we're confronted with quite a different set of circumstances. Many situations can't be dealt with head-on and then forgotten. Where do we run or with whom do we fight when dealing with increasing crime or inflation rates? And if we're not able to fight them and there's no place to flee, how do we get rid of the pressures caused by such situations?

The answer to this question is stress management. If we're unsuccessful in our efforts to cope with stress, we burn ourselves out—our "energy battery" runs low. The overload on our body systems exhausts us and makes us vulnerable to such physical ailments as hypertension, heart disease, ulcers, gastrointestinal problems, asthma, arthritis, cancer, and migraine headaches. These are enemies that are every bit as ferocious as any wild animal faced by Stone Age people.

Stress is a great equalizer. It does not discriminate against age, gender, race, colour, creed, or socio-economic standing. All of us experience at least occasional overdoses of tension and stress in our lives.

1. DO YOU HAVE A STRESS-PRONE PERSONALITY?

Rate yourself based on how you typically react in each of the situations listed below. There are no right or wrong answers. Write down the situation numbers in your notebook and then, beside each number, write the number from the following key that best represents your reaction. Then total your score and consult the scale at the end of the exercise.

3 = Frequently   2 = Sometimes   1 = Never

1. Do you try to do as much as possible in the least amount of time?

2. Do you become impatient with delays or interruptions?

3. Do you always have to win at games to enjoy yourself?

4. Do you find yourself speeding up to beat a red light?

5. Do you hesitate to ask for help with problems?

6. Do you constantly seek the respect and admiration of others?

7. Are you overly critical of the way others do their work?

8. Do you have the habit of looking at your watch or clock often?

9. Do you constantly strive to better your position and achievements?

10. Do you spread yourself "too thin" in terms of your time?

11. Do you have the habit of doing more than one thing at a time?

12. Do you frequently get angry or irritable?

13. Do you have little time for hobbies or time by yourself?

14. Do you have a tendency to talk quickly or hurry conversations?

15. Do you consider yourself hard-driving?

16. Do your friends or relatives consider you hard-driving?

17. Do you have a tendency to get involved in many projects at the same time?

18. Do you have a lot of deadlines at school or in your work?

19. Do you feel vaguely guilty if you relax and do nothing during your leisure time?

20. Do you take on too many responsibilities?

Stress-Prone Personality Scale

Score:

20-30: Individual tends to be non-productive. Life lacks stimulation.

31-50: A good balance exists between the ability to handle and control stress.

51-60: Individual is bordering on becoming excessively tense.

If you're in the higher score categories, it's recommended that you reduce the stress level in your life by taking some of the steps described earlier in this chapter.

W H A T   C A U S E S   S T R E S S ?
▼▼▼▼▼▼▼▼▼▼▼▼▼▼▼▼▼▼▼▼▼▼▼▼▼▼▼▼▼▼▼▼

Some events known to be stressful include:

- Death in the family.
- Divorce or marital separation.
- Personal injury or illness.
- Changes in work responsibilities.
- Trouble with members of the family.
- Change in working hours.
- Change in working place.
- Change in school.
- Change in personal habits.

- A job you dislike.

- Spending time with people who make you feel uncomfortable.

- A problem child or a troubled relationship.

- Feeling torn between what you want to do and what others expect you to do.

- A schedule that doesn't leave any time for you to relax and act naturally.

Stress has been blamed for a lot of things: headaches, heart disease, obesity, drug addiction, high blood pressure, strokes, ulcers, and many other ailments. Stress is not caused by stressful events, however, but by a person's response to these events.

You can't always control what happens to you, but you *can* control your response to what happens. A stressful event for one person is not necessarily stressful for another. If you respond with fear or anger to an event, stress will take its toll. If you can use constructively the energy that you would have used being angry or fearful, maybe you can turn the situation around.

People experience stress when they feel powerless, alienated, or threatened. To combat a feeling of powerlessness, a person needs to take control by:

- Analysing the situation. Don't take things at face value.

- Believing and acting as if you can influence the situation.

- Thinking about how to turn the situation to your advantage.

- Learning the difference between situations and people that you can change and those that cannot be changed.

- Developing options and showing initiative.

- Learning to say "No."

A feeling of alienation, of feeling alone or cut off from other people, can be overcome by making a commitment to use and develop your skills, to reach goals that you set for yourself. Sitting around feeling sorry for yourself achieves nothing.

If situations appear to be threatening, as in the case of changes in your personal, school, or work life, treat the situations as challenges, not threats. After all, change is normal; lack of change means that no growth is occurring. If you treat change as a challenge, it becomes a stimulant to performance, not an upset in your life. And, of course, not all changes are for the worse. Think it through.

Life is demanding, but it's also interesting and challenging. Gain comfort and confidence from your ability to cope.

2. STRESS IN MY LIFE

List six factors that have caused stress in your life. For each, explain how you reacted.

COPING WITH STRESS

▼▼▼▼▼▼▼▼▼▼▼▼▼▼▼▼▼▼▼▼▼▼▼▼▼▼▼▼▼

Exercise is an excellent way of coping with stress. When you're feeling stressed, take several slow, deep breaths; go for a walk; ride a bicycle; take part in a sport; or try yoga. When the muscles in your neck and arms begin to relax, you'll start to feel better.

You can also work off tension by taking up a hobby. Don't just watch television—do something you enjoy that takes your mind off stressful situations.

A technique called *imagery* can also be effective. Think about how you want a situation to turn out and then concentrate on the positive aspects. For instance, you could rehearse in your mind a job interview and concentrate on how well you'll behave, how calm you'll be, and what a good impression you'll make. Positive imagery is like a positive attitude. It pays off in increased confidence.

The level of stress that can be tolerated differs from person to person. For some people, high levels of stress are the spice of life. Through personal experience, they've developed successful ways of coping with stress and using it to their benefit. Usually these people view unexpected events as challenges rather than threats; they're in control of their lives.

The following are some stress management techniques to help cope with stress at school or on the job.

1. When you have a break, get some exercise (take a walk, climb some stairs, etc.).

2. If possible, switch your tasks around, rotating stressful ones with ones that are easier to do.

3. When possible, share your workload if you're handling too much. Asking for assistance doesn't mean you're incompetent but rather that you're a concerned employee who wants to meet company requirements and deadlines.

4. Discuss your workload with your teacher or supervisor. Outline what you feel you can reasonably handle and suggest alternatives for getting the rest of the work done. Agree on a workable arrangement.

5. Concentrate on the positive aspects of school or your job: the hours, the people, the physical environment, the atmosphere, the actual work you're doing, the type of company, the opportunities for promotion, or the chances for self-improvement.

6. Give yourself pep talks. Counter each negative thought with a positive response: "I'm not a failure; I've succeeded at many things"; "I'll be as prepared as I can be under the circumstances."

7. Avoid comparing yourself to others; recognize your capabilities and limitations. Believe in yourself—you can do it!

8. Get moral support by talking in confidence about your concerns with supportive family members and friends.

9. Recognize your limits in relation to energy and time, and set priorities.

10. Stay healthy. Build resistance through regular sleep, physical exercise, relaxation, and good eating habits.

11. Have a sense of humour. Laughter is therapeutic; it's a release from tension.

12. Live a balanced life by allotting time for work, family, and leisure.

WORK-RELATED STRESS
▼▼▼▼▼▼▼▼▼▼▼▼▼▼▼▼▼▼▼▼▼▼▼▼▼▼▼▼▼▼▼▼▼▼▼▼▼

If you find that you're unable to cope with certain stressful work situations after trying the various stress management techniques, you might have to take more drastic action. This could involve changing your attitude, methods, habits—or even your job! Consider some of the following alternatives:

1. Change your expectations of the job and/or of yourself. Maybe you've had unrealistic goals and expectations. Revise or change them so you're not trying to achieve the impossible. Some of your personal needs might never be met through this job. Question yourself about your true values and needs. You might discover a gap between them and what your present job offers.

2. Make a substantial change. You might have to work for change within the organization, transfer to a different job or course, look at retraining possibilities, or look for another job.

3. Map out possible courses of action, taking into account the possible consequences in each case.

4. Seek professional help. Attend workshops or seminars that deal with job dissatisfaction or stress management. Discuss your situation with a counsellor.

5. Take control; make yourself happy—you're the best friend you'll ever have. If you don't like what you're doing or what's happening around you, make some changes. You're the only person totally responsible for your life.

3. HOW TO HANDLE STRESS

In each of the following cases, state what the person should do to reduce stress.

1. A co-worker criticizes Mae for not completing an assignment on time. She thinks she *did* complete it on time.

2. Derek has been working at the same job for three years. His supervisor has often told him that he's doing a good job. Yet other workers hired after him have been promoted. He doesn't understand why he's been passed over.

3. Inga feels she's always overloaded with work. She asks herself, "Am I being given too much work, or am I too slow to handle it?"

4. Damir often argues with his co-workers. He doesn't think it's his fault. However, a friend has told Damir that his supervisor has noticed the arguing and is annoyed.

5. Tanny's supervisor in a retail clothing store criticizes her in public for not keeping her merchandise neat and orderly. Tanny is very hurt and embarrassed.

6. Kenji has been with the same company for five years. He has noticed that many workers who have been with the company three or four years are being laid off. Since his company doesn't seem to be doing much business, Kenji is worried about losing his job.

CHAPTER SUMMARY EXERCISES

▼▼

1. Should stress be eliminated from our lives? Why or why not?

2. Why can some people handle high levels of stress?

3. List some techniques that can help you to cope with stress.

4. In a 250-word essay, describe what is, in your opinion, a stressful situation for a friend or a member of your family. It's not necessary to name the person about whom you're writing. How is that person handling the situation? Name things that the person is *not* doing that might help.

Information for the Workplace

INTRODUCTION
▼▼▼▼▼▼▼▼▼▼▼▼▼▼▼▼▼▼▼▼▼▼

Job safety is the responsibility of both employees and employers. In this unit you will learn what such responsibility involves. This unit also discusses the types of benefits that employees usually receive and various employer policies, in addition to the history and functions of labour unions.

20

Job Safety Concerns

O B J E C T I V E S
▼▼▼▼▼▼▼▼▼▼▼▼▼▼▼▼

After completing this chapter you should be able to:

- Explain employers' and employees' responsibilities in relation to safety in the workplace.
- List possible safety hazards and the steps that can be taken to avoid work-related injury or illness.
- Define the term *workplace accident.*
- Explain the role of workers' compensation.
- Describe the steps required if you are to receive compensation because of a workplace accident.

I N T R O D U C T I O N
▼▼▼▼▼▼▼▼▼▼▼▼▼▼▼▼▼▼▼▼

Safety is defined as freedom from danger, injury, or damage, or the state of being protected against harm. Employers must provide reasonably safe working conditions, and employees must develop an awareness of safe procedures and follow the rules that promote safety. Despite good safety habits, however, accidents occasionally do happen and, when they do, it's important to know the correct procedures to follow. This chapter provides information on safety in the workplace, as well as what to do in case of workplace accidents.

O C C U P A T I O N A L   H E A L T H
A N D   S A F E T Y
▼▼▼▼▼▼▼▼▼▼▼▼▼▼▼▼▼▼▼▼▼▼▼▼▼▼▼▼▼▼

Most workers across Canada are to some degree protected by laws or codes from workplace health and safety hazards. These laws and codes are administered and enacted by the federal and provincial governments and set minimum standards for health and safety in a variety of sectors, including the industrial, construction, mining, forestry, and petroleum industries. In addition to workplace health and safety laws, employees who work with materials, conditions, or equipment considered to be hazardous are covered by legislation and codes relating to these, such as pesticides, chemicals,

X rays, communicable diseases, explosives, environmental contaminants, fire hazards, and the transportation of dangerous goods.

Employers have a legal duty to conduct their operations in a manner that prevents or reduces their employees' risk of injury or loss of health. The basic elements of employee safety programs are specific health and safety policies, defined responsibilities for safety, and measures to maintain safe working conditions, such as inspections, safety training, and first aid training.

Employees themselves have a personal responsibility for carrying out safety procedures to protect themselves and their fellow workers and to wear protective clothing and equipment where this is designated. Employees must police themselves to a certain extent.

Employees are entitled to information about the health and safety hazards of their workplace and about safe performance procedures. For example, the Workplace Hazardous Materials Information System guarantees employees the right to know about controlled or hazardous products (usually chemicals) found in the workplace. This federal and provincial legislation, passed in 1988, requires that suppliers of hazardous materials clearly label all containers that enter the workplace, specifying any dangers or risks, precautions to be taken in handling, and first aid procedures, similar to warning labels found on some consumer products. In some cases, Material Safety Data Sheets must be provided to expand on the information on the labels. Some companies have health and safety committees that act as liaison agents between the organization and employees to gather and provide information.

As a general rule, most employees have a right by law to refuse to perform a job that would endanger their or a co-worker's health and safety. These laws protect the worker from being disciplined for refusing to do such work. Some workers in some provinces, however, don't have this right, if refusal to work would endanger another person.

1. WORK SAFETY QUIZ

Write the numbers of the following statements in your notebook. Then, beside each, write the letter of the answer that you think is correct. If you don't know the answer immediately, think about each alternative and choose the one that seems to be the safest. If more than one answer seems to be correct, indicate this also.

1. Everyone should know the following about fire extinguishers:
   a) How to operate them.
   b) Which types to use on different fires.
   c) Where they're located.
   d) All of these.

2. Injuries often happen to people who:
   a) Always take chances.
   b) Commit unsafe acts.
   c) Ignore safety procedures.
   d) None of these.

3. It pays to develop:
   a) Safety consciousness.

b) Safe habits.

c) Safe attitudes.

d) All of these.

4. Chemicals should be handled only:

a) If they are labelled.

b) If safe handling precautions are explained.

c) If safety and health precautions are followed.

d) All of these.

5. Safety and health information on chemicals should be available:

a) On labels.

b) In Material Safety Data Sheets.

c) From your supervisor.

d) All of these.

6. Machines should be cleaned after use:

a) With a brush or rag.

b) With your hand.

c) According to instructions.

d) None of these.

7. Your work area should always be:

a) Cluttered.

b) Clean and tidy.

c) Dirty.

d) None of these.

8. Scrap materials should be placed:

a) On the corner of workbenches.

b) In provided containers.

c) On the floor near your work area.

d) None of these.

9. Tools should always be:

a) Left on workbenches.

b) Left on machines.

c) Put away when not in use.

d) None of these.

10. Spilled chemicals should be:

a) Left alone.

b) Handled according to instructions on labels and/or Material Safety Data Sheets.

c) Barricaded off.

d) All of these.

11. Materials and parts should be:

   a) Properly stored.

   b) Stored in designated areas.

   c) Arranged so no one will trip over or brush against them.

   d) All of these.

12. On any job, always use:

   a) The tool that is handiest.

   b) The tool for the job.

   c) A knife instead of a screwdriver.

   d) None of these.

13. Tools should be kept:

   a) Where they belong.

   b) Clean.

   c) In safe working condition.

   d) All of these.

14. Dull, broken, or worn-out tools should be:

   a) Reported to your supervisor.

   b) Used.

   c) Thrown away.

   d) None of these.

15. Cutting tools should never be:

   a) Dull.

   b) Carried in your pocket.

   c) Left lying around the work area.

   d) All of these.

16. Operate a machine only when:

   a) Your supervisor is out of the room.

   b) Told to do so by your supervisor.

   c) You see others operating the same type of machine.

   d) None of these.

17. If you don't thoroughly understand some part of your job:

   a) Ask questions.

   b) Go ahead anyway.

   c) Do nothing.

   d) None of these.

18. Before starting a machine, make sure that:

   a) Long hair and loose clothing are safely tied back.

   b) All machine safety guards are operative and in place.

c) You're wearing safety goggles or other necessary protective equipment and clothes.

d) All of these.

19. When working with power tools:

a) Keep your mind on your job.

b) Turn the tools off when you've finished using them.

c) Use them only according to instructions.

d) All of these.

20. Never leave a machine until:

a) The power switch is turned off.

b) It has completely stopped running.

c) You have cleaned up the work area around it.

d) All of these.

21. When cleaning, oiling, adjusting, or repairing a machine, make sure:

a) You've been fully instructed in such procedures.

b) The power switch is turned off and the machine has completely stopped running.

c) All safety guards and mechanisms are re-installed.

d) All of these.

22. Wear proper safety goggles and shoes, face shields, aprons, and other personal protective equipment:

a) Only when your supervisor is in the room.

b) On all jobs that require them.

c) Only when made to do so.

d) All of these.

23. Before operating a machine:

a) Remove or tuck in loose clothing. Tie back long hair.

b) Roll up your sleeves and secure them.

c) Remove rings, watches, and other jewellery.

d) All of these.

24. When using a machine for a small or fast job:

a) It's not necessary to wear protective equipment.

b) You can rely on machine safety guards for adequate protection.

c) You don't have to worry about loose clothing or long hair.

d) None of these.

25. When handling rough, heavy materials:

a) Wear gloves.

b) Wear safety shoes.

c) Wear a heavy apron.

d) All of these.

26. When welding:

    a) Protection of eyes is not important.

    b) Wear goggles with the proper type, colour, or shade of lenses.

    c) Sunglasses afford adequate protection.

    d) All of these.

27. Horseplay and practical jokes:

    a) Are permissible at all times.

    b) Should be carried on when the supervisor is out of the room.

    c) Are not safety hazards.

    d) None of these.

28. Distracting your co-worker's attention for a moment:

    a) Can cause an accident.

    b) Is permissable when the supervisor is out of the room.

    c) Keeps the co-worker alert.

    d) All of these.

29. All cuts, scratches, burns, or punctures:

    a) Can become infected.

    b) Should be reported to your supervisor.

    c) Should be treated immediately.

    d) All of these.

30. If something gets in your eye:

    a) Ask a co-worker to remove it.

    b) Report it to your supervisor immediately and obtain professional first aid.

    c) Flush the eye with water.

    d) All of these.

31. Acids or caustics can be poured from their containers:

    a) Straight into another receptacle.

    b) According to instructions for safe handling.

    c) When not wearing safety goggles, gloves, or any other required protective clothing.

    d) None of these.

32. Glass tubing should be inserted into rubber stoppers using:

    a) A facial tissue.

    b) A pencil.

    c) A heavy cloth in case the tubing breaks. Safety goggles also should be worn.

    d) None of these.

33. Water should never be poured into a container of:

    a) Sulphuric or nitric acid.

b) Any clear, colourless liquid.

c) Dyes.

d) All of these.

34. If an object is heavy or awkward:

a) Ask for help.

b) Show your strength by lifting it yourself.

c) Complain about having to handle such objects.

d) None of these.

35. In preparing to lift an object:

a) Place your feet close to the load to be lifted, properly spaced for balance.

b) Make sure your back is straight and as nearly vertical as possible.

c) Bend your knees, squat, and grasp the object firmly.

d) All of these.

36. To raise a load, lift by:

a) Straightening your legs.

b) Straightening your back.

c) Straightening your arms.

d) All of these.

37. To change directions while carrying an object, do it by:

a) Twisting the trunk of your body.

b) Changing the position of your feet.

c) Swinging your arms.

d) None of these.

38. In piling materials:

a) When a pile of boxes or bags is more than one metre high, taper the pile in toward the centre.

b) Tie boxes or bags together securely.

c) Block in objects that might roll off the pile or make the pile collapse.

d) All of these.

39. When handling materials, be sure to:

a) Use available mechanical equipment.

b) Wear gloves and safety shoes.

c) Handle them in such a way that they will not strike someone.

d) All of these.

40. Before attempting to lift a load with a rope sling, be sure:

a) To examine the sling.

b) That all hooks, rings, and other fittings are properly secured in place.

c) The rope is adequate for the job.

d) All of these.

41. Before climbing a ladder, make sure that it:

    a) Provides secure footing.

    b) Is extended to its full length.

    c) Is as nearly straight up or vertical as possible.

    d) All of these.

42. In climbing a ladder:

    a) It's not necessary to use your hands.

    b) Use both hands.

    c) Use only one hand to hold on.

    d) None of these.

43. When using a ladder:

    a) Reach out from it only within safe limits.

    b) Stand on the top rung of the ladder.

    c) Reach out as far as you can to avoid having to move the ladder.

    d) None of these.

44. Ladders with damaged rails, steps, or rungs should be:

    a) Used.

    b) Used only in an emergency.

    c) Fixed or discarded.

    d) All of these.

45. When using a stepladder, first open it fully, then:

    a) It is safe to climb.

    b) Set both spreaders before climbing.

    c) Set one of the spreaders before climbing.

    d) None of these.

46. All fire hazards should be:

    a) Reported to your supervisor.

    b) Ignored.

    c) Reported to your co-workers.

    d) All of these.

47. Oil waste and rags should be:

    a) Placed in a cardboard box.

    b) Placed in a metal container.

    c) Left where they are.

    d) All of these.

48. Fire doors, aisles, fire escapes, and stairways should be:

    a) Used as storage areas.

    b) Blocked off.

c) Kept clear.

d) None of these.

49. Injuries happen to people who:

a) Sometimes are innocent bystanders.

b) Don't know safety rules.

c) Wear loose clothing around machinery.

d) All of these.

50. Your safety on the job and elsewhere can best be guaranteed by:

a) Using common sense.

b) Following all instructions carefully.

c) Reading labels on containers and Material Safety Data Sheets.

d) All of these.

Based on information from the Industrial Accident Prevention Association, Toronto, ON.

WORKPLACE ACCIDENTS
▼▼▼▼▼▼▼▼▼▼▼▼▼▼▼▼▼▼▼▼▼▼▼▼▼▼▼▼▼▼▼▼

Victims of workplace accidents are by law entitled to compensation and certain services. A workplace accident is one that arises from or occurs during a job, resulting in injury or illness. Such accidents include injury or illness that results from sustained and unusual effort and from strenuous activities that are a regular part of the job. In addition, a workplace accident might occur during the performance of a related task that is not part of the regular job but necessary to complete a job.

The law states that if a worker suffers an accident while under the employer's control, direction, or supervision, and if the activities are part of the working conditions, the accident is a workplace accident. In line with this, the law assumes that injuries that occur in the workplace while an employee is on the job are occupational injuries, and the employee does not have to prove this. An employer might contest an employee's claim, but it is up to the employer to prove that the accident was not work-related. The following are some examples of possible workplace accidents.

• Working in the woods, a worker is cut while operating a chain-saw.

• A restaurant worker spills hot grease on herself and is burned.

• A nurse who frequently lifts and moves patients develops severe back pain; the condition is caused directly by the nurse's job.

• A bank teller is traumatized by a bank robbery.

• A warehouse worker drops a heavy object on her foot.

WORKERS' COMPENSATION
▼▼▼▼▼▼▼▼▼▼▼▼▼▼▼▼▼▼▼▼▼▼▼▼▼▼▼▼▼▼▼▼

Workers' compensation provides compensation for employees who can't work because of workplace accidents or occupational diseases. When employees are injured in the course of their work they are not penalized, but rather are compensated for their loss of income due to their inability to work.

In theory, workers' compensation covers everyone in the paid labour force; however, in each province and territory certain groups are excluded from coverage, such as, in some cases, workers in charitable organizations, real estate operations, beauty salons, and employment agencies. In many provinces, workers' compensation boards allow employers to apply for coverage of employees who would otherwise be excluded. When starting a job, it would be wise to check regarding your coverage by workers' compensation.

The first workers' compensation Act was passed in Ontario in 1914 as a result of the drastic increase in the number of injured workers due to rapid economic growth and mechanization. Other provinces soon followed suit. All Canadian jurisdictions now have workers' compensation Acts that provide medical rehabilitation services as well as financial benefits.

Prior to the passing of these Acts, injured employees sometimes sued their employers for negligence. When an employee was successful in a bid for compensation, the employer was forced to pay out sometimes large sums of money in damages. On the other hand, thousands of injured employees did not go to court—they and their families were deprived of necessary income and often faced great hardship.

The impetus to start a government compensation scheme came from employees' demands for improved protection and the concern of employers about increasingly costly court settlements.

BASIC PRINCIPLES OF WORKERS' COMPENSATION

Workers' compensation legislation sets out the following provisions.

- Compensation for workplace injuries and illnesses is a guaranteed right, regardless of fault.

- Benefits are based on lost earnings and are paid for as long as the worker is disabled.

- Compensation is administered by a board that is independent of both the government and management.

- Employers pay for the entire scheme through a collective insurance system.

- Injured workers are no longer able to sue their employers for negligence.

Compensation includes:

- Medical treatment and rehabilitation.

- Vocational rehabilitation.

- Temporary and permanent disability payments.

- Survivors' benefits to spouses and dependants in the case of death due to injury.

In case you're the victim of a work-related accident or occupational disease, it's important that you be familiar with the following details.

- Your employer or employer's representative must be notified as soon as possible. If you are unable to do so, a co-worker, union representative, family member, or friend can do this for you.

- You must receive first aid quickly. If necessary, you should be taken to a physician or health care centre, and then taken home if hospitalization is not necessary. The employer is responsible for transportation expenses on the day of the accident.

- The compensation board must be notified of all accidents requiring health care or involving lost wages or disability beyond the day of the accident. In general, all serious accidents must be reported to the body responsible for the administration of the general occupational health and safety legislation in the particular province.

- The employer must record all minor accidents in a register kept for this purpose.

- You must provide your employer with a medical certificate if an absence from work of longer than one day is required.

- Your employer is not allowed to penalize you in any way because you've suffered a workplace accident or exercised a legal right.

CHAPTER SUMMARY EXERCISES

▼▼▼▼▼▼▼▼▼▼▼▼▼▼▼▼▼▼▼▼▼▼▼▼▼▼▼▼▼▼▼▼▼▼▼▼▼

1. List three advantages of having and following safety procedures for (a) the employee and (b) the employer.

2. Name three safety precautions in effect at school or at work.

3. Have you noticed any unsafe conditions at school or at work? If so, list the conditions and outline steps that should be taken to remedy them.

a) Arms	c) Eyes	e) Hands	g) Legs
b) Ears	d) Feet	f) Head	h) Lungs

4. List ways in which you think the following body parts can be protected on the job.

5. If, at your workplace, you didn't wear safety gear to protect the parts of the body listed above, what types of illness or injuries could result? Name at least two injuries for each body part.

6. In paragraph form, explain in what ways you think stress could affect job safety.

7. Describe how you think unsafe working conditions could increase stress.

8. List four possible safety hazards related to your job (or to the type of job you'd like to have) that could result in accidents. After each item, indicate what steps could be taken to eliminate the hazard.

9. Explain why having a clean, tidy working area is a safety precaution.

10. On arriving at work or school, you smell smoke and discover a fire that has already had a good start. List at least three things you should do immediately.

11. Explain why tools, other equipment, and materials should always be put away when not in use.

12. An office environment would seem to be a very safe place. However, what safety hazards might there be in a modern office?

13. What is the correct way to lift heavy objects?

14. What is the most important rule to remember in handling chemicals?

21

Employee Benefits/Employer Policies

OBJECTIVES
▼▼▼▼▼▼▼▼▼▼▼▼▼▼▼▼

After completing this chapter you should be able to:

- Explain what employee benefits are.
- Define compulsory payroll deductions and explain what these deductions cover.
- Discuss some of the employee benefits provided by employers.
- Describe some flexible work scheduling methods.
- Explain the process of employee bonding.
- List the important company policies, rules, and procedures with which you should be familiar.
- Handle employment termination professionally if you resign and be aware of your rights if you are dismissed.

INTRODUCTION
▼▼▼▼▼▼▼▼▼▼▼▼▼▼▼▼▼▼

The primary payment that employees receive for their work is the amount that appears on their pay cheques, but many employers offer other benefits and services to the people they employ. These are sometimes referred to as *fringe benefits* and might include a dental plan, extended health insurance plan, allowance of sick days, pension plan, day care plan, or paid vacation. Two job opportunities that offer equal salaries could provide you with different levels of actual return because of the benefits and services that one of the employers provides for its employees.

Employers and employees share in the cost of some of these benefits. Money is deducted from employees' pay cheques to pay the cost of their contributions. The cost of similar services bought by the employee on an individual basis without the contribution of the employer naturally would be much higher. In addition, the employee would pay income tax on the full amount of income it cost to pay for the service. Usually when the employer contributes toward benefits, employees are taxed only on their own contributions toward the benefits; however, some benefits provided are taxable. This is something you should check with your employer.

Employers are obliged to make deductions not only for taxes but also for unemployment insurance and a government pension plan. What you receive on your pay cheque is your *net* pay; the full total of what you earned is your *gross* pay.

Time-off benefits also are important to employees. Statutory holidays, vacations, sick days, and personal leave days, all with full pay, are offered by many employers.

The scheduling of work is also important to employees. The length of work time, time of day, and days of the week worked all have an effect on employees' morale and quality of life. Some employers offer their workers the opportunity to work a compressed work week, so employees might work the equivalent of five days over a period of four days, working longer hours each day and taking the fifth day off. Other employers offer flexible starting and quitting times. Some employees are obligated to work rotating shifts.

COMPULSORY DEDUCTIONS FOR BENEFITS
▼▼▼▼▼▼▼▼▼▼▼▼▼▼▼▼▼▼▼▼▼▼▼▼▼▼▼▼▼▼▼▼▼▼▼

Compulsory deductions from all Canadian employees' pay cheques are for income tax, the Canada Pension Plan or the Quebec Pension Plan, and unemployment insurance, all of which are forwarded to the government by the employer. In some provinces, compulsory deductions are also made for provincial health care insurance plans.

INCOME TAX

The largest single deduction from employees' pay cheques is for payment of income tax. Canadians have been paying income tax since 1917, when it was brought into effect as a "temporary wartime measure" by Canada's eighth prime minister, Sir Robert Borden. Today, income taxes collected by the government are used to provide many social and business support services.

Employees pay both provincial and federal income taxes. In all of the territories and provinces except Quebec, which collects its own provincial taxes, both income taxes are paid to the federal government (Revenue Canada Taxation), which then passes the money on to the provinces. If you're self-employed, you're obligated to pay income tax on a quarterly basis.

When you start a new job, your employer will have you complete a TDI form. This form lists your expected income for the year and the names and particulars of any dependants (such as a spouse and/or children), and is used to determine the amount of income tax deduction to which you're entitled. The balance after allowable deductions is your estimated taxable income, which indicates to the employer how much tax to deduct from each pay, according to a tax table provided by Revenue Canada.

By the end of February each year, you'll receive a T4 slip from each employer for whom you worked during the previous year. The T4 slips show how much salary you were paid and how much income tax was deducted from it.

Based on the information on the T4 slips, you must complete an income tax return annually and submit it to your Revenue Canada district taxation office by April 30. The calculations you do on this return will tell you whether you must pay additional taxes or whether you're entitled to a refund for having overpaid your taxes.

CANADA PENSION PLAN AND QUEBEC PENSION PLAN

Both the Canada Pension Plan (CPP) and the Quebec Pension Plan (QPP) came into effect in 1966, and are designed to provide pensions for the retired from the earnings of people who are employed. All income-earning people, including those who are self-employed, are required to contribute to either the CPP or QPP.

Both pension plans also provide survivors' benefits (spouses' pensions, orphans' benefits, and lump-sum death benefits) and disability benefits, and payments made by both plans are adjusted on the basis of the Consumer Price Index. The Consumer Price Index (CPI) is a report prepared monthly by the government to keep track of the retail prices of goods and services in Canada, as an indication of how much it costs the average Canadian to live.

Employers and employees contribute equally to the CPP and the QPP. Changes in jobs or residences do not affect the plans in any way.

Pension payments begin at age 65 and are based on a contributor's earnings, calculated in terms of the wage standards existing at the time of retirement.

UNEMPLOYMENT INSURANCE

The first compulsory national unemployment insurance program came into effect in Canada in 1941 to protect workers against loss of income due to unemployment.

Unemployment insurance premiums are payable by both employers and employees and these contributions are based on a certain percentage of the employee's salary, with a maximum contribution allowed per year. These contributions, subsidized by the federal government, are used to pay unemployed workers on a regular basis for a certain period of time.

To qualify for unemployment insurance benefits, applicants must prove that they were previously employed for a certain number of weeks. This proof is a Record of Employment form issued by their former employers.

To receive unemployment benefits, applicants must file a claim stating that they are out of work, are willing to work, and are registered at a Canada Employment Centre. Following a waiting period, individuals are eligible to receive a percentage of their previous weekly insured earnings up to a maximum amount. The length of time for which benefits will be paid varies, depending on how long a person was employed and on the national and regional unemployment rate.

VOLUNTARY DEDUCTIONS AND EMPLOYER-PAID BENEFITS

▼▼▼

GROUP LIFE INSURANCE PLANS

Life insurance, which provides financial protection for your survivors in case of your death, is a common employee benefit in Canada. The employer signs up for a group life insurance plan (which is cheaper than if an individual buys a plan) and pays either all or part of the premium for the employees. If the employees contribute part of the premium, a set amount is deducted from their pay. Such deductions are voluntary, since an employee can choose not to take advantage of the plan.

In many companies, employees are insured according to a formula based on the income of the insured. For example, if the formula was two times the salary, a person earning $20 000 would have a policy that would pay $40 000 to survivors on his or her death; another employee earning $30 000 would have a policy that would pay $60 000.

GROUP HEALTH INSURANCE PLANS

Provincial health care programs provide for most health care expenses but extended group health insurance programs cover those that are not. Membership in a company's group plan might be optional or compulsory, depending on the terms and conditions of the plan. Premiums are usually paid in the form of payroll deductions.

Extended health insurance plans usually reimburse part or all of the cost of prescribed medication and specific services such as ambulances, private nursing care, physiotherapy, psychotherapy, and dental care.

SHORT- AND LONG-TERM DISABILITY PLANS

As discussed in the previous chapter, workers' compensation coverage that employers must carry provides for employees in cases of work-related injury or illness. In addition, most employers grant paid sick leave for employees who must miss work due to non-occupational illnesses or injuries. This sick leave is for a limited time only, however, so most employers have short- and long-term disability plans to ensure that employees are covered in case of extended health-related absences from work.

Most disability insurance plans are administered and financed by the employer. A cumulative plan allows the employee to accumulate sick leave days from year to year. A non-cumulative plan is one in which credits are not transferable from year to year.

Another arrangement is a sickness indemnity insurance plan. Premiums are paid (usually all or in part by the employer) to an outside agency or insurance company. The benefits of these plans are usually limited to a certain length of time and are preceded by a waiting period during which no payments are received by the employee, a condition that is often waived in cases of accident. The waiting period is specified because these plans are designed to pay out for longer-term disabilities and illnesses, not for short-term ones such as the flu or a cold. Usually the benefits paid are a percentage of weekly earnings. Some employees receive the benefits of a combination of sick-leave days and a sickness indemnity insurance plan.

Long-term disability plans are designed for employees who are disabled for a prolonged length of time. The payments from these plans, usually a percentage of income, are often preceded by a long waiting period. These payments are usually made only until normal retirement age is reached.

EMPLOYMENT INCOME SECURITY

Some employees have the protection of supplemental unemployment benefits when a layoff occurs, which means that unemployment insurance benefits are added to by the employer from money previously paid to a special fund. As long as the fund remains solvent, participating employees are assured of an income almost equal to their working wages.

PRIVATE PENSION PLANS

Some employers contribute money to private pension plans for their employees, to supplement the pensions provided by the CPP or QPP. In non-contributory plans only the employer contributes to the pension. In contributory plans both the employer and the employee are required to contribute.

Private pension plans are not as flexible as the CPP or QPP, which remain in effect even if an employee changes jobs. Some private pension plans are terminated if an employee leaves the organization (although the money the employee invested is returned), unless the employee has what are called *vested pension rights.* Vested pension rights means that the former employee retains the benefit of the contributions that she or he made to her or his pension. Such rights usually come into effect after several years of service. A portability clause allows the employee's pension rights to be transferred to another employer.

Where will the money come from when your retirement arrives? Some pensions are paid out of the current income of the company. This is called an *unfunded plan.* Funded plans are funds accumulated in advance from the employer and employee. This money, plus interest, covers the cost of the pensions that the fund will be required to pay out. Private pension funds are by law administered by a trust company or by an insurance company, to ensure that employees' funds are protected if a company goes out of business and to prevent misuse of pension funds by companies.

Some private pension funds offer employees the opportunity to retire before the age of 65. Usually, however, there is a penalty in the form of reduced pension benefits, since statistically the employee will be drawing benefits for a longer period of time.

PAID TIME-OFF BENEFITS

Wages paid for time periods when an employee is not actually working are referred to as *time-off benefits.* These can include rest and meal breaks, wash-up time, sick days, personal leave days, and time off for family emergencies. Vacation length is usually based on length of service, although all employees are entitled to at least two-weeks' vacation after one year of full-time service.

The granting of leaves of absence for pregnancy, birth, adoption, extended illness, accidents, etc., is sometimes part of a company's personnel policy. Union contracts sometimes outline specific cases. These leaves are generally granted without pay.

FLEXIBLE WORK SCHEDULES

Flexibility in the scheduling of work is an important social and economic benefit for employees. Shorter work weeks, flextime, and job sharing can give employees choices that can enhance their personal lives. These types of policies benefit the employer by improving employee morale and productivity, and reducing absenteeism in the workplace.

Shorter work weeks compress the hours of a five-day work week into four days, which means that employees work longer hours during those four days. For some workers, having to work longer hours on four days is worth the pleasure of a three-day weekend.

Flextime allows employees some flexibility in when they start and finish their work days. The work day is not longer or shorter. Employees are usually expected to be present during some core hours of the day so that there is continuity in the work being done.

In job sharing, two or more employees share the duties and responsibilities of one full-time job. For example, two employees might make an arrangement with their employer for one employee to work at the job in the morning and the other in the afternoon, or for one to work certain days of the week and the other to work the rest of the days, or for each to work alternate weeks.

Job sharing offers a flexibility that is particularly welcomed by parents who want to give more time to their children's care and yet don't want, or can't afford, to stay home full-time. One possible disadvantage for employers is increased administration duties, but on the other hand, they have employees who are usually more relaxed and happy with their lifestyles and therefore are more effective. Also, employers don't like to lose good employees and permitting them to job share reduces this possibility.

BONDING
▼ ▼ ▼ ▼ ▼ ▼ ▼ ▼ ▼ ▼ ▼ ▼

Bonding is a form of insurance that protects an employer against financial loss due to employee theft or misconduct. Whether the employer or the employee pays for the bond depends on the type of bond and the individual employer.

In the event of a loss due to a dishonest act by a bonded employee, the employer will be reimbursed by the insurance company that provides the bond. The bonded employee will then be required to repay the loss to the bonding company. Specific requirements and procedures for bonding will vary, depending on your circumstances, the job you'll be doing, and the policy of the company that provides the bond.

A variety of types of bonds is available, but the two types that can be obtained by individuals are surety and individual fidelity bonds. Surety bonds are most common and are often required by law for certain types of jobs, such as those done by tradespeople, salespeople, and truck drivers. Obtaining such a bond is often dependent on the applicant's financial position.

Individual fidelity bonds can be purchased to provide protection from loss due to dishonest acts on the part of specific employees, for example, people who have previously been convicted of such offences. As a condition of holding such a bond, annual assessments of the employee's performance might be required by the bonding agent. The amount of a fidelity bond and its cost depend primarily on the type of job, how much money is being handled, and the control the employer exerts through office and bookkeeping procedures.

PROCEDURE FOR OBTAINING BONDING

When you find out that a bond is required, ask the employer which company it uses to bond its employees. You can then approach the bonding company directly.

In some situations, you might need to go through an agent or broker who deals directly with the bonding or surety company. Agents themselves do not issue bonds but will support and process applications for bonding. The agent will give you an application form to complete. For your application you might need references from a clergyman or a previous employer, for example, stating that you're trustworthy and reliable. The application form also might ask for information about previous employers and about your financial status. The completed form, along with the required letters of reference, are then submitted to the bonding company.

If you need an agent, look in the Yellow Pages of the telephone directory under "Insurance Brokers" to see which companies handle bonding in your area.

The next step in the process involves investigation by the bonding agent of your background and status. The investigation can include contacts with friends, neighbours, and relatives, as well as an examination of your financial records. If strong recommendations are made in the letters of reference, this type of inquiry might not be required.

In summary, the decision whether to bond depends primarily on the job description, type and amount of bond applied for, and references. Usually, if your employer also is willing to support your application for bond, the company will look on that favourably.

Adapted from Employment and Immigration Canada. PLACE. *Guided Steps to Employment Readiness.* "Part E: Personal Needs." © Minister of Supply and Services Canada, 1984, Unit 20. Reproduced with the permission of the Minister of Supply and Services Canada, 1990.

1. BONDING QUIZ

1. Define the term *bonding*.

2. Who pays for the bond?

3. Name the types of bonds available to individuals and explain each in your own words.

4. List the procedures for obtaining bonding.

5. Why might you need references when applying for bonding?

6. What happens in the event of a loss caused by a dishonest bonded employee?

KNOWING AND OBSERVING COMPANY POLICIES
▼▼▼▼▼▼▼▼▼▼▼▼▼▼▼▼▼▼▼▼▼▼▼▼▼▼▼▼▼▼▼▼▼▼▼

Employees are sometimes not fully aware of their employer's policies, rules, and procedures. Sometimes this is the fault of the employer in not providing the information, but often it is due to the employee's failure to read information that the company has provided. Rules define the obligations of the employer and the employee to each other and should be carefully read and followed. The following guidelines will help you to be a better employee.

1. Find out the rules. Read all information provided about your job and company policies and benefits. Keep this written information so that you can refer to it when the need arises. Do not discard such information or ignore it. Before accepting a job you should inquire about basic company policies and procedures and then reconfirm these once you start the job. Either obtain printed information from the personnel or human resource department or write down the details in a notebook about:

   a) Working hours:
      - Starting and leaving times.
      - Number of hours per day.
      - Overtime policies.
      - Breaks.

   b) Leave Policies:
      - Holidays.
      - Vacation length and timing.
      - Sick leave.
      - Accident leave.
      - Compassionate leave.

   c) Employee benefits.

   d) Health and safety regulations.

   e) Union organization and agreement details.

   f) Grievance (complaint) procedures.

   g) Rules about privacy and confidentiality of information you learn at work.

2. Organizations usually have unwritten rules that you'll learn about only by observing the behaviour of other employees and listening to them. This can range from how to address certain senior company officials to what to wear to work. Keep your eyes and ears open!

3. If you don't understand a rule or feel that it's being enforced unfairly, ask your supervisor or co-workers for an explanation informally before grumbling or filing a formal complaint. Often an informal chat can resolve the situation.

4. Even when you disagree with a rule or policy, it's your obligation to follow it until it's been changed officially. You can and should make your complaint known, but if you just ignore the rules, you can be fired.

EMPLOYMENT TERMINATION

IF YOU RESIGN

You're expected to give notice to your employer when you decide to resign from a job. It's wise to give this notice in writing as well as verbally. One of your most valuable references in the future could be from your employer, and any employer would hesitate to recommend a former employee who left without allowing some time for the finding of a replacement.

In some provinces, the employer has a right to insist that you give notice. Employees working under federal labour legislation are not obliged to give any notice at all. Most union and individual contracts throughout Canada contain a clause stipulating a notice period before you can leave a job.

So, no matter what reason you might have for leaving the job, resign in a professional manner. If possible, give at least two-weeks' notice. Finish any projects you might have started, and leave your work area organized and tidy for the next person. Give the personnel/human resource department an address at which you can be reached. Remember, you might want to work for the same employer at some time in the future.

IF YOU ARE DISCHARGED

Under the Canada Labour Code, employees who are discharged are entitled to severance pay equal to regular wages for a specific time period if the employee has not been given notice and if the dismissal was not for just cause. Just cause could include such behaviour on the part of an employee as willful misconduct (such as theft), disobedience, or neglect of duty. In such cases, the dismissed employee would not be entitled to either notice or severance pay.

Some union contracts contain clauses that require the employer to pay severance compensation to the discharged employee according to a formula that takes into consideration the amount of time that the employee has worked.

For higher-income executives, severance pay sometimes equals six-months' to a year's salary. Some employees have fought and won legal battles to receive larger compensation because they felt they were unjustly discharged.

When an employee is discharged or quits, the company is required to furnish the employee with a Record of Employment. This is an official document that is required if an employee wants to apply for unemployment insurance. This paper is important even if the employee has not worked the number of weeks that are required to receive benefits. The required number of insurable weeks of employment can be accumulated with weeks of work from several employers. This is an important record that should be kept in a safe place.

Claimants of unemployment insurance who are fired or who have quit their jobs are penalized by having their benefits withheld for a prescribed number of weeks. Claimants have the right to appeal decisions about their claims to a tribunal if they feel that they are being unduly penalized.

CHAPTER SUMMARY EXERCISES
▼▼

1. Name some employee benefits offered by employers.

2. What compulsory deductions are made from wages?

3. Why is it less expensive for an employee to belong to a group life insurance plan than to buy it as an individual?

4. Name four benefits that a group health insurance plan might cover that a provincial health plan might not.

5. How is the amount of a pension received by a retired employee from the Canada Pension Plan or the Quebec Pension Plan determined?

6. Name some usual paid time-off benefits.

7. What protection does a supplemental unemployment plan offer employees?

8. What is severance pay?

9. List important company policies that you should know about.

10. How can employers give employees more flexibility in the hours they work? Explain your answer.

11. What is a Record of Employment form? Why is it important?

Labour Unions

OBJECTIVES
▼▼▼▼▼▼▼▼▼▼▼▼▼▼▼▼

After completing this chapter you should be able to:

- Explain what a union is, how it functions, and the issues it handles.
- Describe how and why unions first came into existence.
- Define the terms *collective bargaining* and *collective agreement* and explain the purpose of each.
- Discuss what grievances are and how these are handled in unionized organizations.

INTRODUCTION
▼▼ ▼▼▼▼▼▼▼▼▼▼▼▼▼▼▼▼▼▼

Labour unions in Canada are recognized as institutions with important economic and social functions, concerned not only with wages and working hours but also with more far-reaching issues. Unions attempt to have a voice in all phases of employee-employer relations, including employee safety and benefits, unemployment, disability insurance, retirement pensions, workers' compensation and other forms of social welfare, and unfair employment practices.

Unions are also involved in the reformation of social and political policies, expanding their original focus to issues dealing with poverty, discrimination of any type, the environment, housing, and the need for improvement in the health care system. Unions also are active in the area of job training and retraining, trying to help solve the problems created by the advance of technology, which has resulted in the disappearance of some jobs and the creation of new jobs for which additional training is required.

What were working conditions like before unions? How is a labour union formed? How do unions operate? All of these questions will be answered in this chapter.

HISTORY OF LABOUR UNIONS IN CANADA
▼▼

When our society was based on an economy that was primarily agricultural, many people worked for themselves as farmers or in small shops. However, as technology advanced, many smaller businesses were unable to compete in the marketplace against the cheaper-priced goods that were mass-produced by larger businesses.

People who had previously produced some of the goods that their families required went to work for these businesses, creating an even larger market for commercially manufactured goods. Wages were usually low and working hours long, often twelve hours a day, six days a week. Working conditions generally were poor and often jeopardized the health and safety of employees. The tasks employees performed were usually monotonous and physically demanding. Complaints were few, however, because the employees were afraid of losing their jobs.

In addition, until as recently as the beginning of this century, child labour was common. Today, child labour is defined as the regular employment of children under the age of fifteen or sixteen, but in the late eighteenth century it was generally assumed that children from about the age of seven should be employed full-time outside their homes. These children worked long hours— often thirteen to sixteen hours a day with little or no time off—in bad and often hazardous working conditions. Young children were particularly of value in the mines, where their small size enabled them to work in narrow, low passages that adults couldn't enter. And, of course, children could be paid far less than adults, so factories, mills, and farms welcomed the cheap labour provided by children. The children's parents were usually extremely poor and had no choice but to send their children out to work, warning the youngsters that they must do everything they were told, without question, because employment was so hard to find and the family's welfare depended on them.

The jobs these children did were, for the most part, dead-end, menial occupations, with no hope of advancement, so they were doomed to lives as poor as those of their parents. Education for other than the children of wealthy families was considered to be of little importance in Canada until the late nineteenth century and the early part of this century.

Finally, workers decided that something must be done and began to band together to demand fair treatment from employers. In the United States, unions began developing in the 1830s, followed in the 1860s by the United Kingdom and Canada. The purpose of these unions was to identify unfair wage levels, too-long work hours, unsafe or inhumane working conditions, and, in general, unacceptable treatment by employers. Where at one time individual employees had been afraid to speak up, suddenly employers were faced by the protests of all of the members of a certain trade and often of related trades, accompanied by threats that production would be stopped if problems weren't solved to the employees' satisfaction.

LABOUR UNIONS TODAY
▼▼▼▼▼▼▼▼▼▼▼▼▼▼▼▼▼▼▼▼▼▼▼▼▼▼▼▼▼▼▼▼▼▼

Unions operate on the same basic principle today, bargaining for such items as:

- Fair wages that take into account the rising cost of living.
- Job security.
- Safe, clean working conditions.

- Recognition of seniority in relation to promotions, layoffs, rehiring after layoffs, and choice of working hours and vacation times.
- Discontinuance of favouritism and similar injustices to employees.
- Proper grievance procedures to enable employees to present justified complaints to unbiased committees.
- Agreements that provide extended maternity and sick leaves, and regular yearly vacations.
- Satisfactory retirement programs.

Today's labour unions play an important role in the working world. Union members account for more than 37% of the non-agricultural, paid labour force. Even non-unionized employees can thank the work of the unions for the general improvement in working conditions and employee benefits. For example, wages are higher because both unionized and non-unionized companies compete for the same skilled and qualified employees.

Many of the occupations you might consider for your future are unionized or involve working closely with members of a union. Some of the Canadian unions with the largest membership are the Canadian Union of Public Employees; the National Union of Provincial Government Employees; the Public Service Alliance of Canada; the National Automobile, Aerospace and Agricultural Implement Workers' Union of Canada; the United Food and Commercial Workers' International Union; and the United Steelworkers of America.

1. INVESTIGATING OTHERS' OPINIONS OF UNIONS

1. Interview someone who belongs to a union. Ask the following questions and add some of your own. Prepare a brief report of your findings.

   a) What is your occupation?
   b) What is the name of your union?
   c) What does your union do for you?
   d) What do you think would happen if there wasn't a union?
   e) How is your union organized?
   f) Who makes the decisions for your union?
   g) How does a strike affect you?

2. Interview someone who does not belong to a union, asking the following questions and adding some of your own. Prepare a brief report.

   a) What is your occupation?
   b) Would you like to belong to a union?
   c) How do you and your co-workers handle problems you encounter at your workplace?

HOW UNIONS OPERATE
▼▼▼▼▼▼▼▼▼▼▼▼▼▼▼▼▼▼▼▼▼▼▼▼▼ ▼▼▼▼▼▼▼

Labour unions are made up of people who work in similar occupations or organizations. The main function of each unit is collective bargaining, which means that representatives of the employees and of the employer sit down and bargain for improved wages, benefits, and working conditions. The agreement reached between the two sets of representatives is called a *collective agreement*, a legal document that lists the items agreed to by both sides during negotiations.

Unions must meet a number of legal requirements before they can represent their members. The vast majority of workers in Canada come under provincial jurisdiction. While the provisions of the law vary somewhat from province to province, they are in most essential ways very similar. A limited number of workers, such as those engaged in interprovincial transportation, communications, and a few other industries, as well as federal employees, are under federal jurisdiction.

HOW A UNION IS FORMED
▼▼

The following steps are involved in the formation of a union.

1. Identification of the group of employees that the union is to represent, such as people who work in certain trades or people who work in the same industry or in related industries. An auto workers' union, for example, might represent not only the people involved in the actual manufacture of vehicles but also people in related industries, such as tire and battery company employees.

2. An invitation is extended to the identified group of employees by the union organizers. Employees who want to join sign an application form and make a small initial payment of dues or pay an initiation fee to indicate their commitment.

3. When the union has the support of the majority of qualified employees, an application for certification is made to the appropriate labour relations board. Certification means that the union is granted official recognition by the government and is entitled to enter into collective bargaining on behalf of its members.

4. Once certification has been granted, the members of the new union elect their own officers, such as president, vice-president, secretary, and treasurer. The elected officers are in charge of all of the activities of the local union and are governed by its constitution. The members pay dues, part of which are kept by the local union and part of which go to the national or international union to which most local unions belong.

Various types of services are provided by the national and international unions, such as assistance in negotiations with an employer. The local union also has the benefit of the expertise of staff such as lawyers, economists, and other research specialists. Education is undertaken by the larger union in the form of brochures, newsletters, and training programs for local union officers.

Aspects of the operation of national and international unions are addressed at conventions held periodically, to which each local union is entitled to send delegates. These delegates help to decide the terms of the union constitution, make budgetary and policy decisions, and elect officers.

2. RESEARCHING UNION RELATIONSHIPS

Identify a local union and then do research to find out if this union belongs to a national or international union. Your teacher will help you to get started on this project. Record the correct names of both the local union and the larger one, making sure that you have the spellings correct, the number of members in both unions, and the types of industries represented by both.

COLLECTIVE BARGAINING
▼▼▼▼▼▼▼▼▼▼▼▼▼▼▼▼▼▼▼▼▼▼▼▼▼▼▼▼▼▼▼▼▼

A union can begin collective bargaining when it has the support of the majority of the employees and has received official certification. The most common procedure followed is for the members of the local union to hold a meeting, or more often a series of meetings, to decide on the proposals that will be made to management, the representatives of the employer. Members are selected to act on the bargaining committee. A negotiator or a specialist might be provided by the national or international union to provide consultation on wage scales, employee benefits, and negotiation strategies.

The contract proposal advanced by the union might cover a wide variety of issues. Wages and job security are the most common, but by no means the only, concerns. Suggestions might be advanced relating to vacations, pension plans, extended maternity and sick-leave benefits, cost of living allowances (COLA), medical insurance, seniority provisions governing promotions, and grievance procedures. The members of the local union vote on exactly what proposals are to be made. The elected bargaining committee then arranges to meet the representatives of management.

The spokesperson for management might be the head of the company, the director of the personnel department, or other company officials, usually depending on the size of the company.

Bargaining is often a slow process. The proposals advanced by the union might be met by counter-proposals from management, followed by a period of discussion, and often by concessions being made by each side. Periodically the two groups engaged in bargaining report back to their superiors; in the case of the union, the bargaining committee reports to a membership meeting, where it might receive additional instructions.

Approximately 90% of the time, voluntary agreement is finally reached between management and the employees. The terms of the agreement are then written into a contract. This contract governs the wages, hours, and other conditions of employment in that particular company for a specified period, normally between one to three years.

PROBLEMS IN THE BARGAINING PROCESS

If the two parties find it impossible to reach an agreement, then government assistance is provided under the labour laws of the various provinces and by federal legislation. The assistance given varies somewhat from province to province but usually is as follows.

1. A conciliation officer, usually an official of the government's labour department, is appointed. This person meets with union and management representatives to determine the nature and extent of their differences. If possible, the conciliation officer helps the two sides to resolve their differences, and a contract is signed.

2. If the first step fails, a conciliation board is often established, usually made up of a representative of the union, a representative of

management, and a chairperson selected by these two representatives. If the two sides can't agree on the selection of a chairperson, one can be appointed by the Minister of Labour. The conciliation board conducts hearings,

listens to both sides' arguments, and then prepares a report. If agreement can be reached at this stage, a contract is signed. If not, employees are in a legal position to strike, after a time period specified by law.

S T R I K E S
▼ ▼ ▼ ▼ ▼ ▼ ▼ ▼ ▼ ▼ ▼ ▼

The final decision as to whether there will be a strike rests with the employees concerned. First the union members vote on what action should be taken. In many cases, an agreement is reached and a contract is signed without any strike action. Strikes result in only about 10% of contract negotiation situations.

When a union does strike, employees usually picket their place of employment to draw attention to their problem. Some unions are required by law to provide essential services in the case of a strike, such as police protection and medical services. A strike means hardship for the employees, management, and the public: the employees need their wages, the company will lose money if operations are discontinued, and strikes always disadvantage the public in some way.

When a company hires non-union workers to replace the unionized workers during a strike, the replacements are sometimes referred to as *scabs*. Some provinces have anti-scab laws that prevent management from hiring non-union labour to fill union positions. In these cases, other members of the company (including management) are often forced to carry on operations by performing the tasks of the unionized workers, even if they're not fully qualified to do so.

Union members vote to strike or to end a strike at the local union level. Sometimes a strike is ended when management obtains an injunction, a court order that ends the strike. Any employees who continue to strike could be fined or lose seniority.

3. REPORT ON STRIKES

Are union employees currently on strike in your area? Why did the employees decide to strike? If a strike is not occurring in your area now, read the newspapers to see if one is underway elsewhere and write a report about it. If all else fails, do research and a report on past strikes. Your local library or newspaper office could be a source of information.

G R I E V A N C E S
▼ ▼ ▼ ▼ ▼ ▼ ▼ ▼ ▼ ▼ ▼ ▼ ▼ ▼ ▼ ▼

Employment contracts are intended to provide an orderly plan for dealing with most labour-management interactions. One of the most important sections of the contract is the one that specifies methods for the settlement of grievances, which are employee complaints that their rights are not being respected.

While every province has legislation that protects the rights of employees (see Chapter 10 regarding prohibited grounds of discrimination in employment, for example) and specifies minimum wages and working condition standards, many issues arise that don't fit precisely into certain legal categories. When this is the case, members can turn to their unions for assistance.

Grievances can concern a number of matters: safety of working conditions, appropriate rates of pay, changes in job description (meaning that an employee might be expected to do tasks that were not specified when that employee was hired), unfair dismissal, etc. If an employee has a complaint about a matter that's a violation of the terms of the contract, she or he has the right to file a grievance with the union.

When a grievance is filed, steps are usually taken first to settle it within the department where the worker is employed. Key people in the settlement effort might be the supervisor of the department and the union shop steward, the person who is usually the head of the local union. The shop steward is one of the employees who has been chosen by his or her co-workers, through the union, to represent the interests of those who work in his or her section.

If a settlement is not reached at this stage, the matter is taken to a higher level involving more senior union officers and company officials. If after this process no agreement is reached, the matter can be placed before a third party from the outside called an *arbitrator* or before several people on an arbitration board. Sometimes a case is heard by a judge from the Department of Labour. The decision given is then binding on the company, the employee, and the representative union.

UNION MEMBERSHIP AND DUES

Whether all employees are required to join the union depends on the terms agreed on by the employees who are already members of the union. The term *closed shop* refers to a company that hires only union members. In a *union shop*, employees are required to join a union after a specified period of time. Even part-time employees such as summer employees are required to pay dues if they work in a union shop, although they might not be required to join the union. In an *open shop*, employees aren't required to be or to become union members.

The term *Rand Formula* refers to a provision whereby the employer deducts a portion of the salaries of *all* employees in a bargaining unit, even if they are not union members, to be given to the union as union dues. This is called *checkoff*. It was named for a decision handed down in 1946 by Mr. Justice Ivan Rand of the Supreme Court of Canada while he was arbitrating the first strike after World War II, which took place at the Ford Motor Company in Windsor, Ontario. The major issue in this strike was for union recognition, and Rand's decision marked a significant step forward in union-management negotiations.

Under the Rand Formula, employees aren't required to actually join the union but they are required to pay union dues. This plan is based on the philosophy that all employees benefit from the activities of the union and should, therefore, contribute to its maintenance. It should be remembered that, with reference to all of these plans, the union is required to obtain and prove the support of a majority of the workers before it can attain a position to gain such provisions.

CASE STUDY

FORMATION OF LOCAL 18 OF THE CANADIAN UNION OF DELIVERY WORKERS

After work one day, four drivers of the ABC Courier Company met for coffee and, in the course of their conversation, decided that something had to be done about the way they were being treated at work. The drivers' wages varied but it seemed that wages averaged a measly $5.60/h (for those who talked about it). It also seemed that the boss's favourite drivers got much higher wages.

Another problem seemed to be the company's expectation that, with last-minute notification, the employees would willingly work overtime. This happened frequently and inconvenienced many of the drivers and dispatchers. Most of the dispatchers were women, single mothers and others who had to get home to handle family responsibilities. Also unfair was the requirement that the dispatchers be on the job half an hour prior to their shifts but were not paid for this time. To top it all off, employee benefits were non-existent.

Employees who complained or frequently refused to work late or come in early were notified that they were "redundant" or "not flexible enough"—and fired. Jobs were hard to come by, so the employees grudgingly accepted the situation.

The issue of favouritism also aroused great resentment. Unless you played up to the boss or supervisors, you didn't get anywhere. The boss's favourites got better pay and the best delivery routes.

Eventually the situation became intolerable. The employees were tired of being treated unfairly and taken for granted. Over coffee, the four drivers decided to seek the help of a union organizer. They called the offices of the Canadian Union of Delivery Workers and arranged to meet with a union official in secret the next night.

After that meeting, a committee of ABC Courier Company employees was formed. The committee had to go to all employees' homes—also secretly—to ask them to sign union cards and pay a small fee. Many employees were afraid to sign up, but the organizing drive was very successful and 43 out of 60 employees signed.

The union made an application to the government for certification as the bargaining agent for all of the employees of the ABC Courier Company. ABC's management was not happy. They tried to correct some past wrongs and even increased all of the employees' wages, but the damage had already been done. The government received the application and issued a vote order at the workplace. Weeks later the government sent a representative to the ABC office and set up a polling station. The employees voted in secret to determine if they wanted a union. The union won certification because 70% of the employees voted to join the union.

QUESTIONS

1. List five complaints of the drivers and dispatchers of the ABC Courier Company.

2. Which drivers and dispatchers do you think would not want to have a union? Explain your answer.

3. List some of the ways in which a union could help the drivers and dispatchers of the ABC Courier Company.

4. Why was ABC management unhappy about the union applying for certification? What did they try to do? Why did they not succeed?

---

4. UNDERSTANDING UNION FUNCTIONS

1. In terms of the workplace, what is a union? How does your dictionary define the word *union?*

2. Explain what a grievance is and give examples of the types of grievances you think employees might have.

3. Name some company policies and benefits that might be particularly important to female employees.

4. Explain the process of collective bargaining.

5. Do you think that employees who provide essential services should have the right to strike? Explain your answer. Name two essential services and explain the effects of each going on strike.

6. Would you like to belong to a union? Why or why not?

CHAPTER SUMMARY EXERCISE
▼▼

In your notebook, write each statement below and fill in the word or phrase from the following list that best fits.

a) grievance
b) shop steward
c) COLA
d) negotiating
e) injunction

f) strike
g) employee benefits
h) seniority
i) certification
j) closed shop

k) picket
l) collective bargaining
m) checkoff
n) collective agreement
o) conciliation

1. A refusal to work because a satisfactory contract cannot be negotiated is called a/an ___.

2. An employer and employees who are trying to come to an agreement are ___.

3. A legal step that can be used by an employer to end a strike is called a/an ___.

4. A/an ___ lists the agreements between an employer and a union relating to wages, working conditions, fringe benefits, etc.

5. The ___ is the union worker elected by co-workers to represent them in dealings with management.

6. Dental plans, pension plans, sick-leave plans, etc., are called ___.

7. A company that won't hire non-union workers is called a/an ___.

8. The method of settling a dispute between an employer and employees by bringing in a third party is known as ___.

9. One method of collecting union dues is ___.

10. ___ is a legal requirement for a group to become a union.

11. Workers on strike usually ___ their place of work.

12. A unionized employee has the right to file a ___ if some part of her or his contract is not honoured.

13. In a unionized organization, ___ is taken into account when promotions are being considered.

14. A method of determining wages, hours, etc., through direct negotiation between the union and the employer is called ___.

15. ___ is the short form for "cost of living allowance."

Adapted from Ontario Ministry of Education. *Work and Employability Skills Program*, 1982, p.94.

U N I T

6

Creating Work Opportunities

I N T R O D U C T I O N
▼▼▼▼▼▼▼▼▼▼▼▼▼▼▼▼▼▼▼▼▼▼▼

At this point you've already thought about a specific career and might have certain expectations of what your job and future will be like. If these expectations are to be realized, you'll need to develop certain skills, including the ability to use your initiative. Decision-making skills are also discussed in this unit. This chapter concludes with a look at entrepreneurship, which involves the use of all of your job skills, the ability to take charge, and the courage to take risks.

Creating your own work opportunities is not as difficult as it might sound. While working for someone else, this is achieved by doing the best you can at any task, watching for opportunities to take the lead. By using your initiative and learning new skills, you will gain confidence in your ability to make worthwhile decisions.

Using Your Initiative

O B J E C T I V E S
▼ ▼ ▼ ▼ ▼ ▼ ▼ ▼ ▼ ▼ ▼ ▼ ▼ ▼ ▼ ▼

After completing this chapter you should be able to:

- Appreciate the value of showing initiative.
- Assess your own level of initiative.
- Identify ways in which you can show initiative.

I N T R O D U C T I O N
▼ ▼ ▼ ▼ ▼ ▼ ▼ ▼ ▼ ▼ ▼ ▼ ▼ ▼ ▼ ▼ ▼ ▼ ▼

The verb *initiate* is defined as meaning "to cause the beginning of," and employers appreciate employees who demonstrate this ability by thinking carefully about their jobs, deciding what needs to be done, and doing it without repeated instructions. Independent thinking often leads to suggestions from employees about faster, more effective, or less expensive ways in which tasks can be accomplished. This benefits not only the employer but also the individual employee, whose job record is enhanced. An alert, willing attitude will help you to see where you can take the initiative in the future.

1. ASSESSING YOUR INITIATIVE

When employers are asked to name the quality that they value most in their employees, they usually answer that it is initiative. Showing initiative in your job involves using good judgment in solving problems. To assess your ability in this regard, answer the following questions. If you don't have a job, base your answers on the way you have participated in various clubs, on sports teams, etc.

In your notebook, write down the numbers of the questions. Then, beside each, write your answer based on the following key.

N = No   Y = Yes   NS = Not Sure

1. Do you make an effort to learn about the objectives and products of the organization for which you are working? This would include asking your supervisor or other employees about the organization's structure, products, and services, and reading employee manuals, organization newsletters, and annual reports.

2. Are you versatile and adaptable? This would be shown by such actions as willingly learning new jobs, taking over for others who are unexpectedly absent, etc.

3. Do you try to improve your skills and qualifications? You can do this by learning new skills from other workers, getting involved in your organization's in-house training programs, teaching yourself new skills in your spare time, or taking upgrading courses at your local college or university.

4. Do you show a positive attitude toward your job? This would include taking pride in doing your job well, not complaining about the work or the people you work with, and willingly staying late to finish an urgent task.

5. Are you a problem solver? This would include noticing problems when they arise, reporting them to your supervisor, and coming up with solutions to overcome the difficulty.

6. Do you try to improve the quality of the projects on which you are working? This would involve understanding the purpose of your work, making suggestions about new and better ways to perform a task, and making sure that the quality of your work is high.

7. Are you able to present your solutions to problems to other employees in a non-threatening manner, being assertive but not aggressive?

If you've answered "No" or "Not sure" to any of these questions, you might need to learn to show more initiative on the job.

Adapted from Guidance Centre, University of Toronto, in co-operation with Employment and Immigration Canada. PLACE. *Guided Steps to Employment Readiness.* "Part D: Doing Well on the Job." © Minister of Supply and Services Canada, 1984, p. 17. Reproduced with the permission of the Minister of Supply and Services Canada, 1990.

2. ASSESSING OTHERS' INITIATIVE

Interview three people who are employed. Find out how they or their co-workers show initiative at their place of work. Prepare a brief report that gives each person's job title and then list the ways in which each person shows initiative.

3. YOU DECIDE

Showing initiative can lead to job promotion and bonuses. Pretend that you're the head supervisor of the Physical Therapy Unit of the Clearbrook Hospital. The human resource manager has told you that you can promote two people in your department to supervisory positions. She has also given you $1000 in bonus money to distribute among the workers on the basis of how well they have shown initiative. An individual can receive any amount up to $1000. Read the employee descriptions below and decide whom you would promote and how much bonus money you would give to each. Explain the reasons for your decisions.

Marissa: Works overtime when asked. Often helps patients on her own time. Does not participate in hospital social activities.

Lazlo: Seldom has to be told what to do. Has missed work often, usually because of family problems. Absences irritate co-workers. Enrolled at a local community college in a two-year program that will qualify him for a higher position in physical therapy.

Simone: Works very well alone on the job. Usually does not help other co-workers except when asked. Has thought of new ways to get the job done more efficiently.

Huan: Does not watch the clock; if the job requires extra hours, works them cheerfully. Is thinking of looking for a higher-paying job at another hospital.

Lisa: Gets along very well with co-workers but has quite a few disagreements with supervisors. Volunteers to come in on days off if the hospital is short-staffed.

4. CLUES FOR ASSESSING YOUR INITIATIVE*

Answer "Yes" or "No" to the following questions.

1. Do you wait until you are told before beginning a new task?

2. If you think something is being done wrong, do you think that it's someone else's problem?

3. Do you think that doing your job well is all that should matter to your supervisor?

4. Do you resent being asked to take over for another employee who is absent or overworked?

5. Do you avoid suggesting changes because you feel no one will listen or that it probably isn't a very good idea anyway?

6. Do you try to avoid talking to your supervisor?

7. Do you avoid working extra hours if you are asked?

8. Do you get to work barely on time and leave as soon as you can?

If you've answered "Yes" to more than one of these questions, it's possible that you're unwilling or unable to show initiative. If you'd like to show more initiative but aren't sure how to go about it, the following guidelines might help.

---

*This exercise and the next section are adapted from: Guidance Centre, University of Toronto, in co-operation with Employment and Immigration Canada. PLACE. *Guided Steps to Employment Readiness.* "Part D: Doing Well on the Job." © Minister of Supply and Services Canada, 1984, pp. 91-93.

G U I D E L I N E S   F O R
S H O W I N G   I N I T I A T I V E
▼▼▼▼▼▼▼▼▼▼▼▼▼▼▼▼▼▼▼▼▼▼▼▼▼▼▼▼▼ ▼

1. **Keep a broad perspective**. Maintain an understanding of the organization for which you work. Read the organization's publications, newsletters, catalogues, and annual reports. These will help you identify the purpose of the company. Learn about the operational structure of the organization. Keep your eyes and ears open to find out what other people

in the organization are doing and why. This will help you to be aware of current issues and to understand how your own work fits in.

2. **Learn to assess priorities**. Not all tasks you do are equally important. Learn which duties are most important and those that are secondary. When you are pressed for time, you will then know which things you should do first. Read your job description carefully. It is probably organized with the most important duties listed first. When you first start a job, ask your supervisor to tell you what your priorities should be.

3. **Adapt to change**. If your supervisor asks you to perform a new task or to change your daily routine to meet a sudden need, a person with initiative will respond to the new challenge promptly. This type of behaviour will demonstrate a willingness to learn and a commitment to the needs of the organization.

4. **Solve problems**. Almost every day, workers are faced with problems that need solving. Some people report every new problem to their supervisor and follow the instructions they receive. People with initiative, however, find a solution themselves before taking the issue to their supervisor. For example, if you were concerned that a project deadline would not be met, you shouldn't ignore the potential problem in the hope that it will disappear or be dealt with by someone else. You should report the possibility to your supervisor after determining that you've done everything possible within your area of responsibility.

5. **Build a reputation for being reliable**. If you've been assigned a task, it's up to you to get it done satisfactorily and on time. There are usually difficulties in getting a job done and some people always blame external circumstances for failure to complete jobs. People with initiative look for ways around problems because they recognize that they are responsible for their work.

6. **Show a willingness to learn**. Leaders have the self-confidence and eagerness to keep on learning. They learn from reading, by taking evening courses, and from their own and other workers' experience. Seek to expand your area of competence by asking questions when you don't understand. Observe and listen to others, and try new things. Everyone makes mistakes; people with initiative learn from them.

INITIATIVE HAS ITS BENEFITS
▼▼

Further guidelines for showing initiative are as follows.

1. Have positive relationships with your co-workers.

2. Develop habits that help to maintain positive relationships.

3. Make sure your work is up to the standards that are expected of you. If you are unsure what the standards are, find out.

4. Be aware of your personal appearance.

5. Build a reputation for being reliable.

6. Understand your employer's goals and purposes.

7. Be alert for possibilities to improve your situation.

8. Don't procrastinate.

9. Examine your options. There is never only one way to do something.

10. Never say that there's really nothing you can do about a situation. There's always something that can be done.

CASE STUDY

Pam is the Business Department manager at Supreme Chemical Company. Among her many tasks she has the responsibility of putting all of the money away in the safe at the end of the day. In addition, she has to secure the area, which includes locking all doors and turning out the main lights.

One Friday afternoon, Pam was suddenly called home because of a family emergency. As he was leaving the building, Riad, a secretary in the Personnel Department, noticed that the day's receipts had not been put in the safe. Before leaving, he put the money in the safe, locked the doors, and turned out the main lights.

QUESTIONS

1. In what way did Riad show initiative?

2. How will his initiative benefit Pam?

3. How will his initiative benefit the entire Business Department?

4. How will Riad benefit by showing initiative?

5. How might Riad's initiative benefit the Personnel Department even though he helped the Business Department?

CHAPTER SUMMARY EXERCISE
▼▼▼

Do you show initiative on the job? Or, if you don't have a job yet, do you exhibit characteristics at home or school that suggest you *would* show initiative on a job?

If you have a job, describe in detail your job responsibilities. Then write down the numbers of the following initiative items in your notebook and, beside each, the number in the key that best represents your level of initiative at your workplace.

If you don't have a job, think of situations in which effort or work is expected of you; for example, at home, where house or yard chores are assigned to you or at school in school work or extra-curricular activities. Describe one such situation in detail and then write down the numbers of the initiative items and the number from the key that apply.

If possible, have someone else look at your answers to see if he or she would rate you the same way.

5 = Excellent   4 = Good   3 = Average
2 = Below Average   1 = Need a Lot of Improvement

1. Am willing to work, not just put in time.

2. Help others on the job, at home, or at school.

3. Keep busy when my regular tasks are done.

4. Do extra work when needed.

5. Put in extra time if needed.

6. Do positive things to help improve the spirit of my friends, family, or co-workers.

7. Take courses or subjects that improve my job performance.

8. Suggest new and better ways to improve task performance.

Decision-Making Skills

OBJECTIVES
▼▼▼▼▼▼▼▼▼▼▼▼▼▼▼▼▼

After completing this chapter you should be able to:

- Explain the importance of effective decision making.
- Define the decision-making process.
- Use this process to devise solutions for fictitious problems.
- Use this process to solve your own problems.

INTRODUCTION
▼▼▼▼▼▼▼▼▼▼▼▼▼▼▼▼▼▼▼

Every day we make choices and decisions. Most of these decisions involve little effort: which way to walk home, what to eat for breakfast, what to wear. We've had to make the same decisions before, have the information we need to make these decisions, and risk little if we later regret our decisions.

As you assume more responsibility for yourself and others, the decisions you make will sometimes be more complicated. Decisions about which college or university to attend, which job to take, which car to buy, with whom you will live, and whom you will hire will require effort and care.

Indecision is a major component of stress. Avoiding making a decision sometimes causes a feeling of uncertainty that can be far more stressful than living with the consequences of our decisions. Making decisions gives us the power to develop options. Being indecisive, letting other people decide for you, or avoiding making a decision until there is only one option left can sometimes leave you feeling as if you have no choices.

In this chapter a strategy is outlined that will improve the effectiveness of your decision making. Making important decisions becomes easier as you gain more experience and self-confidence.

THE DECISION-MAKING PROCESS
▼▼▼▼▼▼▼▼▼▼▼▼▼▼▼▼▼▼▼▼▼▼▼▼▼▼▼▼▼▼▼▼

Before making a decision, ask yourself:

1. Is this my decision to make or am I making a decision for someone else?
2. Should I be sharing the responsibility for this decision with other people?
3. Am I being rushed or pressured to make a decision?

When you have answered these questions to your satisfaction, you are ready to begin the decision-making process, which is as follows.

Step 1: Define the problem.

Carefully examine the problem to make sure you understand it. Write the problem down, stating all the facts. For example, if you are constantly short of money, you could define the problem as being the fact that you spend too much or that you need to earn more money. You might need the help of others in defining the problem.

Step 2: List all possible solutions to the problem.

After careful thought and necessary research (including talking to other people, if necessary), write down all of the possible solutions to the problem. Don't try to make a final decision at this point.

Step 3: Evaluate all of the possible alternatives and choose the best solution.

Don't jump to conclusions and choose the first solution that seems to make sense. Look at the problem from every possible angle and assess each alternative in every possible context. Avoid procrastinating but don't make hasty decisions. Use the information you gathered, your intuition, and your past experience to come to a workable decision that reflects your values and goals.

Step 4: Develop a plan of action.

Write a list of the steps you need to take to implement your plan.

CASE STUDY

Jolene usually liked her job at a sporting goods store, but today she was irritated. Her manager had left early again and for the fourth time in just two weeks she would have to close the store at the end of the day. In the past, Jolene had to close only once or twice a month. Closing meant that she had to wait until all the other employees had left, then check the day's cash receipts and make out the work schedule for the next day. These additional responsibilities would take at least an hour and a half to complete. Because of these extra duties, Jolene had asked her manager for overtime pay and a promotion to assistant manager, but her manager only said, "I'll think about it."

Jolene wants to do something about this job problem, so she has decided to use the decision-making process.

JOLENE'S DECISION-MAKING WORKSHEET

Step 1: Define the problem.

My manager doesn't recognize that my additional hours and responsibilities are worth overtime pay and a promotion.

Step 2: List all possible solutions to the problem.

1. Quit and find another job.

2. At an appropriate time, talk to my manager again about my added job duties and responsibilities. Present her with a written statement showing actual dates, hours, and duties performed. This statement will also express my desire to be promoted to the position of assistant manager, with an increase in pay. I'll also ask my manager, in a way that isn't embarrassing to her, if she has the authority to give me the promotion or at least the overtime pay. If the discussion with my manager doesn't go well, I might decide to find other work.

3. Go over my manager's head and talk to the store owner about this problem.

4. Say nothing else about the situation, continue to do my work, and hope that my manager will recognize my value.

Step 3: Evaluate the alternatives and choose the best solution.

I have selected Solution 2 because:

1. I like my job and don't want to quit. This approach seems to be the most positive because it allows for two-way communication. The company's and my points of view can be discussed. Talking over the facts with my manager will most likely ensure a better work future for me.

2. Another reason is that I have expenses and several monthly bills to pay. I want my financial credit rating to remain strong. If it's necessary to leave, I would want to have found another job first.

Step 4: Develop a plan of action.

By September 30 I'll have made an appointment to speak with my manager. I'll have my written statement about this situation prepared. Included in this written statement will be all of the dates and hours of work, that I've put in, plus the responsibilities I've had to assume. This will support my claim that I deserve overtime pay and a promotion. I must be sure that my appointment is at a time when the manager can take the time to discuss and help solve this problem.

QUESTION

Do you think Jolene made a good decision? Explain your answer.

---

1. TIMING DECISION MAKING

We make decisions every day. Some decisions are so routine that we hardly think about them. Other decisions are more important, so we might take a long time thinking about them. On the next page is a list of decisions that you probably have faced or will face during your lifetime. Rank these decisions according to the amount of time you expect to spend on each, using the following key.

1 = Routine; I wouldn't spend much time thinking about this before doing it (or not doing it).

2 = I'd give this decision an average amount of time and thought.

3 = I'd think about this carefully. I would take plenty of time before making this decision.

DECISION:

1. To go to work.

2. To blame someone.

3. What to have for lunch.

4. What time to get up in the morning.

5. What to do on a weekend.

6. To tell someone you're angry about something.

7. To change jobs.

8. What type of car to buy.

9. To ask someone for a date.

10. What to spend extra money on.

11. What clothes to wear.

12. What to do after high school.

13. To go to school.

14. Which school to attend after high school.

Look back at how you ranked your decisions. You'll probably notice that some very important decisions are surprisingly easy to make and don't take much time at all. The decision to go to work, for example, is certainly an important one. Yet working people make this decision every day without even thinking about it as a decision at all.

CASE STUDIES

CASE STUDY 1

Three years ago, Mr. Singh established a specialized work experience education program designed to train hotel and motel managers. Although the program got off to a slow start, he now has more than twenty trainees placed in a variety of good training positions and has the full support of sponsoring managers of all of the major hotels and motels in his area.

Two weeks ago Mr. Singh introduced a learning goal idea to his trainees. He took a full hour to explain the concept in detail and then asked the students to list their goals on a form he had prepared and turn them in the following week.

One of the students, Michael, took the form and tossed it into a drawer at home. Why should he fool around with such a dumb procedure?

In Mr. Singh's opinion, Michael is a completely disorganized person who seldom takes things seriously. He feels that Michael was attracted to the program because of the prospect of working in an elegant, luxurious hotel. Michael is a handsome young man who likes fancy cars, fancy clothes, and an exciting social life. By his own admission Michael feels that a career as a hotel or motel manager will give him the "freedom and social contacts necessary for the type of lifestyle I want."

The following week, when Mr. Singh picked up the forms completed by his students, Michael was the only one who failed to produce one. Mr. Singh told Michael he would give him one additional day. The following day Michael turned in the completed form, but on reading it, Mr. Singh discovered that Michael had not taken it seriously. The goals he had put down were poorly written, general in nature, and gave clear evidence that Michael had not taken more than ten minutes to write them.

QUESTIONS

1. What action, if any, should Mr. Singh take to convince Michael of the importance of having learning goals?

2. Should Michael's work experience supervisor be involved in the problem? If so, in what way?

3. If Michael fails to take the learning goal concept seriously, should he be dropped from the program? Explain your answer.

CASE STUDY 2

Mrs. Kristiansen is the head of a business work experience education program that is highly successful. For the last five years there has been a long waiting list of qualified trainees who want to enrol. Last summer Mrs. Kristiansen convinced Mr. Renaud, the manager of an accounting firm, of the advantages of having a trainee. Her chief argument was that the co-operative education program would provide Mr. Renaud with a constant supply of temporary and long-term help.

Mr. Renaud agreed to use the program on a trial basis and, through the office manager, set up an excellent progressive program. The trainee would work directly under the chartered accountants in the office and would eventually receive training in all areas of accounting. If the program worked, Mr. Renaud would employ additional trainees the following year.

After interviewing three students from the program, Mr. Renaud chose Sal, a quiet young man who was very serious about becoming a skilled chartered accountant. Two weeks after Sal started at the firm, he came to Mrs. Kristiansen with a problem. "Mrs. Kristiansen, no matter what I do there, it's wrong. I'm getting the needle from all directions. Everybody seems to resent me." On investigation Mrs. Kristiansen made the following discoveries.

1. The office manager and the accountants resented the fact that Sal had been given special treatment over two other part-time university students who also wanted to become chartered accountants and were there before Sal.

2. The accountants resented the extra time they had to spend training Sal and delegating work to him. They felt they were hired to deal with clients, not to be teachers.

QUESTIONS

1. What would you recommend that Sal do in an attempt to overcome this resentment?

2. What might Mrs. Kristiansen do to help Sal?

3. What might Mr. Renaud do to improve the learning climate for Sal and to guarantee that the co-operative education program is successful the first year?

CASE STUDY 3

Despite the fact that Abby has done well in school, is well-respected by her teachers, and has numerous girlfriends, she is surprisingly immature in comparison with others her age. Although she claims to have tried many times, she has never been able to land any type of part-time job on her own.

In an effort to help her, Abby's counsellor recommended her to Miss Kent, a very popular teacher and co-ordinator of a general office work experience education program. On learning that Abby was a business student with very good inputting and general office skills, Miss Kent admitted her to the program and helped her to find a trainee position in the office of a small factory. Here, Abby would receive general office training. In Miss Kent's opinion, the job would have the following advantages and disadvantages.

Advantages	Disadvantages
Excellent learning environment.	Office old and shabby.
Regular, guaranteed hours.	Industrial neighbourhood.
Modern equipment.	Minimum pay.
Good moral support available.	No other young people employed.

Two weeks after Abby reported to her supervisor, Miss Kent noticed that Abby seemed depressed. In talking with her after class, Miss Kent discovered that Abby was deeply discouraged with her work situation. As she put it, "Miss Kent, all I do is work, work, work, while my friends seem to have all sorts of fun in their jobs. Besides, it's not going to help my personality to be around old people all the time."

QUESTIONS

1. What would you guess is the primary cause of Abby's negative attitude toward her job?

2. Do you feel that her negative attitude is justified?

3. What approach should Miss Kent use to help Abby?

CASE STUDY 4

Rick is a highly energetic, independent, and hard-working individual with good mechanical aptitudes. Although he is still living at home with his parents, he has earned the money to pay for his clothes, car, school supplies, and incidentals since he was fourteen years of age. His pride and joy is a sports car that he had customized to his own artistic specifications. His goal is to have his own shop someday where he can specialize in customizing foreign cars for clients.

Rick was accepted in an auto body repair work experience education program two months ago. He is a trainee in a quality body and repair shop in his home town. The owner of the rather small shop, Mr. Walesa, is delighted with Rick's ability to learn quickly and to assume responsibility. As a result, Rick has been pushed far ahead of his planned learning schedule.

Rick is not doing very well in school, however. He is failing a course in English and one in practical mathematics. Ms. Montano, the co-ordinator, had a short talk with Rick three weeks ago, but Rick didn't seem to respond. He continued to miss some of his classes, his concentration has been poor, and he is farther behind in his assignments than ever.

Yesterday, Ms. Montano made a special trip to talk to Mr. Walesa about the problem. She explained that, under the co-operative education plan, school work and on-the-job learning must be given equal attention by the student. In Rick's case, this was particularly important because he expected eventually to operate his own business.

Ms. Montano made the following request: "I'd like you to talk to Rick about the importance of his English language skills in dealing with his customers, both now and in the future. A well-spoken person gives a customer confidence, as does a well-written business letter. Perhaps you can also help him to realize that, without some practical mathematical skills, his business will certainly fail."

QUESTIONS

1. Did Ms. Montano, the co-ordinator, do the right thing?

2. If you were Mr. Walesa, Rick's sponsor, how would you have reacted to Ms. Montano's request?

3. If you were Mr. Walesa, how would you handle the matter with Rick?

CHAPTER SUMMARY EXERCISE
▼▼▼▼▼▼▼▼▼▼▼▼▼▼▼▼▼▼▼▼▼▼▼▼▼▼▼▼▼▼▼▼▼▼▼▼▼▼▼

Apply the decision-making process to the following case studies. In each case:

• Define the employee's problem.

• List all possible solutions.

• Evaluate the alternatives and choose the best one.

• Detail a plan of action.

You could set this up in your notebook as follows.

Step 1: The problem:

Step 2: Possible solutions:

Step 3: Best solution:

Step 4: Plan of action:

1. Lately Tak has been under a lot of financial pressure. It seems he never has enough money for the things he needs. Tak goes to university full time, and on weekends and some week nights he works for the minimum

wage at a local restaurant. In the summers he works as a lifeguard and swimming instructor also. He lives in a very inexpensive apartment on a quiet street near the hospital where he takes some courses. After two more years of university he will graduate as an physical therapist. He is looking forward to having a secure income.

2. David works in a large office building in the suburbs. He is a customer service representative. At work he often feels tired and has headaches. Some of the other workers complain of the same symptoms. During his two-week summer vacation he feels in the best of health. When David returns to work after the holidays, his symptoms return. He suspects that the building's inadequate air circulation system might be the cause of his problems.

3. Eva has had a permanent part-time job as a circulation clerk in the college library for three years. She is well-liked by staff and students. Eva is pleasant with the library users and follows the library policies. Eva's supervisor, Linda, is not officially in charge of hiring circulation staff but often makes strong recommendations to her supervisor. Often Linda's friends and family are hired. A full-time position will soon be available. People are aware that Eva is going to apply. The vacation schedule is posted and Eva realizes that a more recent part-time worker, one of Linda's friends, has been given the vacation weeks that Eva requested. Eva is resentful of Linda but is aware that she must be careful if she wants the full-time job.

4. Denise is a server at Mario's Steak House. She is often annoyed with Leo, one of the assistants. The servers rely on the assistants to make their jobs easier. The assistants clear the tables, keep the water pitchers full, and sometimes help the servers to make salads and carry plates. The servers give the assistants a share of their tips at the end of the evening. The tips reflect the service the assistants have given. Leo covers the tables served by Denise, Jocelyn, and David, the head waiter. David gives Leo big tips, so Leo spends more time on David's tables. Denise is tired of Leo's treatment of her. She is left with more work and has had some complaints from customers. On the nights when she works with Yuri, another assistant, her job is much easier and she gets better tips.

5. On his first full-time job as machinist, Jack found himself working with several men who were much older. They were nice, but generally they left Jack alone and didn't offer to help him as much as they could have. Jack was young, and they had seen many first-time workers come and go. Since the machine department was small, Jack knew that he must earn his older co-workers' confidence. If the men decided to make things rough for Jack, it would be more difficult for him to keep his job.

6. You might know of a job problem at your place of work. Write down the details of the problem and, using the decision-making process, explain how you think the problem could be solved.

Entrepreneurship

O B J E C T I V E S

▼ ▼ ▼ ▼ ▼ ▼ ▼ ▼ ▼ ▼ ▼ ▼ ▼ ▼ ▼

After completing this chapter you should be able to:

- Define the term *entrepreneur.*
- Describe the characteristics and values that entrepreneurs usually possess.
- Ascertain if you have the potential to become an entrepreneur.
- Detail the steps involved in becoming an entrepreneur.
- Develop a business plan if you decide to become an entrepreneur.

I N T R O D U C T I O N

▼ ▼ ▼ ▼ ▼ ▼ ▼ ▼ ▼ ▼ ▼ ▼ ▼ ▼ ▼ ▼ ▼ ▼

An entrepreneur is a person who creates a new product or service, or improves an existing product or service, and then sets up a business organization to market it. *Successful* entrepreneurs recognize what consumers want—or might want—and then provide a good product or service for sale at a reasonable price.

Small businesses set up by entrepreneurs are thriving in Canada today. In fact, more small businesses are being established and succeeding than are large businesses. And, outside of government, small businesses are leading medium-sized and large businesses in:

- Providing more jobs for other people.
- Accounting for more sales.
- Developing more new goods and services.
- Promoting the growth of smaller communities.
- Replacing imports from other countries with goods produced in Canada.
- Increasing the amount of goods exported to other countries.

People of any age can choose to become entrepreneurs. Some start while they're still in school, others midway through their lives, and still others after retirement from regular jobs. Some entrepreneurs are consultants who provide other businesses or governments with the knowledge or skills they have acquired in a variety of trade, technological, or professional fields. Others are inventors of new products or services, and still others are people who recognize the value of a new product or service and work at developing markets for these. Since inventors often lack marketing or business management abilities, they usually develop enterprises in association with people who do have such skills.

WHO CAN BECOME AN ENTREPRENEUR?

▼▼▼▼▼▼▼▼▼▼▼▼▼▼▼▼▼▼▼▼▼▼▼▼▼▼▼▼▼▼

Anyone can become an entrepreneur given the right circumstances and enough desire—entrepreneurs are made, not born. However, people with certain personality traits and with particular values and backgrounds are more likely to become entrepreneurs. For example, studies have shown that entrepreneurs are independent, self-reliant individuals with initiative, decision-making skills, drive, energy, and a need for personal achievement. Also, people who grow up in families in which parents or other relatives are in business for themselves often develop entrepreneurial traits because they see first-hand that it *can* be done and learn how to go about it.

1. DO YOU HAVE WHAT IT TAKES?

Studies have revealed that entrepreneurs share similar attitudes. Answer the following questions either "Yes" or "No" to discover if you have a natural aptitude for entrepreneurship.

1. Have you enough stamina to work long hours?
2. Is achievement important to you?
3. Are you self-confident?
4. Do you like to be in control?
5. Are you persistent?
6. Can you cope with uncertainty?
7. Are you willing to take moderate risks?
8. Can you work on several projects at the same time without becoming irritated?
9. Do you usually complete any task you start?
10. Do you think you are a realistic thinker and planner?
11. Do you welcome challenges?

If you answered "Yes" to most of these questions, you have some of the characteristics of an entrepreneur.

Source: Alberta Career Development and Employment. *Are You Cut Out to Be an Entrepreneur?* 1988.

2. VALUES AND NEEDS*

To analyse whether your values and needs are similar to those that are characteristic of entrepreneurs, write the following statements in your notebook, completing each with your preferred response from the choices given.

*This exercise and the following two are adapted from: Alberta Career Development and Employment. *Are You Cut Out to Be an Entrepreneur?* 1988. Based on William E. Jennings, Gary Rabbior. *Entrepreneurship, A Primer for Canadians.* Canadian Foundation for Economic Education, 1985.

1. When you're faced with a tough decision, you:

   a) Consult a friend.

   b) Consult an expert.

   c) Try to work it through by yourself.

2. You are motivated most by:

   a) Challenge.

   b) Public recognition.

   c) Money.

3. You believe your success depends most on:

   a) Others.

   b) Your own skill and hard work.

   c) Luck.

4. At work you place highest value on:

   a) Competence and efficiency.

   b) Control over your own schedule and activities.

   c) Doing new and creative projects.

5. You want to make a profit so that:

   a) You will have enough money to expand or develop new ideas.

   b) You can get rich.

   c) Your success is obvious to yourself and others.

6. Given the chance, you'd most likely choose a business:

   a) Where the risks are as high as the possible rewards.

   b) That had a good combination of moderate risk and enticing challenge.

   c) With low risks and easy work.

7. When it comes to leisure activities:

   a) You always do what your friends are doing.

   b) Sometimes you choose to go without them.

   c) You spend most of your time alone.

No entrepreneur possesses all of the common traits. If you agreed with five out of seven of the answers given at the end of this chapter, you are high in entrepreneurial potential.

3. PERSONAL CHARACTERISTICS FOR SUCCESS

Choosing from the following list, and including the number for each item, write in your notebook the eight characteristics that you think are most important for entrepreneurial success. Then choose the eight characteristics that you think are least important. The characteristics that you haven't chosen are the ones that you consider to be moderately important for success as an entrepreneur. Are there some characteristics that you don't have? If so, list them.

1. High energy
2. Good health
3. Need to achieve
4. Willing to risk
5. Creative
6. Innovative
7. Competitive
8. Persistent
9. Patient
10. Flexible
11. Well organized
12. Good leader
13. Need for power
14. Desire for money
15. Need for close friends
16. Self-reliant
17. Self-confident
18. Ability to relate to others easily
19. Good communicator
20. Tolerance for uncertainty
21. Independent
22. Positive outlook
23. Sense of purpose
24. Courage

Entrepreneurs who answered this quiz agreed that the following abilities were of great importance:

8) persistent, 17) self-confident, 22) positive outlook, 3) need to achieve, and 11) well organized.

Characteristics chosen with less frequency but also rated as very important were:

1) high energy, 16) self-reliant, 21) independent, 10) flexible, 23) sense of purpose, 4) willing to risk, 24) courage, and 20) tolerance for uncertainty.

Least important to all of those who answered this quiz were:

13) need for power, 14) desire for money, 15) need for close friends, 12) good leader, 9) patient, and 5) creative.

The rest of the abilities fell in the area of important but not absolutely necessary for success.

4. PERSONAL PROFILE

Take a look at your past and then, in table form as shown below, list ten of your accomplishments and the skills and attributes you demonstrated to achieve these. For example: started a preschool, collected the most money for the Canadian Cancer Society, won an art prize in Grade 11. A list of some skills and attributes follows the example. Include any others that you think are appropriate.

Example:

Accomplishments	Skills or Attributes
1. Started a preschool	Administer, create, lead, persistent, energetic, organized

Skills			Attributes		
act	compose	examine	ambitious	dependable	inquisitive
administer	conduct	explain	artistic	determined	intelligent
advise	control	fix	assertive	diligent	kind
analyse	create	found	attractive	efficient	loyal
arrange	decide	gather	calm	energetic	mature
assemble	define	handle	capable	firm	neat
budget	display	improve	caring	flexible	organized
build	draw	lead	competent	frank	persistent
calculate	drive	learn	creative	honest	polite
coach	edit	manage	decisive	industrious	
communicate			productive	quick	

STEPS TO BECOMING AN ENTREPRENEUR
▼ ▼

Once you've decided that you have the necessary characteristics and values of an entrepreneur, you still require:

- A good business idea.
- The skills and training to build a business around this idea.
- A good business plan.

THE BUSINESS IDEA

Definition of what makes a good business idea is difficult, but some Canadians have provided good examples. J. Armand Bombardier, for example, met a need for a vehicle that would travel well over snow by inventing the snowmobile—inventing a new sport at the same time! The enterprising group who invented the board game Trivial Pursuit is another example. Their game is now famous internationally and the inventors are millionaires. And then there's the young man who felt that his grandmother's mustard was better than anything on the market, made up a batch in the family kitchen, sold it to a few neighbourhood stores, and now heads a large condiment manufacturing operation.

Success didn't come overnight for any of these entrepreneurs but, in all cases, they felt they had a good idea, they were willing and able to spend the time and energy necessary to find out how to manufacture and market their products, and they all weathered many difficulties before they achieved their goals.

To be successful, the product or service an entrepreneur provides must be something that people are ready and able to buy. That means that it must meet a present need or be something that people will want, even though it's new. Also, you have to be able to make the product or service available at a price that people are able and willing to pay. Ensuring that there's a market for your idea is an important first step.

SKILLS AND TRAINING

Ideally, an entrepreneurial plan should be based on skills and training that a person already possesses. So the best way to be ready to follow up on a good idea is to gain as many different types of skills and training as possible at the time of your life when these are most readily available—while you're in school. Then, when an entrepreneurial opportunity presents itself, you'll have less to learn to take advantage of it and much more chance for success.

Consider this: unless you're able to team up with other people, as an entrepreneur you'll have to be your own manager, public relations representative, bookkeeper, buyer, and salesperson—and that's without even taking into account the technical end of whatever endeavour you choose!

THE BUSINESS PLAN

Once you decide that you have a good business idea and are ready to go into business for yourself, you must develop a business plan. The following guidelines will be useful.

1. Analyse your strengths and weaknesses, both personal and educational. Are there weak areas that might cause your venture to fail? What steps can you take to remedy these?

2. Research the market for your product or service. Who will your customers be? Where can they be found? Will you have to relocate? Will these customers be willing and able to pay the price you'll be asking? Visit any competitors. If you're setting up in another area, you could ask them for advice.

3. Choose a business location. Can you operate from your home or do you need premises in a particular type of location?

4. Determine financing requirements. How much will you need to start your business? Where will you obtain the money?

5. Develop a production plan if you plan to manufacture a product. How should the production process be laid out? What equipment will you need?

6. Develop a personnel plan. Can you operate the business by yourself? If not, how many people will you need? With what talents? What jobs will each person do?

7. Develop a marketing plan. How will you let potential customers know about your business? Will you use personal selling methods or advertising and sales promotions?

8. Decide whether you're going to register your business as a sole proprietorship (you own the business by yourself), a partnership (you share the profits and risks with one or more other people); or a corporation (ownership of the business is divided into shares, and the owners of these shares are called *shareholders).*

9. Determine the types of financial and general business records and reports you'll need. How should they be prepared? What are their purposes?

10. Develop a financial projection of your first three years in business and a detailed statement for the first year. How much cash do you expect to flow in and out of the business? When can you expect to start making a profit?

11. Determine insurance needs. Will you need some type of insurance to protect your business assets, employees, or customers?

12. Prepare a report that details your entire business plan so that you can raise money if necessary or convince others to join you in your venture.

Based on Alberta Career Development and Employment. *Are You Cut Out to Be an Entrepreneur?* 1988, and Canadian Foundation for Economic Education. *Entrepreneurship, A Primer for Canadians*, 1985.

5. THE BOTTOM LINE

If you've ever thought about having your own business, this exercise will help to familiarize you with some of the serious considerations involved. Even if you've never contemplated such a move, pick a business that you think you'd enjoy and be good at and answer the following questions. In each case, explain your answer.

1. What type of building/office/storage facilities will I need for my business?

2. Where should my business premises be located? Should I be on a busy street where lots of potential customers will pass by? in a mall? in an industrial area? in an office building?

3. Will I have to rent or buy my business premises, or can I operate from my home? If I operate from my home, are there any legal or municipal zoning restrictions?

4. Will I be able to operate this business on my own or will I need help? Who can provide this help? Will I have to pay someone to help me?

5. What laws or regulations will apply to my business? Will I have to have a licence of some sort? take special precautions on my business premises? obtain insurance of some type? bond myself and/or my employees?

6. Will my new business yield enough income right away for me to cover all businesses expenses and have enough left for personal expenses? If not, how will I survive until it does?

ASSISTANCE FOR WOULD-BE ENTREPRENEURS

▼▼

The federal and all provincial governments offer a substantial amount of assistance to people interested in starting their own businesses. Information is readily available, usually at no cost, in the form of publications, audio/visual material, and kits. For example, the Federal Business Development Bank (FBDB) provides a set of four pocketbooks called *Minding Your Own Business* and also has do-it-yourself kits related to several business fields. Also, some provinces have set up Enterprise Centres and some also have toll-free business startup "hotlines"—telephone numbers you can call for general business information.

Loans are available through the FBDB and other federal departments, as well as through various provincial departments across Canada.

To find out more about the resources available for entrepreneurs, check the *Government of Canada* listings in your telephone book for the number for the FBDB and check the provincial government listings for a general information number through which you'll be put in touch with the appropriate department.

You could also contact your local Chamber of Commerce or Board of Trade for information about courses available in your area and other available local resources.

CHAPTER SUMMARY EXERCISES

1. Answer the following questions in your notebook.

   a) What is an entrepreneur?

   b) Is it a good time to be considering becoming an entrepreneur? Explain your answer.

   c) Do you have to be a particular age to become an entrepreneur?

   d) What type of person is most likely to become a successful entrepreneur?

   e) Besides certain characteristics and values, what else so you need to become an entrepreneur?

2. Name a new product or service that you think is an example of a good business idea, explaining your reasoning in detail.

3. Think of a business that you'd like to start, describe the business, and list the skills and training that would be necessary to operate it.

4. In point form, describe what a business plan involves.

ANSWERS TO EXERCISE 2 (page 217)

1b)   2a)   3b)   4c)   5a)   6b)   7b)